DEATH IN AMERICAN TEXTS AND PERFORMANCES

To all the dead who inspire us
as artists, characters, and personal friends

Death in American Texts and Performances
Corpses, Ghosts, and the Reanimated Dead

Edited by

LISA K. PERDIGAO
Florida Institute of Technology, USA

and

MARK PIZZATO
University of North Carolina-Charlotte, USA

ASHGATE

Published by
Ashgate Publishing Limited
Wey Court East
Union Road
Farnham
Surrey, GU9 7PT
England

Ashgate Publishing Company
Suite 420
101 Cherry Street
Burlington
VT 05401-4405
USA

www.ashgate.com

British Library Cataloguing in Publication Data
Death in twentieth-century American texts and performances: corpses, ghosts, and the reanimated dead.
1. Death in literature. 2. Death in the theater. 3. American literature–20th century–History and criticism.
I. Perdigao, Lisa K. II. Pizzato, Mark, 1960–
810.9'3548'0904–dc22

Library of Congress Cataloging-in-Publication Data
Perdigao, Lisa K.
Death in twentieth-century American texts and performances : corpses, ghosts, and the reanimated dead / Lisa K. Perdigao and Mark Pizzato.
p. cm.
Includes bibliographical references and index.
ISBN 978-0-7546-6907-4 (alk. paper) – ISBN 978-0-7546-9602-5 (ebook : alk. paper)
1. American literature–20th century–History and criticism. 2. Death in literature.
3. Ghosts in literature. 4. Death in mass media. I. Pizzato, Mark, 1960– II. Title.

PS228.D43P47 2010
810.9'3548–dc22

2009020943

ISBN: 9780754669074 (hbk)
ISBN: 9780754696025 (ebk)

Mixed Sources
Product group from well-managed forests and other controlled sources
www.fsc.org Cert no. SGS-COC-2482
© 1996 Forest Stewardship Council
FSC

Printed and bound in Great Britain by
TJ International Ltd, Padstow, Cornwall

Contents

Notes on Contributors

Anne Fletcher is Associate Professor of Theatre at Southern Illinois University Carbondale. Her work has appeared in *Theatre Journal, Theatre Symposium,* and *Theatre History Studies*. She has chapters in the *Blackwell Companion to American Drama*, edited by David Krasner, *Experimenters, Rebels, and Disparate Voices*, edited by Arthur Gerwitz and James Kolb, *Interrogating America through Theatre and Performance*, edited by Iris Smith Fischer and William W. Demastes, *Brecht, Broadway, and Unites States Theatre*, edited by Chris Westgate, and *The Encyclopedia of Modern Drama*, edited by Gabrielle Cody and Evert Sprinchorn. She is the author of *Rediscovering Mordecai Gorelik: Scene Design and the American Theatre* (2009).

Jorge A. Huerta is the Chancellor's Associates Professor of Theatre *Emeritus* at the University of California, San Diego. He is a professional director and a leading authority on contemporary Chicano and US Latino theatre. Dr. Huerta has edited three anthologies of plays: *El Teatro de la Esperanza: An Anthology of Chicano Drama* (1973); *Nuevos Pasos: Chicano and Puerto Rican Drama* (with Nicolas Kanellos, 1979, 1989); and *Necessary Theatre: Six Plays About the Chicano Experience* (1987, 2005). Huerta published the first book about Chicano theatre, *Chicano Theatre: Themes and Forms* (1982), which is now in its second edition. Huerta's latest book, *Chicano Drama: Society, Performance and Myth*, was published in 2000.

Belinda Kong is Assistant Professor of English and Asian Studies at Bowdoin College. Her teaching and research focus on Asian-American and Asian diaspora literature, with particular emphasis on the Chinese literary diaspora. She is currently at work on a book manuscript about diasporic fiction of the 1989 Tiananmen movement.

Kathryn Nicol is currently an Irish Research Council for the Humanities and Social Sciences Post-Doctoral Fellow at University College Dublin, where she also teaches contemporary American fiction. She received her PhD from the University of Edinburgh, and has also spent time there as a Research Fellow at the Institute for Advanced Studies in the Humanities. She has previously published essays on Toni Morrison's fiction, racial passing, and visual culture. Her forthcoming works include a collection of essays on the fiction of Kathy Acker and the transnational. She is currently working on a monograph on the fiction of Toni Morrison.

Lisa K. Perdigao is Associate Professor of English at the Florida Institute of Technology. Her book on representing death in fiction, *From Modernist Entombment to Postmodernist Exhumation: Dead Bodies in Twentieth-Century American Fiction*, is forthcoming from Ashgate. She has published articles in book collections on Adrienne Rich's poetry, Toni Morrison's fiction and prose, Caribbean women's writing, and children's and adolescent literature and has an article forthcoming in the MLA collection on teaching William Faulkner's *As I Lay Dying*.

Mark Pizzato is Professor of Theatre at UNC-Charlotte, where he teaches both theatre and film courses. His publications include *Ghosts of Theatre and Cinema in the Brain, Theatres of Human Sacrifice: From Ancient Ritual to Screen Violence* and *Edges of Loss: From Modern Drama to Postmodern Theory*. He has a new book forthcoming on "neurotheatre," regarding gods, angels, and devils evolving in the human brain, through prehistoric cave art, stages of Western drama, recent cinema, and television. He has also written a number of plays. Short films, produced from his screenplays, have won Minnesota Community Television and New York Film Festival awards.

Andrew J. Price is Professor in the English Department at Mount Union College, where he holds the Mary W. and Eric A. Eckler Chair in American Literature. He teaches courses in American literature, gender studies and critical theory. His current research has focused on body studies, gender and whiteness. His most recent publication is "'Monsters' and 'Face Queens' in Harry Crews's Body," *Upon Further Review: Sports in American Literature*, edited by Michael Cocchiarale and Scott D. Emmert.

Jon D. Rossini is Associate Professor in the Department of Theatre and Dance at the University of California, Davis. He is the author of *Contemporary Latina/o Theater: Wrighting Ethnicity* as well as essays in *Gestos, American Drama, Journal of American Drama and Theatre, Text & Presentation, The Dictionary of Literary Biography*, and chapters in the collections *Mediating Chicana/o Culture* and *Codifying the Nation*.

Alasdair Spark is Director of Quality at the University of Winchester. He has published articles on a variety of topics such as the Vietnam War, Science Fiction, Conspiracy Theories, and 9/11. He is currently working on a book on the Apollo moon landings.

Elizabeth Stuart is Pro Vice-Chancellor of the University of Winchester. She is the author of many works on theology and sexuality. For many years she ran the MA in the Rhetoric and Rituals of Death at Winchester.

William S. Waddell is Professor of English at St. John Fisher College in Rochester, New York. His publications and professional presentations have focused primarily on modern and contemporary American poets, including Robert Frost, Robert Lowell, Denise Levertov, and Adrienne Rich. He is the editor of *"Catch if you can your country's moment": Recovery and Regeneration in the Poetry of Adrienne Rich.*

Ian W. Wilson is Assistant Professor of German and Humanities and Chair of the German Studies Program at Centre College in Danville, Kentucky. He is in the early stages of a project involving issues of ambiguity, obscurity, and illegibility in the works of Elfriede Jelinek. His most recent publication is "Greeting the Holocaust's Dead? Narrative Strategies and the Undead in Elfriede Jelinek's *Die Kinder der Toten*" in *Modern Austrian Literature* 39 (2006).

Acknowledgements

Mark Pizzato wants to thank UNC-Charlotte for a reassignment of duties leave in spring 2009, which helped him with time to finish his part in editing this book.

Excerpts from "Epilogue," "Fall 1961," "Florence," and "For the Union Dead" from *Collected Poems* by Robert Lowell. Copyright © 2003 by Harriet Lowell and Sheridan Lowell. Reprinted by permission of Farrar, Straus and Giroux, LLC.

Introduction

Lisa K. Perdigao and Mark Pizzato

Each of us faces death in private, personal ways. Yet we also encounter death in relation to our culture's aesthetics of mortality, through traditional and new media. From the page to the stage to the screen, twentieth and twenty-first century American texts and performance media are vexed sites for representing death, demonstrating both transcendent possibilities and mortal limitations. This collection explores the modern and postmodern aesthetics of death, through corpses, ghosts, and reanimated bodies in literary, performative, and cultural contexts. Corpses, as abject objects, display the loss of a living person. Ghosts insist on the opposite, that a spirit continues beyond the body. The reanimated dead, in various other forms, may combine (or express the gap between) these contradictory modes of un-being. Such representations of death are analyzed here across different genres, as we examine the ways that poets, novelists, dramatists, and film/TV-makers struggle with the presence of the dead in their texts. This is not a comprehensive survey of the twentieth century. Nor do we explore the two World Wars, with their international demands for sacrifice. Instead, this volume features other sites of American death, looking back through a post-millennial viewpoint. It considers how texts and performances respond to the crisis of representation that is always involved in re-presenting death.

Various works of recent scholarship—Karla FC Holloway's *Passed On*, Anissa Janine Wardi's *Death and the Arc of Mourning in African American Literature*, Sharon Patricia Holland's *Raising the Dead*, Elisabeth Bronfen's *Over Her Dead Body*, Alessia Ricciardi's *The Ends of Mourning*, Jahan Ramazani's *Poetry of Mourning*, and Clifton Spargo's *The Ethics of Mourning*—examine the linguistic representations of the dead in twentieth-century American literature, as building toward our current ambivalence about death. This collection extends that gaze to consider how representations of death in theater, film, and television compare with those in literary texts. Such performances highlight the problems and possibilities of representing dead bodies not only through language, but also through actors' mortal bodies onstage or their seemingly immortal images onscreen.

In *Images of the Corpse*, Elizabeth Klaver writes, "Historically, the dead body in the West has always been fraught with all sorts of cultural vexations about spectacle, taboo, violence, and, perhaps surprisingly, research" (xii). Research into the body, for Klaver, quite literally leads her to examine the trope of autopsy. Focusing on how autopsy becomes a model for critical inquiry *into* the dead body, Klaver argues that death "becomes exposed as culturally constructed, an agency laden with the significance of social legibility and utility for the living" (xii). Yet, as much as we come to understand death as a cultural construct, it also remains beyond the limits of intelligibility. Discourses about death may become deconstructionist exercises, textual spaces filled with unsettling binaries. As Michael Mendelson writes, "however inconceivable, utter, and absolute 'not-being' may be, the vestiges are always there to haunt us, the pain of the void always there to goad us, in a manner that obliges us to take seriously what we seem incapable of lucidly and coherently conceiving" (192). In this collection, we consider the haunted vestiges of American history, through its literary and performative representations, not only in ghostly figures, but also in other ways. There is an insistence upon corporeality in some of the works explored here, an unwavering gaze at the corpse. Yet we shall look, too, at various modes of reanimating the dead: through a war monument, racial rebellion, and new technologies of postmodern media.

Our discussion of mortality concerns the performativity of different media, as crucial to the modern and postmodern rituals of death. According to Holloway, "The twentieth century rehearsed, nearly to perfection, a relentless cycle of cultural memory and black mourning" (7). This can be seen in popular culture with the mass marketing of flowers, caskets, and plots by mortuaries—as well as in the high art of James Van Der Zee's funereal photography, which seemingly preserves the corpse. The marketing of death, making it accessible and controllable to the living, shapes the way Americans conceive of this elusive and evasive concept. Thus, the performances of death in literature, television, and film offer aesthetic frames for examining how funereal rites and acts of memorialization re-present the dead in everyday life. For example, William Carlos Williams's poem, "Tract," calls for no black, no polish, no glass, no upholstery, no little brass rollers, "small easy wheels," "no top at all," no wreaths, "especially no hot house flowers," yet some "common memento," "his old clothes," "a few books perhaps," but no silk hat—rejecting traditional markers of the funeral. Peter Schmidt states that this rhetoric "does not reject artifice, but rather contrasts honest and dishonest artifice—a rite that acknowledges the facts of nature versus a rite that does not" (36). What happens, however, when texts and performances stress the significance of such markers or, in contrast, strip away meaning from the corpse, from the rituals associated with death and acts of remembrance? Crossing genre lines, this collection considers how a range of texts represent the cold materiality of death in the corpse, a figurative transcendence in the ghost, and a return of voices and presences in the reanimated dead.

Theatre theorists have also explored the cultural rites of death—in funerals, cemeteries, and stage dramas. In *Cities of the Dead*, Joseph Roach considers the funeral body as performing "the limits of the community called into being by the need to mark its passing" (14). Roach investigates the "performance genealogy" of various sites of death in New Orleans and London, over the past several hundred years, to consider the kinesthetic imagination of "exemplary histrionics" in theatre and everyday life, throughout the circum-Atlantic world as a "vast behavioral vortex" (26–30). More recently, Marvin Carlson has used the term "ghosting" for the overlapping of past and present onstage, as the memories of prior actors in the same role (or of the same actor in another role) haunt the spectator's imagination during a show. Likewise, Alice Rayner argues that "the ghost is not so much the essence of theatre as it is an inhabitant of all its elements," since it is a "theatrical way of seeing double" (xv, xxi). These approaches relate also to Herbert Blau's notion of "ghosting," regarding his own work as a theatre director—with the actor's material body dying as it lives, while playing a living or dying character, in front of a "live" audience also moving toward death (*Take Up*, chapter 5; *To All Appearances* 195). Thus, the performance of death onstage stresses the audience's own proximity to death, in a more corporeal way than poems, novels, or screen media—as Jon Rossini's essay considers in this volume. "Of all the performing arts, the theatre stinks most of mortality" (Blau, *Blooded Thought* 132).

Whether in literature, on the stage, or onscreen, the representation of death presents a gap between artifice and nature—a performance (or reenactment) of loss that may bring meaning but cannot recover the body's transient past. The poststructuralist recognition of this absent presence, in art and rituals of ordinary life, allows a language, albeit paradoxical, for such sites of irreconcilable crisis. Elisabeth Bronfen writes about the funeral as "supported by consolatory literature, grave inscriptions, monuments and the keeping of mementos of the dead," so that "Finality could be denied because continuity was excessively staged" (87). The staging of death here, as a deconstructive paradox, echoes Blau's sense of ghosts appearing through the actor's body in live theatre. The funeral rite, although a performative act of remembering the past, also relies on the corpse as a present object (or its palpable absence in some cases). Remembrance itself is ephemeral, yet seemingly evades loss, as a "form of masking death ... [through] the world of memory" (Bronfen 87). Thus, the paradox of the ghost troubles these borders, between the (corpo)reality of the dead and the work of memory. Jeffrey Andrew Weinstock writes, "Because ghosts are unstable interstitial figures that problematize dichotomous thinking, it perhaps should come as no surprise that phantoms have become a privileged poststructuralist academic trope. Neither living nor dead, present nor absent, the ghost functions as the paradigmatic deconstructive gesture, the 'shadowy third' or trace of an absence that undermines the fixedness of such binary oppositions" (4). Here, the deconstruction of the line between the living and the dead reads like that of the distinction between materiality and discourse. The representation of the dead—as corpse, ghost, or reanimated body—thus highlights what is always already at work in representation. As Sharon Patricia Holland says, "The dead truly acknowledge no boundary" (171). By offering various essays on poetry, fiction, and theatre, with examples from film and television as well, this collection disturbs such borders, too, as it considers how death is represented across genres, in both language and performance, as the presence of an absent presence.

While performances onstage lend themselves to a specific materiality of representation and the possibility of "ghosting," literary texts suggest alternate (and perhaps contradictory) responses to the absent, yet present dead. In poetry, the elegy is a traditional form that laments loss. Yet this form also exposes a paradoxical relationship between the living and the dead as the speaker's apostrophe continually reasserts absence. In fiction, when the plot turns toward death, the representation of a character's dying often provides a moving moment, yet stalls the transaction of the narrative. For example, in *The Great Gatsby*, the characters (including the narrator Nick Carraway) stop to stare at Myrtle Wilson's dead body and Nick fails to find a language to describe the sight.[1] In drama, the performance of death—or the presence of absence through ghostly characters— complicates and complements what is at work in other genres. Thus, Barbara Johnson defines a "performative language" in poetry involving, in the case of the elegy, a prosopopoetic performance, a return of the dead through the speaker's linguistic reflections. However, in theatre, film, and television, dead and dying bodies are also presented through the actor's materiality, onstage or onscreen. The enactment of death onstage (with the actor's "live" body also moving toward death) reveals a potential presence beyond the gap in poetry or novels: between language and the dead body. Cinema narrows this gap even further as death is represented in new ways through advances in technology. It can be reversed, upset, rewound, and replayed. Contemporary television also offers new vantage points for viewing the dead body through a fascination with forensics (in *Law & Order*, *CSI*, *Crossing Jordan*, and *Bones*), with rituals surrounding death and interment (in *Six Feet Under* and the "reality" show *Family Plots*), and even with death-defying logic (in the quantum-leaps of *Tru Calling*, *Dead Like Me*, *Rescue Me*, and *Pushing Daisies*). These too become intertexts for the development of death's representations in poetry, fiction, and drama.

Twentieth-century texts not only suggest a turn from Victorian aestheticization to decaying material but also demonstrate the ways in which the contexts of that century revolutionized how we conceive of the body, with its mortal vulnerability and possibilities for augmentation. As bodily strategies continue to shift (through scientific and medical discoveries as well as technological developments), the representations of death in American texts and performances reveal a narrative about the culture's responses to dying, as well as changing notions of aesthetic limits and possibilities. This is especially insightful given recent reminders of death in television news: from 9/11 to the "War on Terror," Hurricane Katrina, and the Virginia Tech massacre, as well as rising death tolls in Afghanistan and Iraq.

In their introduction to *Death and Representation*, Elisabeth Bronfen and Sarah Webster Goodwin write,

---

[1]   In *Fictional Death and the Modernist Enterprise*, Alan Warren Friedman cites R.W.B. Lewis's statement that "twentieth-century literature 'began on the note of death'" (21). But Friedman goes on to argue that "modernist fiction reflects society's refusal to countenance death's quotidian presence: deathbeds and dying were elided; death was past or future but rarely present, confronted, and mourned. When formally enacted, death's processes shifted from Victorian aestheticization (the death of Little Nell) to decaying material (Kafka's 'Hunger Artist'; Hemingway's 'Snows of Kilimanjaro')... [as] the beautiful death became the elided or the dirty death."

The question might be asked, Who or what represents the corpse? In this question's linguistic ambiguities lie many of the theoretical difficulties we are concerned with here. On the one hand, it can mean, How do we represent the point at which a body becomes a corpse? What is the truth-value of the technological response(s) to this question? And even here we might well ask who "we" are who are doing the representing, to what audience, for what purpose. How is a corpse represented differently for the purposes of law, of mourning, of the news media, of aestheticization in a symbol? (6)

The literature and performance texts explored by the current volume engage these questions by representing corpses, ghosts, and other deadly reanimations in a variety of media. Representations of death always already necessitate an apostrophe—from the living character's vantage point—or a prosopopoetic whereby the writer constructs the voice of the dead. In either case, the absent presence of the dead marks the narrative with loss, a gap that can never be fully bridged, even with "live" bodies onstage or apparently immortal projections onscreen. And yet, the limits and possibilities of representing death in literature and performance also weave a cultural narrative of America in the twentieth and twenty-first centuries: making art out of loss for insight, propaganda, or entertainment.

As the two World Wars signified a changing of the guard—from Victorian[2] to modernist and postmodern literatures—the catastrophe of 9/11 and subsequent terrorist warfare necessitate a new consideration of the functions today in death's representation. The American landscape has changed, complicating our view of loss, mourning, and violence. 9/11 presented monuments of loss through the barren landscape of "Ground Zero," flag-draped coffins, and the "Portraits of Grief" published in the *New York Times*. The losses that Hurricane Katrina brought to Louisiana, Mississippi, and Alabama have also been symbolized by a subtle shift of language—from rescue to recovery—in the drive to account for those lost, to bury the dead, and yet rebuild beyond them. The hurricane-ravaged landscape also defied the past performances of burial rites, as flooded cemeteries opened their graves and exhumed their bodies. Images of coffins floating down city streets signified that the landscape itself was rejecting a traditional narrative of death and burial. Likewise, in American texts and performances, there are representations that challenge what has become naturalized and ritualized in relation to the dead. The essays in this collection explore how artists articulated this space of loss, constructing a new language to represent death, dying, and the dead body—as they approached and entered our new millennium.

The first section, "Studying the Corpse," considers the physicality of the dead body—in stage, screen, and narrative performances. Jorge Huerta examines the flag-draped coffin onstage, and the fictional body contained within it, to consider

---

[2] Cf. Frank, who highlights how the questions of "*whose* death and *whose* mourning" are represented in the "multiplicity of discourses through which nineteenth century Americans sought to elegize and to communicate with the dead" (11).

how the Chicano drama *Dark Root of a Scream*, by Luis Valdez, performs death and dying, through both myth and politics, in the Vietnam era. Mark Pizzato's analysis of Amiri Baraka's play *Dutchman,* through Anthony Harvey's film adaptation, considers the "live" body dying onstage or immortalized onscreen, as erotic and murderous, in relation to its inheritance of racial perceptions, prejudices, and conflicts, from nature to culture. Jon Rossini then explores how Don DeLillo's play *The Day Room* elides the representation of death in its performance. Yet, in two later works, a play *Valparaiso* and novella *The Body Artist*, Rossini finds DeLillo reconceiving performance as a means of making death materially present. Alasdair Spark and Elizabeth Stuart look at another performance medium, contemporary television, through the series *Six Feet Under*, and its "corpse of the week"—in relation to *The Gate's Ajar* series of novels a century before. According to Spark and Stuart, the post-9/11 narrative of *Six Feet Under* is both modern and postmodern, as it shows the inevitability and yet randomness of death contained in the viewing of the corpse.

The next section, "Tracing Ghosts," focuses on the figuration of death through spectral tropes. Instead of looking at the corpse as a site of speculation and potential crisis, the essays in this section consider how the ghost employs figurative language, showing cultural attitudes toward death—and toward a possible world or way of being beyond it. But the diverse spaces of these essays also serve to redefine our living American culture. Anne Fletcher considers the staging of ghosts (as spectral grave bodies) in the classic American drama, *Our Town*, by Thornton Wilder. Yet, she connects such modernist characters, in a play from 1938, set at the turn of the century, to the concerns of our postmodern era—through Buddhism, time theory, phenomenology, and acting theory. Belinda Kong's chapter then asks: What does it mean for a ghost to dream, and to dream in a non-native country? Kong explores this question of displaced desire via a reading of Lan Samantha Chang's 1998 novella, *Hunger*, in light of contemporary Asian-American women's writing (and the trickster figure of Chinese mythology). Overturning a longstanding tradition within this literature to foreignize the Asian immigrant, Chang uses the spectral voice of the immigrant mother to suggest an interlingual model of desire without lack and, by extension, a vision of Asian-America's diasporic future. Also looking at uncanny desires, Ian Wilson considers John Edgar Wideman's representation, in *The Cattle Killing*, of African American culture remembering itself with regard to the spectral legacy of slavery. For Wilson, ghosts (especially female ghosts) are metaphorically transformative, reflecting a series of returns, after death, to meaning. But ghosts also reflect the spectral characters within our brains. Mark Pizzato ends this section by comparing the stage and screen versions of *Proof* (by David Auburn and John Madden), a tragicomedy about mental illness, mathematical genius, and patriarchal ghosts in the twenty-first century. With these examples, Pizzato considers how stage and screen media continue the evolution of human higher-order consciousness, through ghostly and godlike illusions that also have effects in the Real.

The final section, "Reanimating the Dead," examines various figures, voices, and spaces between the corpse and the ghost. Reversing the teleology of death by moving toward a prosopopoetic that, in effect, posthumously represents death from the other side, it considers works that approach death in paradoxical terms. William Waddell's study of Robert Lowell's "For the Union Dead" considers how a certain culture remembers (and reconstitutes) the war dead through monuments and a poetic language built upon loss. Grave markers (and Lowell's poetry) not only point to the corpses lost on the battlefield during the American Civil War, but also become ways of reanimating the dead in the twentieth century. Kathryn Nicol then examines cultural remembrance from another perspective—the politicization of death in Toni Morrison's works. Like Waddell, Nicol explores how war, catastrophe, and suicide enable characters to articulate their national and individual identities through narrative tragedy. However, in his reading of *White Noise*, Andrew Price argues that Don DeLillo offers a critique of narrative form and, in a sense, marks the death of traditional narrative. Lisa Perdigao further relates such mortal terms to postmodern film and television, arguing that these performance texts present death not only as imminent and pervasive, but also as the point of origination. Hence, the artistic work of film and television, at the turn of the millennium, becomes an act of reanimating the dead, as well as recovering meaning—through new, retrospective media.

Between and across genres, the literary texts and performance media considered in this volume signify how absence is felt, how it is made meaningful in and by language. As writers conceive the dead land and attempt to locate it as a site of loss, they face the impossibility of total recovery or transformation. In language and in gesture, the works explored here attempt to re-member the dead—sometimes in their corporeal form or, in other cases, as illusive and allusive presences. While fiction, poetry, drama, film, and television struggle to represent what is both intangible and concrete in the "weight" of loss, comparisons of such genres may also inform how we come to understand representation in a larger sense. Human language has long been directed at the ghostly abstractions of thought, through a troubling awareness of the mortal body moving toward its endpoint. Representations of death in American texts and performances not only suggest recent ways of understanding the dying process, but also expose a crucial matrix of language, identity, and meaning—haunting our world with stories of corpses and ghosts returning to life.

Works Cited

Blau, Herbert. *Blooded Thought: Occasions of Theatre*. New York: PAJ Publications, 1982.
——. *Take Up the Bodies: Theater at the Vanishing Point*. Urbana: University of Illinois Press, 1982.
——. *To All Appearances: Ideology and Performance*. London: Routledge, 1992.

Bronfen, Elisabeth. *Over Her Dead Body: Death, Femininity, and the Aesthetic*. New York: Routledge, 1992.

Carlson, Marvin. *The Haunted Stage*. Ann Arbor: University of Michigan Press, 2001.

Frank, Lucy E. Introduction. *Representations of Death in Nineteenth-Century US Writing and Culture*. Ed. Frank. Aldershot: Ashgate, 2007. 1–12.

Friedman, Alan Warren. *Fictional Death and the Modernist Enterprise*. Cambridge: Cambridge University Press, 2008.

Goodwin, Sarah Webster, and Elisabeth Bronfen, eds. *Death and Representation*. Baltimore: Johns Hopkins University Press, 1993.

Holland, Sharon Patricia. *Raising the Dead: Readings of Death and (Black) Subjectivity*. Durham: Duke, 2000.

Klaver, Elizabeth, ed. Introduction. *Images of the Corpse*. Madison: University of Wisconsin Press, 2004. xi–xx.

Mendelson, Michael. "The Body in the Next Room: Death as Differend." *Images of the Corpse*. Ed. Elizabeth Klaver. Madison: University of Wisconsin Press, 2004. 186–205.

Rayner, Alice. *Ghosts: Death's Double and the Phenomena of Theatre*. Minneapolis: University of Minnesota Press, 2006.

Roach, Joseph. *Cities of the Dead*. New York: Columbia University Press, 1996.

Schmidt, Peter. *William Carlos Williams, the Arts, and Literary Tradition*. BatonRouge: Louisiana State University Press, 1988.

Weinstock, Jeffrey Andrew. Introduction. *Spectral America: Phantoms and the National Imagination*. Madison: University of Wisconsin Press, 2004. 3–17.

Williams, William Carlos. *Selected Poems*. Ed. Charles Tomlinson. New York: New Directions, 1985.

PART I
Studying the Corpse

Chapter 1

A Representation of Death in an Anti-Vietnam War Play by Luis Valdez: *Dark Root of a Scream*[1]

Jorge A. Huerta

If we do not act, we shall surely be dragged down the long, dark, and shameful corridors of time reserved for those who possess... strength without sight.

Dr. Martin Luther King, Jr., 1968

Today, the sixteenth of September, the day of independence for all Mexican peoples, I declare my independence of the Selective Service System. I accuse the government of the United States of America of genocide against the Mexican people... of creating a funnel which shoots Mexican youth into Vietnam to be killed and to kill innocent men, women and children.

Rosalío Muñoz, 1969 (217)

I might even get killed. If I do, they'll bring me back here in a box, covered with the flag.....

"Johnny," *Soldado razo* Luis Valdez and the Teatro Campesino, 1971
(Valdez, *Early Works* 123)

The 1960s and 1970s were a turbulent time in the history of the United States, especially for its marginalized citizens. The incipient Civil Rights Movement of the 1950s rallied people from all ethnicities and walks of life, and by the mid-1960s many of those same people marched against what they perceived to be an immoral war in Vietnam. A "conflict," as it was dubbed by the politicos, had become, by 1968, a full-fledged war that tore families and communities and the country itself apart. Few people outside the Latino communities knew then and fewer still know today, that a disproportionate number of Chicanos were dying in Vietnam (Guzman 12–15).[2] Also little-known outside the barrios, Chicana and Chicano activists were marching and rallying, hoping to alert the community

---

[1] I would like to acknowledge the assistance of my graduate Research Assistants, Ashley Lucas and especially Jade Power, in the completion of this article.

[2] For more on the Chicana/o experience in Vietnam and on the home front, see Mariscal, *Aztlán*.

to the gross injustices of the war as thousands of Chicanos were being drafted. Misinformation was the norm, but activists and artists from all communities were not standing-by; they would not let themselves be silenced by the government from protesting the slaughter.

One such activist was Luis Miguel Valdez, an undergraduate student leader at San Jose State College, California, in the early anti-Vietnam War Movement. Valdez was a popular and charismatic speaker on campus and in the community during the early 1960s, who initially aligned himself with Castro's Marxist Revolution. As a member of the first group of US students in the "Venceremos Brigade"[3] to Cuba in 1964, Valdez was energized by the revolutionary fervor he and his friend, Roberto Rubalcava, witnessed. The two wrote: "The Mexican in the United States has been, and continues to be, no less a victim of American imperialism than his impoverished brothers in Latin America" (Valdez and Steiner 215). In his analysis of this statement, Jorge Mariscal observes, "Valdez and Rubalcava situated Chicano issues within the larger context of Latin American history, and argued that 'the example of Cuba will inevitably bring socialist revolution to the whole of Latin America'" (*Brown* 110). As the son of migrant Mexican farm workers, Valdez knew all-too-well a life of poverty, displacement and struggle in his own country. He witnessed hardships daily and aligned himself with his fellow Mexican, Filipino, and Chicano farm workers. But Valdez's world-view was also informed by his Yaqui mother who inspired interest in his indigenous roots from an early age; this would influence his later creative and political work as well.

Valdez's first full-length play, *The Shrunken Head of Pancho Villa*, was produced at San Jose State College in 1964 while he was a student.[4] I believe it is important to begin with this play because it is Valdez's first such effort and also because it stands in sharp contrast to the aesthetic journey the playwright would undertake during the next three years. Between 1964 and 1967 Valdez developed two distinct theatrical forms, the *acto* (in collaboration with his troupe) and his own vision, the *mito*, or myth. In the playwright's words, the acto is the Chicano "through the eyes of man," while the mito is the Chicano "through the eyes of God" (Valdez, *Early Works* 11). It is his first mito, *Dark Root of a Scream* (1967),[5] which is the focus of this study, for it signals the beginning of Valdez's fascination with Aztec and Maya mythical iconography re-configured within a contemporary

---

3   *Venceremos* means "we will overcome."

4   San Jose State College is now called San Jose State University, and is a part of the 23-campus California State University system.

5   For another discussion of this mito, see Diamond.

Mechicano[6] setting.[7] What I intend to do here is to discuss this *mito* as an example of one playwright's Mexican/Chicano view of Death in a time of great crisis for the country as well as for the Chicanos and Mexicans living in the United States.

A Search for Identity: The *Shrunken Head of Pancho Villa*

In his preface to the published version of *The Shrunken Head of Pancho Villa*, Valdez prepares the reader and production team for the style he envisions: "The play therefore contains realistic and surrealistic elements working together to achieve a transcendental expression of the social condition of La Raza en los Estados Unidos [Mexicans/Chicanos in the United States].... In short, it must reflect the psychological reality of the barrio" (154). This play revolves around the central figure of Belarmino, a character *who has no body* and claims to be the lost head of Pancho Villa. For the twenty-four-year-old Valdez, the Chicano reality could only be expressed through the surreal (a bodiless head) juxtaposed with characters and situations that are also extensions of reality.

One of the most perplexing images in this play is created by the cockroaches that grow ever larger, crawling all over the walls, in true surrealistic fashion. Worse, Belarmino's sister, Lupe, feeds these repulsive creatures to him and eventually eats them as well. You do not have characters eating cockroaches in your play without expectations. Expectations that your audience members will not soon forget the imagery, and the hope that they will think about what they have just witnessed. I believe this is Valdez's metaphor for what he terms "the psychological reality of the barrio": confusion created by displacement.

The young writer employed exaggeration for political reasons. Belarmino claims to be the head (posthumously decapitated) of the Mexican revolutionary, Pancho Villa, and politicizes the hero, Joaquin, who represents the revolutionary Chicano. Joaquin is the most sympathetic character, the misunderstood "vato loco," a disenfranchised street youth in constant trouble with the authorities and in conflict with his brother Domingo, who transforms into "Mr. Sunday" in his

---

6   The term, "Mechicano" refers to both the Mexicans from Mexico and the native-born Chicanos living in the US. The experiences of growing up in the US as a marginalized Chicano are different from the experiences of having been raised in Mexico, where class, not national origin, distinguishes the individuals. When both the Mexicans and the Chicanos experience the same kind of treatment they can be called "Mechicanos."

7   Now that Latinas and Latinos are becoming the fastest-growing group(s) in the United States, attention must be paid to the distinctions between the three largest groups: the Chicanos, Puerto Ricans, and Cubans. Each group has its own cultural practices and religious beliefs, from the hybrid of African-Christian faiths that permeate the Caribbean to the combinations of indigenous and Christian faiths that one finds in Mexico and other parts of Central and South America. I urge the reader not to conflate these three groups as I discuss the Chicano and Mexican view of Death.

total rejection of Mexican and Chicano culture. After spending time in jail for robbing supermarkets to feed the poor, Joaquin comes home without a head. The juxtaposition of the bodiless head and the headless body is clear: combine them for a complete, revolutionary man. It is the playwright's hope that the confusion he perceives in the barrio will be replaced by a political consciousness, his "psychological reality" more informed by an awareness of marginalization than by Freudian analysis. Valdez's characters and the situations in which they find themselves are representative of the playwright's dislocation, which he believes is universal to working class Mechicanos.[8]

In Valdez's early vision, the mystery of Belarmino's condition is not determined by supernatural forces, but, rather, by the playwright in his attempt to educate, to entertain and to horrify. Years after the first production of the play, Valdez told an audience that his older brother was the model for Mr Sunday and that he (Luis) is represented in the character of Joaquin. He then admitted: "people didn't exactly get it... the horror, the horror of watching a brother become a stranger and the horror of watching somebody get their head cut off" (Valdez, *Keynote Address*). In the fall of 2005 Valdez revealed that his first play was actually influenced by Ionesco and the absurdists, something I had never previously read or heard from him.[9] Whether surreal or absurd, for the young playwright his play was a visceral response to the loss of a brother to total acculturation through denial of his Mexican heritage, and the loss of cultural identity through brainwashing symbolized by decapitation. There is one actual death in this play when the alcoholic father apparently gets killed by a train. But the metaphoric death of the brother, Domingo/Mr Sunday, was a more powerful and enduring image in much of Valdez's (and subsequent Chicana and Chicano playwrights') works. In many ways, this experiment in playwriting set the tone for all of Valdez's later works, none of which can be termed realistic.

Taking the Revolution to the Fields of California

After graduating from San Jose State College in 1964 Valdez joined the San Francisco Mime Troupe under the direction of Ron Davis. This Marxist collective introduced Valdez to street theatre, to *commedia dell'arte* with a social message. In the fall of 1965 he and a group of striking farm workers founded the Teatro

---

[8]   As seen in his later play, *I Don't Have to Show You No Stinking Badges* (1985), Valdez believes dislocation affects middle class Chicanos as well. While he was a student, however, Valdez's references were to the working class Mechicanos of his immediate experience.

[9]   Luis Valdez was speaking at a tribute to him and his company for forty years of social, artistic work at his alma mater, San Jose State University, on 27 October 2005. The Teatro Campesino documented this day-long event, which was organized by San Jose State University, Professor Ethel Walker, Ashley Lucas, and me.

Campesino as the cultural and educational arm of Cesar Chavez and Dolores Huerta's fledgling farm workers' union. Much has been written about the early days of the Teatro by this author and many others. Most importantly, the aesthetic trademark of the early group became the collectively created actos Valdez guided as he and his farm workers-cum-actors improvised scenarios aimed at getting other farm workers to join the Union. Using minimal props and costumes, while wearing masks and signs around their necks to identify their place in the social strata ("Farm Worker," "Boss," "Scab," and so on), the Teatro actors educated and entertained their fellow union members and prospective members.[10]

Valdez and the Teatro members made the difficult decision to leave the ranks of the farm workers' union in 1967 in an attempt to focus on their craft. This was especially important for the director/playwright, who needed the time to write his own plays. The Teatro would never abandon the farm workers' issues and many subsequent works would feature farm workers and their families in crisis. But you cannot run a fledgling theatre company and a growing farm workers' union as well. The call to write beckoned Valdez and he answered it as he began to develop his mitos, which meant a return to his indigenous roots.

The Chicano Artists Discover the Aztecs

Before turning to *Dark Root of a Scream*, I believe it is important to trace the roots of a Mexican/Chicano view of Death. The subject of death and the mystery that surrounds it have been around as long as there have been people to witness and wonder at the moment someone dies. The Big Question—Where do they go?—can only be answered by theology or myth. Some cultures believe in an afterlife, others see death as the end of life. Today, we refer to someone having "passed away," which connotes a journey, a passing to the "hereafter" of some kind, to "the Other Side." In a classical European world-view, we recall the myths of the Greeks with their Hades and their River Styx. Christian thought changed that concept and offers a variety of scenarios for an afterlife. But to understand the Chicanos' views of life and death, one must turn to the indigenous cultures of Mesoamerica. That is what the Chicano artists began to do in the 1960's: create or re-create a Chicano mythos based on Mexican and Pre-Columbian heroes and myths.

Most prominent and visible among Chicano artistic expressions of the early period were the murals painted on public buildings, meeting halls, housing projects, and the like all over the southwest.[11] Many of these murals portrayed

---

[10]   The acto form continues to be a staple of incipient Chicano theatre groups around the country, for it is based on the experiences of the creators and reflects the struggles of whoever attempts to create their own statement against any form of oppression, from police brutality to biased judges and racist police, etc. For more on the early Teatro Campesino's actos see Huerta, *Chicano Theater* 14-27, and Valdez, *Early Works* 6–134.

[11]   For more on the Chicano murals see Griswold del Castillo et al. and Tréguer.

revolutionary icons such as Cesar Chavez, Che Guevara, or Pancho Villa. Others recreated Mexico's Patron Saint, the Virgin of Guadalupe, or Aztec and Maya pyramids and mythical figures in an effort to give their Chicano brethren a sense of their ancestors' rich history. However, a mural or painting can only tell the viewer so much. And even though "a picture is worth a thousand words," those words may be lost if the person viewing the image has no references, no connections to that image. Study a painting of Quetzalcóatl, the "Feathered Serpent," and you may only see what appears to be a snake with feathers. The snake as symbol has many meanings, of course, but what of the feathers? Where are the wings? What does it all mean to a contemporary Chicana/o who has probably been taught through Christian narratives that indigenous religions are pagan and that the snake is a symbol of evil?

Given the various recreations of indigenous symbols I have seen on numerous murals in barrios throughout the US, it becomes clear that if visual artists do not provide a narrative, it is up to the writers, poets, songwriters, and playwrights to give those images and concepts a place in the Chicano imaginary. In his introduction to a special issue of *El Grito* dedicated to Chicano drama in 1974, Herminio Rios-C wrote: "It is indeed impossible to understand many Chicano literary works without a knowledge of Nahuatl [Aztec] and Mayan mythology. Many Chicano writers are exploring this part of our history and are actualizing it in terms of contemporary realities" (6).

Something strange happens when the Mechicana/o playwright has to educate audiences about their Mexican history and mythologies, substituting Aztec or Maya beliefs for the more familiar European myths. As Herminio Rios-C stated a generation ago, Mechicano audiences do not automatically recognize or identify with Aztec and Maya gods and goddesses. Indeed, most people cannot pronounce names like Quetzalcóatl, Itzamná, or Coyolxhaqui, much less identify with them. But that was the challenge to those playwrights who wanted to bring the gods back to their contemporary Mechicano audiences: to transform Zeus into Itzamná, substitute Guadalupe with Tonantzín and replace Mount Olympus with Teotihuacán. That is what Luis Valdez chose to do, setting a mythico/historical quest for himself and his communities.

The Aztecs and Death

In the words of David Iguaz, "Death in ancient Aztec Mexico formed an integral part of daily life and was considered just a further stage in the continuation of life towards the individual's final resting place. Death was to be found everywhere in the form of sacrificial rites, religious rituals, mourning celebrations and funerary festivities" (Iguaz 63). In his seminal book on the Mesoamericans, *Pre-Columbian Literatures of Mexico*, Miguel León-Portilla writes of the Aztecs: "There is also ample proof in the codices and Náhuatl poetry that the Ancient Mexicans gave considerable thought to death.... [T]here are many references to death in battle, death of the victims who were sacrificed..." (83). León-Portilla notes that in their poems the Aztecs saw death as both a dreaded mystery and as a kind of release. One poem begins:

> Given over to sadness
> We remain here on earth.
> Where is the road
> that leads to the Region of the Dead,
> the place of our downfall,
> the country of the fleshless?

and ends with the following image:

> I will have to go down there;
> nothing do I expect.
> They leave us,
> given over to sadness. (León-Portilla 85)[12]

León-Portilla then contrasts this poem with the following, more hopeful vision:

> Truly I say:
> certainly it is not the place of happiness
> here on earth.
> Certainly one must look somewhere else,
> where indeed, happiness will exist.
> Or only in vain have we come to the earth? (86)[13]

The third example of an Aztec death poem cited by León-Portilla fits the theme of Valdez's play even more.

> Thus the dead were addressed,
> when they died.
> If it was a man, they spoke to him,
> invoked him as a divine being,
> in the name of pheasant;
> if it was a woman, in the name of owl;
> and they said to them:
> "Awaken, already the sky is tinged with red,
> already the dawn has come,
> already the flame-colored pheasants are singing,
> the fire-colored swallows,

---

[12] Quoted by León-Portilla from the *Cantares Mexicanos*, fol. 14r.

[13] Quoted by León-Portilla from the *Cantares*, fol. I V.

already butterflies are on the wing."
For this reason the ancient ones said,
he who has died, he becomes a god.
They said: "He became a god there,"
which means that he died. (62)[14]

Not only the dreaded mystery and hopeful release of death, but also its divine dimension, as expressed by the Aztecs, can be found in Valdez's play–along with its Mayan roots.

The Quiché Maya and Their *Popol Vuh*

In 1968, the year after the first production of *Dark Root of a Scream*, a Mexican anthropologist, Domingo Martínez Parédez, published his controversial book, *El Popol Vuh tiene razón: teoría sobre la cosmogonía, preamericana* [*The Popol Vuh is Correct: A Theory of Precolumbian Cosmogony*]. The *Popol Vuh* is perhaps the most discussed of pre-Columbian writings because it stands alone as a Quiché Maya book of origins. Martínez Parédez raised the eyebrows of the academy by declaring that this book, previously viewed as myth, in fact explained the creation of the solar system according to scientific theories adapted centuries later by European scientists.[15] Most important to Valdez, and to this study, Martínez Parédez reveals that the Maya word, *mucnal*, means both "to bury a body" and "to plant the corn" (153).[16] Thus, to the Maya, as to other indigenous peoples of Mesoamerica, there was, in this sense, no death. The treatise by Martínez Parédez would become important to Valdez as he further developed his Mexican-indigenous view of life and death.

The Twentieth Century Mexican and Death: Two Views

Just as indigenous myths influenced Valdez and other Chicana/o artists, we must also take into consideration an extension of those beliefs in Mexican culture as expressed in the Dia de los Muertos [Day of the Dead], November 2nd. On this day families commune with the dearly departed, cleaning and decorating their graves and then eating a meal "with the dead." Although non-Mexicans may find

---

[14] Quoted by León-Portilla from the *Códice Matrinsense de la Real Academia*, fol. 195 r.

[15] From an informal discussion with Luis Valdez in the spring of 1973.

[16] "[M]ORIR es BAJAR, y esto es innegable, porque el cuerpo BAJA a la sepultura y a ésta se llama MUCNAL–ENTERRAR MAIZ." ["To die is to go down, and this is undeniable because the body is lowered into the grave and this is called *mucnal*—to plant the corn." My translation.]

this practice rather morbid, for Mechicanos it is a responsibility and an honor. In Mexico and in Mexican barrios in the US, street vendors sell skeleton toys, sugar candies in the shape of skulls, and other reminders that we all look alike, rich or poor, fat or thin, beneath the skin.

As seen in the engravings of José Guadalupe Posada, the Mexican sees Death as both comic and tragic, as just another state of being.[17] In their earliest posters, the Teatro Campesino used Posada's delightful engravings of cavorting skeletons and in later productions staged entire plays with characters dressed as *calaveras* (skeletons), causing one confused critic to refer to the play as a "Halloween program" (Sullivan, "El Teatro" 9). But death has a special meaning to the modern Mexican. As Octavio Paz stated many years ago:

> The word death is not pronounced in New York, in Paris, in London, because it burns the lips. The Mexican, in contrast, is familiar with death, jokes about it, caresses it, sleeps with it, celebrates it; it is one of his favorite toys and his most steadfast love. True, there is perhaps as much fear in his attitude as in that of others, but at least death is not hidden away: he looks at it face to face, with impatience, disdain or irony. (57–58)

More recently, another well-known Mexican author, Carlos Fuentes, in speaking about the first quintessential Mexican picaresque novel, Juan Rulfo's classic, *Pedro Páramo*, wrote: "Because of this novelist, we have been present at our own death. We are better able to understand that the life/death duality does not exist, that the life-or-death option does not exist, that Death is in fact part of life, that everything is life" (63). Even death is life, as Luis Valdez shows us in his mito.

Dark Root of a Scream

When Valdez's *Dark Root of a Scream* was initially produced in 1967, the playwright/director and his troupe were removing themselves from the daily struggles of organizing farm workers. Whereas the first actos dealt with unionizing issues, Valdez knew that he must move beyond the farm workers' problems to deal with the concerns of the majority of Mexicans and Chicanos who were (and are) urban. The troupe had not moved too far away from its roots in Delano, California, but Valdez needed that symbolic distance to re-focus his creative energies and delve into the mysteries of life and death on a mythic level. Therefore the mito became a re-imagining and re-articulation of the Chicanos' indigenous cultures and mythologies. Death was never too far from the workers' realities as they stood their ground at the edges of the corporate farms they were striking against, facing guards wielding clubs and shotguns. To these humble workers fighting for decent wages and better living and working conditions, the possibility of imminent death

---

[17] For samples of Posada's prints, see Berdecio and Applebaum 2–19.

was real. Furthermore, Chavez and his followers knew that the indiscriminate use of pesticides in the fields was causing deadly diseases among the workers. The young playwright's response was to evoke the Mesoamerican redeemer, Quetzalcóatl, in *Dark Root of a Scream*.

The title for this mito was inspired by a line at the ending of Federico García Lorca's *Bodas de sangre*, known to English-speakers as *Blood Wedding*. In the final scene, the Mother is mourning the death of her last surviving son:

> these two men killed each other for love.
> With a knife
> with a tiny knife
> that barely fits in the hand,
> but that slides in clean
> through the astonished flesh
> and stops at the place
> where trembles, enmeshed,
> the dark root of a scream. (99)

In the original language the last two lines read:

> donde tiembla enmarañada
> la oscura raíz del grito. (662–63)

The word, *enmarañada*, can be translated as "tangled" or even "confused," terms which I think better serve the immensity of the moment than "enmeshed." The scream is tangled, confused, just as we might imagine the final moments of the mito's Chicano hero, Quetzalcóatl González, a fallen Chicano solider known to his friends and family as Indio.

Not all cultures have wakes and most do not hold their wakes in a living room, but in this mito the action takes place at a wake. Here Valdez is recalling the rural custom, especially in Mexico, wherein the deceased is, indeed, laid out in a coffin in the family home. Joseph Roach's splendid study, *Cities of the Dead*, has much to teach us about death and dying, and especially about "the feathered peoples," the indigenous cultures of the Americas and their culture clash with the European conquerors. Roach's description of "mortuary ritual," focusing here on funerals, can also be applied to a wake:

> In any funeral, the body of the deceased performs the limits of the community called into being by the need to mark its passing. United around a corpse that is no longer inside but not yet outside of its boundaries, the members of a community may reflect on its symbolic embodiment of loss and renewal. (14)

Roach's reference to "loss and renewal" fits our mito perfectly, for that is what Valdez is portraying here, the loss of a young Chicano but the hope for renewal through the climax of the piece.

According to Valdez's stage directions, the setting for his mito is "a collage of myth and reality" (*Root* 3). The central image is an indigenous pyramid whose different levels represent the Chicano's progression from earthly to spiritual. The pyramid changes as it ascends from a composition of "iron and the hard steel of modern civilization–guns, knives, automobile parts; others reveal a less violent, more spiritual origin–molcajetes [Mexican stone mortars], rebozos [shawls], crucifixes, etc." These earthly objects blend into indigenous symbols as the pyramid rises, crowned with conches, jade, and feathered serpent heads. Although this is not indicated in the published script, in a 1971 production of this play the lighting shifted from the street to the wake as the dialogue undulated from one side to the other. Though the play can be produced without a complex lighting plan, the 1971 production benefited greatly from the spectacle.

From the beginning of this play, with its symbolic setting, the audience is aware that it is witnessing a non-realistic vision. The curtain rises on the fantastic setting and the two tableaux of characters at the base of the pyramid. Stage left is the wake, with a priest, an older woman, and a young woman. These three are entering through a curtained doorway and they freeze as the action immediately shifts to the street scene and the three *vatos* who draw our attention. The vatos are typical Chicano street youths in dress and demeanor, but their faces are made up to look like their nicknames: Gato (Cat), Lizard, and Conejo (Rabbit). These nicknames echo the barrio custom of giving someone a name that fits his or her character (such as "Smiley") or physical features (such as "Tiny"). The makeup and costumes of the three youths reflect their animal characteristics and recall indigenous attitudes toward their animal types. Lizard is a sexual animal, snake-like and obsessed with the physical. Gato is cunning and evil, the major antagonist in this play. Conejo is kind and softhearted, yet the wisest of the three. He is the main connection with the dead soldier and, like his sister, whom we will presently meet, Conejo defends the fallen warrior.

In a meticulously planned and well-timed technique, the action shifts from side to side. The undulating rhythm is at first slow, then builds to a point where the dialogue of the two separate scenes is melded into what seems a single conversation. This duality of scenes and dialogue is a metaphor for the redeemer-figure, Quetzalcóatl, for the feathered serpent represents the coming together of the terrestrial (the serpent) and the heavenly (the quetzál bird). The kindly Quetzalcóatl is the giver of life and symbol of divine transcendence over the mundane. Here, Valdez is rediscovering ancestral philosophies. He finds a sharper focus in this play as he creates a modern mito that compares the god and cultural hero Quetzalcóatl with a contemporary Chicano leader of the same name. *Dark Root of a Scream* is basically a history lesson, but the premise on which it is based creates a fascinating drama.

While *The Shrunken Head of Pancho Villa* was constantly moving forward with crises and continual entrances and exits of characters, *Dark Root of a Scream* is much more dependent upon the past to move the action forward. It is the story of the dead soldier, and his past is recalled by the characters in the two scenes as they discuss his life. What could become a boring biography is kept interesting by Valdez's constant use of colorful, witty dialogue and the contrast of the two settings. The opening line, delivered by Lizard, "Come on, ese, let's toke up" (3), immediately identifies these other-worldly characters as contemporary vatos, smoking that ever-present symbol of their defiance, marijuana. Their dialogue tells us who they are and that they knew Indio. We learn that Conejo's sister was Indio's girlfriend. The scene shifts suddenly to the opposite side of the stage where the priest says, "That's it, easy does it, Señora Gonzales. No sense in getting hysterical about these things" (4).The priest, we discover, is not Mexican or Latino, though he does speak Spanish when he communicates with the mother. His opening remarks establish him as somewhat cold, an outsider who feels that he knows what is best for his barrio parishioners. Though he speaks the language, he obviously has little understanding of the people. The true mourners are the mother, Dalia, and her brother, Conejo. The attitudes of the other three range from the indifference of the priest to the hostility of Gato. The Valdezian family in crisis is reduced to a suffering mother-figure who has lost everybody: her husband and her three sons. The first son died in World War II, the second in Korea, and the last lies in a coffin beside her. Now the mother is left with mere extensions of her son: Dalia and Dalia's brother, who was his friend. The family has, in effect, crumbled, and we find these vestiges of a once-proud people in verbal combat with the others to protect the image of the dead Chicano.

At the beginning of Scene IV, the mother finds blood dripping from the flag draped over the coffin. This discovery makes her think that her son is alive in the coffin, and she shouts, "¡Mi hijo esta vivo! [My son is alive!]," foreshadowing the major premise of the play: Quetzalcóatl lives (5). She faints from the stress of this discovery, and the action shifts quickly to the next scene on the street. In the following scene the dialogue begins to alternate between settings and characters. At first, the transition is subtle. The boys are discussing another dead soldier whose body had already begun to reek of death at his funeral and Gato remarks: "I bet Indio smells like that." Immediately, the scene shifts to the wake, where the priest offers the stricken mother a cloth soaked with alcohol and says: "Here, madre, smell this" (6). Though the numbering of the scene does not change, the focus remains on the wake rather than the street. Scene VI then switches back to the street, and we continue to learn about Indio's past. Once again, in Scene VIII, the dialogue fuses, this time as if the two conversations were identical.

The boys discuss Indio's given name and Conejo says, "Quetzalcóatl, the feathered serpent," to which the priest adds: "Quetzalcóatl Gonzales. What a name for an American soldier. I wonder what it means? The first part, of course. Everyone knows what Gonzales means" (8). Conejo then answers the question as if he had been asked by one of the vatos. The conversations have become one now and, though the characters are separated in time and space, their discussion clarifies the differences in objectivity about the dead soldier. Scene IX illustrates the different levels of communication between the characters as Conejo and Dalia answer questions for the priest and Lizard.

PRIEST: How did Indio come to have a name like that?
CONEJO: His father name him that.
PRIEST: Oh yes, his father. How did his father–?
DALIA: He was a teacher in Mexico.
CONEJO: His name was Mixcóatl-Cloud-serpent.
PRIEST: I see. A nationalist, eh?
LIZARD: So what, man? Over here he was a wetback, a farm laborer just like everybody else.
PRIEST: A political exile, no doubt.
CONEJO: He knew a lot about Mexican history. Quetzalcóatl used to be a god for the Indians a long time ago.
LIZARD: Sure, man, the Apaches. (8)

Both the priest and Lizard hold negative attitudes toward Indio and his culture, which are bred of ignorance and insensitivity. The priest represents the Church's outright hostility toward indigenous beliefs. But the street youth is indicative of another form of cultural bias. Lizard can only think of "Apaches" when the image of an Indian comes to mind, the product of John Wayne movies and television stereotypes. Lizard's line is also an example of Valdez's juxtaposition of the serious with the sardonic, the ridiculous with the sublime. Like many immigrants to this country, Indio's father left his country an educated man, only to become another common laborer.

As the scenes evolve and the dialogue continues to undulate from one group to the other, the discussion centers around the god Quetzalcóatl, the Toltec leader named after him, and the Chicano named after both. Valdez does not bother to distinguish between the myths surrounding the Toltec leader Ce Acatl Topiltzin Quetzalcóatl and the god after whom he was named, for the central theme is the parallel between the indigenous figure, whether god or man, and his contemporary incarnation.[18] It is Valdez's intention to draw comparisons between the indigenous myth and the Chicano mito as his characters describe the corresponding qualities of each. Like the indigenous figure, Indio was a man of peace who worked to stop street violence and restore the Chicanos' pride in their heritage and culture. Indio was a contemporary leader who was drafted in the prime of his cause, a victim of the racism the priest accused him of. This juxtaposition is interesting, for the audience knows that it is the priest, not the Chicano, who is basically racist in his inability to comprehend the youth's motives for trying to help his people.

---

[18]   As Miguel León-Portilla demonstrates, there are various versions of the life and times of Quetzalcóatl. See pages 31–33; 37–42, 109–112 and 127–130.

In an interesting parallel, Valdez shows both the god, Quetzalcóatl, and Indio, the young Chicano, being betrayed by priests. Conejo tells the boys that the legendary Quetzalcóatl was deceived by evil priests who despised him because he would not permit human sacrifice. They thus got him drunk and showed him who he really was in a mirror. Shamed, Quetzalcóatl fled on a raft of serpents, promising to return. Likewise, Indio was betrayed by the priest and Mexican Americans in his parish who did not allow him to use the church hall for meetings. When Indio got drafted, he consulted with the priest about what to do. The priest tells Dalia: "He was considering fleeing the country, but he knew he'd never be able to return as a community leader" (12). Gato responds in the other scene: "Big community leader. That draft notice showed him to his face who he was, like a mirror." Gato's reference to the mirror immediately recalls the original Quetzalcóatl's downfall and parallels the Mesoamerican practice of human sacrifice with the sacrifice of human beings in Vietnam.

The vatos decide to go to the wake after Gato and Lizard have a scuffle. Gato is clearly the other's superior, and the emotional climax of the threatened knife fight is comically dissipated by Lizard's cocky strut offstage after he has composed himself. Lizard's exit is juxtaposed with the priest's next line: "Now we will pray" (15) as the scene shifts back to the wake and the requiem for the dead. The three youths appear at the door and clumsily enter the service. Gato sits by Dalia and attempts to get fresh with her, while the priest chants, "Quetzalcóatl, your humble servant," and the others repeat, "Bless him, Señor" (15). The service is halted when the youths repeat, "Your humble *serpent*," and the priest discovers Gato's lascivious advances toward Dalia. Pandemonium breaks out and the priest rushes out for the police with Lizard close behind him. Gato tells Conejo to try and stop him, and the intensity builds until the mother lets out a blood-chilling wail and attacks Gato. This stops Gato; then, as the mother sobs over her son's coffin, Lizard enters dressed in the priest's cassock.

Once again there is a mixture of pathos and the grotesque as Lizard tells the others that the priest is running down the streets "in his shorts" (18). Suddenly he notices the mother and Dalia at the coffin; they have discovered more blood dripping onto the floor. As the boys decide who is going to open the coffin, the mother steps up to it and pulls up the lid. Conejo looks in and says, "It's... feathers!" Lizard reaches in and pulls out "a brilliant headdress of green feathers and a cloak of Aztec design" (19). He puts these ancient vestments on and asks: "How do I look, ese?" as drums begin to beat in the background. They all look toward the coffin and Lizard, looking very much like an Aztec priest atop a ceremonial pyramid, reaches into the casket, pulls out something, and lifting it in his hands screams: "Indio's heart!" (19). The stage directions tell us that "the heart gives out light in the descending darkness" and the play ends.

In the 1971 production mentioned above, the scrim behind the pyramid dissolved, revealing the silhouette of the mythical Quetzalcóatl in his indigenous finery, looming above everything as the heart emitted a pulsating light in Lizard's hands. Just as he had promised, Quetzalcóatl had returned. In his review of that production, Dan Sullivan asked: "Is that a dead soldier or a dead god lying under the American Flag in the funeral parlor? If a dead god, is he dead forever? If a dead soldier, need there be others?" Sullivan recognized Valdez's genius in this production and noted that his plays "seem to spring from a far more comprehensive view of life than most Americans can manage without confusion" (Sullivan, "Homecoming" 6). *Dark Root of a Scream* evoked many images and called upon its audience to go back and forth in time and space just as the action had. In Valdez's mito, that bleeding, pulsating heart must be likened to the Sacred Heart of Jesus, which represents eternal life, not death, in Roman Catholic beliefs. The light that emanates from the heart is energy; it lives and so, too, does Quetzalcóatl.

I believe that *Dark Root of a Scream* remained for several years Valdez's finest dramatic achievement, but it was seldom produced. The cost of an adequate production and the unique and specific spectacle required to produce this play made it virtually impossible to tour to the usual barrio locations. Also, within a few years the war ended, causing the play to lose its immediacy. But during the 1980s, in the Reagan years, the US was intent on suppressing leftist movements in Central and South America and this mito became topical again. El Teatro Campesino produced *Dark Root of a Scream* in 1985, under the direction of Tony Curiel, its Associate Artistic Director. That production toured to the New York Shakespeare Festival's "Festival Latino," in tandem with its acto complement, *Soldado razo*, mentioned earlier in this chapter.[19] While Curiel and his production team did not alter the text to reflect the United States' surreptitious military actions in Latin America, anyone could see the metaphor.

Most recently, with the advent of George W. Bush's war in Iraq, the Teatro Campesino remounted *Dark Root of a Scream* in 2004 and adjusted the situation. This production was directed by Kinán Valdez, Luis and Lupe's youngest son, in the Teatro Campesino's playhouse in San Juan Bautista, California. In this adaptation the Madre has lost her first son in Vietnam, her second in the first Gulf War and Indio in Iraq. Although statistics show that Spanish-surnamed soldiers are not dying in disproportionate numbers in Iraq, they are dying and being wounded, to be sure. In a very topical reference in the 2004 adaptation, Indio, it appears, is not a citizen. Conejo tells the others, "The recruiter told him he'd get his *papeles* [papers] faster if he went."[20] In an effort to recruit more soldiers, this occurs today and many dead soldiers are awarded their citizenship posthumously.

It may be that the ending of this play leaves most audience members with more questions than answers. Yet, for those who believe the Mesoamerican philosophy, there is no death, only life-as-struggle, represented by Indio's pulsating heart. It is also important to consider the following interpretation of the significance of the blood and water that streamed from the crucified Christ's wound: "*Desde los primeros siglos... ha sido costumbre meditar sobre el costado abierto de Cristo y el misterio de la sangre y agua, y se ha visto a la Iglesia como naciendo de esa*

---

[19]   While the acto impressed *Village Voice* critic Michael Feingold, the mito did not.

[20]   From a typescript in my collection.

herida, del mismo modo como Eva nació del costado de Adán" (*Enciclopedia Católica*).[21] ["From the first centuries... it has been customary to meditate about Christ's open side and the mystery of the blood and the water, and the Church has been seen as having been born out of that wound, in the same manner as Eve was born of Adam's rib."] Could it be that Valdez is suggesting that Indio's blood, dripping from that coffin, can inspire a movement, a church of a different kind and purpose? If the pulsating heart still lives, does not Indio?

Perhaps Indio had to die, a sacrificial victim of late capitalism and what President Eisenhower called in 1961 the "military-industrial-complex." What Valdez invokes with this young Chicano's death is the uselessness of war in general and the Vietnam War in particular. Although Indio's life has been cut short, his fate must remain a lesson to other Chicanas and Chicanos not to go blindly into conflicts that will result in useless death and destruction. With this mito the playwright was taking a very anti-American position at a time when many Americans, of every stripe and color, were not proud of what the government was doing in the name of "America" and "freedom." Sadly, the same could be said of millions of Americans today. Although the Vietnam War is now a part of history, conflicts continue throughout the world and the play is still an important philosophical and artistic statement.

Works Cited

Berdecio, Roberto and Stanley Applebaum, eds., *Posada's Popular Mexican Prints*. New York: Dover, 1972.

Diamond, Betty. "Brown-eyed Children of the Sun: The Cultural Politics of El Teatro Campesino." Ann Arbor: University Microfilms, 1977. 160–171.

Enciclopedia Católica. http://www.enciclopediacatolica.com/d/devocioncorjesu. htm (Accessed 10 October 2009).

Feingold, Michael. "Festival Latino: Raza Sharp," *Village Voice* (20 Aug. 1985):109.

Fuentes, Carlos. *This I Believe*. Trans. Kristina Cordero. London: Bloomsbury, 2004.

García Lorca, Federico. *Blood Wedding*. Trans. James Graham-Lujan and Richard L. O'Connell. *3 Tragedies*. New York: New Directions Publishing, 1955. 34–102.

———. *Bodas de sangre*. *Obras completas*. Madrid: Aguilar, 1980.

---

[21] Cf. San Ambrosio, Expositio Evangelii secundum Lucam, 2, 85-89; Concilio Vaticano II, Lumen Gentium, 3; Sacrosanctum Concilium, 5, N.T. "Sin embargo, no existe constancia alguna de que durante los primeros diez siglos se haya rendido culto al Corazón herido." ["It goes without saying that there is no doubt that during the first ten centuries the wounded Heart was worshipped." My translation.]

Griswold del Castillo, Richard, Theresa McKenna, and Yvonne Yarbro-Bejarano, eds. *Chicano Art: Resistance and Affirmation, 1965–1985*. Los Angeles: Wight Gallery, 1991.

Guzman, Ralph. "Mexican-American Casualties in Vietnam," *La Raza* I (1970): 12–15.

Huerta, Jorge. *Chicano Theater: Themes and Forms*. Ypsilanti, Michigan: Bilingual Press, 1982.

Iguaz, David. "Mortuary Practices Among the Aztec in the Light of Ethnohistorical and Archaeological Sources," (Part I), *Papers from the Institute of Archaeology*. 4 (1993): 63–76.

León-Portilla, Miguel. *Pre-Columbian Literatures of Mexico*. Trans. Grace Lobanov and Miguel León-Portilla. Norman: University of Oklahoma Press, 1989.

Mariscal, George, ed. *Aztlán and Vietnam: Chicano and Chicana Experiences of the War*. Berkeley: University of California Press, 1999.

——. *Brown-Eyed Children of the Sun: Lessons From the Chicano Movement, 1965–1975*. Albuquerque: University of New Mexico Press, 2005.

Martínez Parédez, Domingo. *El Popol Vuh Tiene Razon: Teoría sobre la cosmogonía preamericana*. Mexico: Editorial Orion, 1986.

Muñoz, Rosalío. "Speech Refusing Induction." *Aztlán and Vietnam: Chicano and Chicana Experiences of the War*. Ed. George Mariscal. Berkeley: University of California Press, 1999.

Paz, Octavio. *The Labyrinth of Solitude: Life and Thought in Mexico*. New York: Grove, 1961.

Popul Vuh. Trans. Ralph Nelson. Boston: Houghton, 1976.

——. Delia Goetz and Sylvanus G. Morley from translation of Adrián Recinos, Norman: University of Oklahoma Press, 1969.

Rios-C, Herminio "Introduction." *El Grito*. (June-August 1974).

Roach, Joseph. *Cities of the Dead: Circum-Atlantic Performance*. New York: University of Colombia Press. 1996.

Sullivan, Dan. "El Teatro Campesino in a Halloween Program." *Los Angeles Times* 3 November 1970: IV, 9.

——. "Homecoming of a Dead GI," *Los Angeles Times* 25 September 1971: II, 6.

Tréguer, Annick. *Chicanos: Murs peints de États-Unis*. Paris: Concours de l'Université de la Sorbonne Nouvelle, 2001.

Valdez, Luis. *Early Works: Actos, Bernabé, and Pensamiento serpentino*. Houston: Arte Público Press, 1990.

——. "Eighteen Years After the Founding of El Teatro Campesino." Keynote address, 1983. Unpublished typescript in collection of Jorge Huerta.

——. *Dark Root of a Scream. West Coast Plays 19/20*. Los Angeles: California Theatre Council, 1986. 1–19.

——. *I Don't Have to Show You No Stinking Badges. Zoot Suit and Other Plays*. Houston: Arte Público Press, 1992. 21–94.

——. *The Shrunken Head of Pancho Villa. Necessary Theater: Six Plays About the Chicano Experience.* Ed. Jorge Huerta. Houston: Arte Público Press, 1989.

Valdez, Luis and Stan Steiner, eds. *Aztlán: An Anthology of Mexican American Literature.* New York: Vintage Books, 1972.

Chapter 2
Skins of Desire in Evolution:
The Black and White Murder Film,
Dutchman

Mark Pizzato

According to DNA evidence, all humans on earth today descend from Africans who developed their genes in various ways across that continent or migrated through the Arabian Peninsula and South Asia (50,000 years ago) to Australia, or through the Middle East and Central Asia (45–30,000 y.a.) into Europe, and eventually (20–10,000 y.a.) through Siberia to the Americas (Wells).[1] The differences today in human physical features and skin tones derive from that worldwide migration of our species and the successful genetic mutations of our ancestors, diverging in different climates. Dark skin protects the body's sweat glands and prevents the loss of folate (a B-vitamin needed for embryonic brain development and sperm generation) to the sun's harsher ultraviolet rays in the tropics (Jablonski and Chaplin; Kirchwenger). People in higher latitudes developed fair skin to absorb more ultraviolet light and its benefit of vitamin D (especially needed during pregnancy and lactation). Thus, the evolution of skin color in different human groups has a biological basis, changing with the migration of our species, and then through the intermixing of "races." Yet we all belong to one family tree with its trunk in Africa. We bear traces of our dead ancestors—and of their bodies struggling to survive in various environments—in the successful genes passed on to us, producing our different skin tones and the advanced brains that we share as human beings.

During the millions of years prior to the migration of current *homo sapiens* across the globe, our brain structure evolved differently from that of other primates. Language abilities "invaded" the left hemisphere of the neocortex: supplementing the brainstem's instincts, limbic system's passions, and right hemisphere's spatial representations of mimetic actions with myth-making interpretations and executive controls in the left (LeDoux 303; Donald; Pizzato, *Ghosts*). Later, interpretations of skin color as "race" developed through each of these areas in the human brain, during cultural interactions that spread certain myths and mimetic performances of identity. Racism against others with darker skin emerged in particular due to the geographical luck of lighter-skinned humans in the Middle East and Europe

---

[1] For critiques of Wells's genetic research, see Gradie and Harpendin.

finding highly productive crops and animals in their regions, during the agricultural revolution 10,000 years ago (Diamond, *Guns*).

In the last 500 years, the migration of Europeans to other continents and their colonization of other peoples spread not only the evils of racism and slavery, but also the Renaissance and Enlightenment ideals of democracy. Eventually, a principle of universal, individual rights for all humans developed. But to what degree can the current ethics of "white" (Western) culture counter its cruel legacy and persistent tendencies of racism—especially through works of art where bodies with different skin tones perform?

In order to address this question through specific representations of black and white bodies onscreen, as living and dead characters haunted by racial ancestry, I will focus on the 1966 black and white film *Dutchman*, by British director Anthony Harvey, made from Amiri Baraka's 1964 drama of the same name. I will apply theories from evolutionary psychology, neurology, and psychoanalysis to this film (and play) about an interracial love affair and murder on a New York City subway car. How does the experience of this drama as cinema, with a white woman seducing and killing a black man onscreen, reflect race and gender relations—not only in the 1960s and today, but also regarding the longer time-scheme of human evolution, from nature's drives to culture's conflicted identifications of skin and sex? Do the screen bodies in *Dutchman*, as living and dead characters, merely express the dangers of racial envy and manipulative passions? Or do they also demonstrate the potential of theatre and cinema to contribute to our cultural evolution as black and white, male and female, within one species?

Desires as Memes

It has become a commonplace notion in postmodern theories of the body that gender, class, and race are performed through socially constructed signifiers. But such masks, costumes, and skins of desire are not just arbitrary signs. They are drenched in a bloody history—relating also to the prehistory of human evolution, with individuals and groups competing to survive and reproduce by conquering new environments. It is both the inheritance of different genetic traits in various human groups, migrating and adapting to diverse environments over tens of thousands of years, *and* more recent historical legacies of interpreting such differences that produces racism out of race in specific cultures. Social conflicts between white and black races in historical and modern times, along with genetic traces of prehistoric human migration and its evolution of different skin tones, hair types, and facial characteristics, show the long-term drama of our species—with the desires and fears of prior generations inherited, to some degree, by each new human brain.

Non-human animals have two primary drives, survival and reproduction, with specific instincts to organize their behavior according to these goals. But human nature evolved a cultural dimension vastly complicating its life or death needs and sexually selective drives with extra desires. Lacanian psychoanalytic theory describes this human situation as a "lack of being" or "want to be" (*manque à être*), which means that each person's desires are the "desires of the Other"—of parents and other authority figures who offer social ideals that give an illusory definition to the individual ego. Biologist Richard Dawkins and psychologist Susan Blackmore develop a related notion of "memes" (without reference to Lacan). Memes are gene-like ideas reproducing in human culture, through the "memeplexes" of social systems that use bodies and brains as their "vehicles." Dawkins coined the term *meme* from the ancient Greek word *mimesis*, which Aristotle discerned as the source of theatre (109–12, 297). He changed the root word *mime* to *meme*, making it sound like "gene"—thus combining the English words "mime" and "me"— in his theory of the "selfish gene." Like Dawkins, Blackmore views memes as influencing the evolution of humans as a species of "best imitators" with our particular theatrical abilities in life and art (129–31). As in Lacan's theory of the conflicting desires of the Other, appearing through and reshaping each person's sense of Self, memes compete for survival as the ideas, identities, and actions of persons in each human generation (extending human genetic success, from nature to culture). Even the idea of "free will," involving individual "human rights," may be a contingent desire and modern meme, stressed by Western culture—not an inevitable goal of our species (Blackmore 241–44; Gazzaniga and LeDoux 159–61). Yet, such ethical desires, like the racist memes they try to counter, have evolved from primal drives that are common to all human brains, according to Lacanian psychoanalysis, evolutionary psychology, and neuroscience.

Despite the radical contingency of the Other's desires and the cultural variability of parasitic memes, both are tied to primal life-or-death and erotic drives in the human animal—and thus to the panic, fear, rage, and lust systems in the brain's paleo-mammalian, limbic pathways and brainstem (Panksepp). Today's interpretations of black or white, male or female skin, on an enemy or a lover, can be traced back through personal and cultural desires to the evolutionary drives that we share as human beings. Such shared drives and competitive, memetic desires of race, class, and gender become expressed in *Dutchman* through plot conflicts and character revelations in a game of erotic seduction on a New York City subway car, en route to an explosion of violent rage by the black man and a ritualized murder of him by the white woman. Thus, *Dutchman* shows the desires of the Other, as parasitic memes, circulating through character's bodily perceptions, and exposing the drives of our species beyond skin color. This reveals the cultural and natural forces—as traces of ancestral dead bodies within the living—continuing to shape black and white, male and female identities in the 1960s and today.

Unlike its progenitor, the 1964 drama by Baraka, Harvey's 1966 film records certain historical actors (Shirley Knight and Al Freeman, Jr.) in specific costumes with particular performance choices, as the white and black characters, Lula and Clay. Audiences of Baraka's drama onstage today would see actors of our current historical habitus presenting their (and other artists') interpretations layered upon the script's indications of race, class, and gender memes. But spectators watching the film see certain memetic expressions of 1966 onscreen, reinterpreted through the personal and cultural desires of an audience now—while ghosted by the actors, designers, director, cinematographer, editor, and spectators of the past. Both historical layers in the 1960s and today, of memetic expression and interpretation, of psychological and political desires, are connected to a common human want of being and its warping of remnant animal drives—which gradually evolved during millions of years in Africa and then during the worldwide migration of human groups, which produced our current variations in skin color.

Much has been written about Baraka's *Dutchman* as an expression of the playwright's shame at assimilation and his rage for a new identity, as he moved from being a Greenwich Village poet with a white wife (Hettie Cohen) to being a black nationalist without her and leader of the Black Arts Movement with his own theatre in Harlem.[2] The early 1960s were a turning point for LeRoi Jones, as he became Imamu Amiri Baraka, shifting away from the Ralph Ellison tradition of black inclusion in the Anglo-American modernist canon, toward the diverse, rebellious powers of postmodern identity politics. Autobiographical interpretations of the play often focus on Clay's final speech, exploding with rage at whites who do not know the murderous desires behind the blues artists they admire. But what about Lula's seduction of (or by) Clay and evocation of this black rage, which she then uses as a justification for assassinating him? Is she merely a signifier of the white Other that Baraka wants to purge from black souls, or is she more complex as his and Clay's antagonist?[3] Does Clay remain just a spokesman for the author and director in the 1960s, or does he become a memetic prism for spectators to perceive in different ways today—through his living and dying as a black body on the subway car?

As a white, male reader of the play and viewer of the film (perhaps like the British filmmaker Anthony Harvey), I identify with both Lula and Clay in various ways: with Lula's desire to connect with black culture and with Clay's drive to connect with a sexy woman. When they first make eye contact, Lula not only flirts with Clay's "male gaze" (Mulvey), while posing on the platform, she also gazes at his black male face, judging his attractiveness through the subway car window. According to Baraka's initial stage directions, Clay "sees a woman's face staring at him through the window; when it realizes that the man has noticed the face, it begins very premeditatedly to smile" (4). Thus, from the beginning of the play, Lula becomes not just an object of male desire (as an "it"), but also an alien force reshaping Clay's subjectivity with a premeditative smile, like the *jouissance* of the (m)Other mirroring the child's earliest definitions of self, joy, and desire (Lacan).

Harvey's black and white film depicts this mirror-stage scene with Lula in a horizontally striped mini-skirt and large sunglasses, displaying her bare legs and exaggerating the size of her eyes. She licks her upper lip while Clay watches her

---

2   See Kumar; Löfgren 424; Piggford; Rebhorn; and Tate. These essays about *Dutchman* (and others cited here) concern the play, not the film, which has received very little, if any, scholarly analysis.

3   Cf. Bergesen and Demastes 225–26.

through his window. She shows her "desire to be desired" (Doane); yet she does not remain a passive object of the male gaze. She acts out, crossing racial and gender barriers by entering Clay's subway car and sitting next to him, "going some other way than mine," as she tells him (7). While embodying the desire of the Other for Clay, as sexy white woman to his assimilated male blackness, she also acts through the memes of sex, class, and race revolutions in the 1960s, which continue in other ways today.

Even if Clay and Lula were of the same race, this would be a provocative opening scene. But the different skin tones of the characters, evolved by their ancestors tens of thousands of years ago for environmental reasons, now become crucial in the cultural interpretations of their gazes—and in the views of spectators watching them. Viewers of the film today see two actors, Freeman and Knight, whose bodies existed a half century ago, nearer to the time of slavery and lynching, during the sexual liberation, civil rights, and black power movements of the 1960s. Lula exhibits an adventurous, perverse desire, breaking the norm for her gender in 1960s America or today, as she clutches Clay's knee and thigh, drapes her legs over his (in the film), and invites him to dance the "belly rub" on the train car with her. Clay, in his assimilationist suit and tie, stays properly in his seat, until his violent outbreak near the end of the play. But Lula transgresses from the beginning, expressing her racist fantasies and drawing out his as well. She uses her right-brain intuitions about Clay, playing with his erotic desires and their memetic perceptions of each other (as well as the audience's of them) to gradually deconstruct his left-brain, whitewashed, "civilized," self control.

Lula demonstrates her own left-brain, mythic dimension (in the playwright's and filmmaker's hands) by eating an apple as she enters the train car. She then offers an apple to Clay—like a modern Eve to a malleable Adam—after wrapping the first in a tissue and tossing it on the floor.[4] "Eating apples together is the first step," she says (11). But she has already teased out the knowledge of good and evil in Clay's gaze, by exposing his cross-racial desire and the sex drive behind it. She says she saw him "staring through that window down in the vicinity of my ass and legs" (7). In speaking this way, Knight also offers her body to the film's present spectators, through the male gaze of its director and the screen as window: "Run your mind over people's flesh." Unlike the viewers of this play onstage, today's spectators of the film *Dutchman* see Knight's legs at a certain point in the past, running their minds over her skin as an immortal photographic fetish from 40 years ago, masking the actress's own aging body in real life (and her later years as a plus-size actress). Freeman's body is likewise fetishized, as fictively living and dead in the drama onscreen, but also real during the 1960s, with a black power that evokes white lust and collective repression by Lula and others on the subway car.

Baraka's stage directions describe Lula as a thirty-year-old white woman, ten years older than the twenty-year-old Clay (3). Harvey's film shows her as closer

---

[4]   Cf. Clericuzio, who calls Lula "more similar to Lilith than to Eve" (117). See also Tate.

to Clay's age.[5] But she still plays a mimetic, seductive, mirror-stage game with Clay, as Eve-like mother goddess or clairvoyant witch,[6] using her right-brain, visuospatial, holistic, devil's advocate intuition to perceive and challenge the left-brain, audioverbal signifiers of his identity (Ramachandran and Blakeslee; Solms and Turnbull). She tells him he looks like "death eating a soda cracker" (8). She perceives him as being from New Jersey, as trying to grow a beard, and as having tried to "make it" with his sister when he was ten (8–9). All of this he indirectly admits, wondering if they have met before or if she knows his sister, or his friend, Warren Enright. She then describes Warren as a "tall skinny black boy with a phony English accent," though she says she never met him (10). She claims to know Clay like the palm of her hand because she knows his "type" (17). She tells him that his three-button suit comes from a tradition that oppresses him (18). She calls him a "murderer" and taunts him with racist terms: "escaped nigger," "liver-lipped white man," "Uncle Tom," and "Woolly Head" (21, 29–32). Eventually, by teasing Clay with the temptations of racist panic and rage, of erotic fear and lust, she provokes Clay into acting out his limbic passions in a final, "Black Baudelaire" speech, physically threatening her and other whites, for which she then assassinates him (20, 33–37).

Throughout the film (and play) Lula uses sexual and racist memes to evoke Clay's limbic passions, as if superimposing the left-brain controls of the white symbolic Other onto his mind, reshaping his right-brain, intuitive, imaginary anxieties and Real drives.[7] She suggests she has done this many times before, with other men. And yet, she is mortal and aging in her prejudiced promiscuity—for she notices a strand of gray hair growing from her head. "A gray hair for each year and type I've come through" (13). Clay calls her a "lady wrestler" when she twists his wrist (11–12), indicating the brute force that will emerge at the climax of their courtship. But Lula challenges Clay with historical and symbolic as well as physical and imaginary memes, while they wrestle over his identity and sculpt theirs together as a mixed-race couple, despite the lynching laws of a racist heritage. "Did your people ever burn witches or start revolutions over the price of tea?" (18). Here Lula implies that her attraction to and rage against Clay evolved from the memes of sexual oppression suffered by other female bodies, now dead, and perhaps her own, in an unspoken, prior trauma—triggering further sacrifices through her witchcraft and personal rebellion.

Evolution through sexual reproduction demands the eventual death of individuals (despite their survival instincts) so that mutations will develop and generations will change, as selected by nature and culture, through animal genes and human memes. Some sacrifices demanded by the memeplexes of specific

---

[5]   Shirley Knight was actually two years younger than Al Freeman and both were in their thirties when the film was released.

[6]   Cf. Löfgren 438–41 and Rebhorn on Lula's blackface mimicry and masks. See also Piggford on Lula as mother and psychotherapist to Clay.

[7]   Cf. Rebhorn on Clay's black male anxiety and masochism.

cultures are explicitly controlling and destructive, such as burning witches or enslaving and lynching blacks. Others are more subtle and seductive, as shown in *Dutchman*. Clay and Lula seduce each other into a fantasy love affair, revealing how their reproductive drives of limbic lust turn upon the memes of desire that they perceive in each other as a black male and white female. Lula also lures Clay into expressing his limbic rage. After subduing her sexually expressive dance in the subway car, he reveals his murderous desires as a former poet, like the blues artists he cites (Bessie Smith and Charlie Parker). Then Lula masters him with a knife. Thus, they both show how the genetic drive of lust can twist, through memetic desires and signifiers, to evoke panic, fear, and rage—resulting in the sacrifice of Clay as a poetic "murderer," by Lula as an actual murderess. Yet, Lula also sacrifices herself, like Clay, to her murderous desires, as the inheritance of white and black memes battle to control these characters' brains and bodies.

Today's mass dramatic media reconfirm certain sacrificial memes, especially through melodramatic formulas of good and evil, stereotyped characters, vengeful violence, and victorious endings (Pizzato, *Theatres*). But theatre and cinema also enable spectators to evolve toward a greater consciousness of and choice in how memes circulate through their brains, bodies, and actions. *Dutchman*, as play and film, may even provide a catharsis beyond Baraka's black power sentiments of the 1960s, showing the sacrificial trap of racial rage, white or black, against the Other.

A Dance of Sex and Death

The memetic ideologies, desires, and drives circulating through the brains and bodies of Lula and Clay bring them together as lovers, yet also turn them against each other as mortal enemies. Why do these characters move, through left-brain interpretations of skin type and character, through right-brain erotic and rebellious fantasies, from love to murder?

According to evolutionary psychologist David Buss, women inherit a genetic legacy of desiring men for security, status, and resources to protect the long-term investment of their female bodies in limited egg production (approximately 400 in a lifetime), in the dangers of pregnancy and human birth, and in the labor of child nurturing (19–27). Men, on the other hand, with an almost limitless production of sperm (millions in an hour) inherit the genetic strategy of short-term gain in spreading many seeds, often desiring young, beautiful women with healthy, childbearing potential. And yet, women may also use a promiscuous strategy to measure their value to various males while seeking a mate or to provide alternative security and resources against the inadequacies of a mate already chosen (86–91). Beyond Buss's genetic argument and sociological data, however, the representation of fertile female bodies and of high-status males still depends a great deal on specific memeplexes in various cultures.[8]

From the start of the film, Clay and Lula are desirable to each other, through the test of their memetic perceptions. Yet their bodies and words also express the tension of conflicting desires and drives. Clay shows his high status by wearing a suit and tie, though he tugs at his tight collar while Lula enters the subway car, unseen by him, under a Dutch Masters cigar ad. He is haunted by ghosts, in suit and skin, as a "Dutchman"[9] inheriting the memes of both colonizer and colonized, while trying to master the lust and rage within his limbic brain, as well as the white woman provoking him. But Lula is more masterful early on. She sits on Clay's newspaper, making him pull it out from under her "ass," while taunting him about staring at it earlier. She not only offers him an apple to eat with her, she feeds Clay a piece that falls from the side of his mouth—flirtatiously, yet with maternal control, telling him he "could be a handsome man" (12). She aggressively puts on lipstick, as if it were war paint, while asking Clay to ask her to his party. She scripts and directs how he should invite her, insisting that he use the exact "lines" she gives him, while making him rehearse the question and cut his "huh's" (16). Lula then puts her bare legs between Clay's dress pants, enticing and dominating his hidden phallic power. She challenges his view of her status and his own: from his earlier male gaze at her as sex object to his current relationship with her—as an assimilated black man being touched by a sexually liberated white woman in an otherwise empty subway car traveling under 1960s New York. "What thing are you playing at, Mister?" (17).

Provoked by Lula, Clay explicitly states his lustful and then murderous passions. After Lula puts her bare legs over his left thigh (going farther in the film than the play's stage directions), Clay warns her that she might excite him "for real" (17). Her mood suddenly changes at this; she shoves him, stands, and walks away, screaming "I bet." Harvey's film creates a bigger break here, between Clay and Lula, than in the play where she just "slumps in the seat." In the film, Clay chooses to follow Lula to a new seat, twice, while the train car darkens and she avoids responding to his attempt at reconnecting: "I thought you knew everything about me? What happened?" Over a minute passes (and Clay asks her again to the party) before she responds, scolding him maternally, "Don't get smart with me, Buster"—while stomping away from him again. The camera breaks the 180-degree rule, flipping twice to the opposite side of the car in this sequence of Clay chasing Lula to various seats. But she becomes seductive once again as he persists in valuing his contact with her. She even pulls down the strap of her dress, briefly

---

[8]   See also Miller's argument that sexual selection has led to the wasteful opulence of the human brain and its cultures, as excessive fitness indicators, like the peacock's cumbersome, energy expensive tail—involving both sexes in our species.

[9]   The play and film title *Dutchman* may refer to the legendary ghost ship *Flying Dutchman* (and Wagner's opera), but also to the theatrical term for a strip of cloth used to hide the crack between the seams of flats (Piggford).

revealing her black bra underneath, as she tells Clay that she knows him like the palm of her hand—the "same hand" that she unbuttons her dress with when she lets it fall down (18). She also calls him "Lover." Yet her love in this drama turns out to be vampire-like.[10] As femme fatale, she is both a vampire-maker and killer, drawing Clay's blood and limbic passions, beyond his right-brain wariness and left-brain control, to reveal his murderous bestiality. And then, she steals his black phallic power, at the climax their love/hate-making, with a knife in his chest. Lula thus demonstrates the sacrifice of her own erotic desire, as well as Clay's, to the white superego demand of controlling the black man—while Clay's right-brain fantasies and left-brain reasoning turn him into a sacrificial actor, too.

However, midway through the *Dutchman* film (at the end of the play's first scene), a happier love story seems to be evolving. Lula defines the primal scene of Clay's parentage as "the union of love and sacrifice that was destined to flower in the birth of the noble Clay," foreshadowing their own fantasy love affair and physical sacrifice that will evoke the memes of artistic black rage and cruel white nobility (20). Lula jokes with Clay, as the "Black Baudelaire," about his invisible-man appearance to others in society, or to the audience of the film and play: "May people accept you as a ghost of the future" (20–21). She then calls him a murderer, but also says she will pretend with him to be invisible and free of their "history"— as they ride the rails of passion and fantasy "through the city's entrails" and thus, in the terminology of their time, "GROOVE!"

Perhaps Lula really wants to be free of white and black history with Clay, but her very attraction to him, through his black skin and her white sexiness, bears the weight of history that cannot be shaken off with a liberating grooviness. As the film's second half begins, Lula kisses Clay, feeding him a piece of apple with her mouth. But the camera swings around them to reveal that others are now on the subway car, too, even as the lovers remain oblivious to them. Lula describes her fantasy with Clay at the future party, "exchanging codes of lust," as she holds his loosened tie (23). A little later, Clay lifts his tie over the top of her dress, then names their divine passion a "corporate Godhead," while she puts her bare arms around his neck and pulls his head into her breasts (24). As Lula extends the fantasy to her "tenement" home, she involves codes of lust not just for the divine but also the animal parts of their incorporated brains, calling Clay her "tender, big-eyed prey." She predicts that they will talk about Clay's "manhood" in her home; it is then that he notices the others in the subway car with them (25).

This presence of the Other temporarily blocks Clay's desire to hold Lula close and fantasize about their future. The silent bodies of other passengers, white and black, remind Clay that he and Lula are not free of their histories and memeplex pressures. He invites Lula to continue the fantasy, but repeatedly looks over his shoulder at the others—as she speaks close to his face, telling him that she will "map" his manhood and they will "screw" (26). Lula also predicts that Clay will

---

[10]   See Baraka, *Home* 216 (also cited by Piggford), on the vampire-like role of white women, "sucking the male juices to build a navel orange, which is themselves."

call her place "Juliet's tomb," bringing the weight of literature as well as history to bear on their deadly love. She says that Clay will declare his "love" for her many times, but he will be "lying" in order to keep her "alive" (27).

Thus, *Dutchman* shows the steps that a black man and white woman take toward desirable fantasies as self and other deceptions. But the degree to which Clay and Lula willfully choose those steps, or become swept away by unconscious drives and historical powers—from eyeing to touching each other, from fantasy love affair to death act—also depends upon spectators' identifications and interpretations. Initially, Clay exchanges gazes with Lula through the window. Then she enters the subway car and he allows her to sit next to him. Yet, powerful memes are already at work at these contact points. The dance of sex and death between Lula and Clay continues toward their apple eating, fantasy affair, interaction with others in the train car, and their final, murderous speeches and actions. Clay does pause early on, in a cinematic close-up, staring at Lula when she calls him a "black nigger" (19). But he has by then followed her to various seats in the car, apparently willing to overlook this and other insults in his drive for pleasure and his desire for status in mating with a beautiful white woman. Lula's awareness of that drive and desire in Clay, as a black male, seems to trigger contradictory impulses in her. She wants to know if she is "exciting" Clay (10). But she also knows his "type," has been with various types before, and is wary of how a relationship may be "gentle when it starts" yet lead to something else (13). Apparently, she has suffered loss and pain with other men, perhaps of Clay's type, and now seeks both love and vengeance through him.

In certain species of spiders and mantises, sexual murder and cannibalism occur as a matter of course (Diamond, *Why* 11). "This cannibalism clearly involves the male's consent, because the male of these species approaches the female, makes no attempt to escape, and may even bend his head and thorax toward the female's mouth so that she may munch her way through most of his body while his abdomen remains to complete the job of injecting sperm into her." Since opportunities to mate are rare for such a male, his genetic instinct compels him to offer himself to the female, sacrificing his life for the sake of feeding her and nurturing his offspring inside her. The female's eating of him also allows "copulation with the male's genitalia to proceed for a longer time, resulting in more sperm transferred and more eggs fertilized" (12).

Clay does not consent to being killed and eaten by Lula. But he does enjoy the fantasy of making love to her, becomes enraged at her embarrassing belly-rub dance on the train car, and then suffers death at her hands after expressing his desire to rip her breasts off and murder her. Lula seduces and kills Clay (perhaps premeditatedly) not to feed the genetic offspring inside her, but to feed the mixed memes of white and black in their subway encounter—and in the audience's minds.

On one level, the film conveys Baraka's desire to purge whiteness from black culture in the 1960s, or his fear of being suppressed by it, as Clay is by Lula after revealing the rage behind the blues. But on other levels, especially with the expanded audience of Harvey's film, *Dutchman* shows the tempting memes of sexual seduction and artistic, yet murderous expression in both white and black brains, as each meets the body of the Other. Limbic drives for genetic reproduction become transformed by right-brain, devil's advocate anxieties and holistic, mimetic desires, plus left-brain executive controls and linear, mythic rationales. This recapitulates the human evolution from nature to culture: from episodic awareness in the animal brain to mimetic skill in *Homo erectus* two million years ago to mythic thought in archaic *Homo sapiens* a half million years ago to the theoretic technologies of current humans, such as theatre and cinema (Donald). Each child passes through these stages, too, absorbing the memes of a particular family and culture, as desires of the Other are reformulated to shape the emerging ego of Self.

Lula and Clay show two selves in competition for memetic progeny, with their offspring continuing also in spectators' minds. Each of the characters' (and actors') brains bears many memes, operating independently in the right and left hemispheres, then converging or interfering as single-minded or conflicting desires (Newberg et al. 21). Such mating and fighting memes within each character also conjoin or struggle with those of other characters seen onscreen. Thus, the genetic reproduction goals and sacrificial demands of animal drives become greatly transformed through the white and black histories born by these characters' bodies, in their mixing and wrestling memes.

With Us or Against Us

Many words and actions of Lula and Clay may seem devilish to viewers. Indeed, the film shows a man in a poster behind them, on the train car wall, wearing a devil costume, as they fantasize about their love affair and then expose their wounded and violent passions. The horns of the devil costume appear over Clay's head, but it is Lula who turns from screwing him in a fantasy future to resentments from the past. She predicts that his love will be a lie to keep her alive. When he does not understand, she says: "Well, don't look at me. It's the path I take, that's all" (27). Lula is driven to repeat her lies as an "actress," drawing on a black male's passions, with and against her, to keep her alive, to nurture the memes of loss, rage, rebellion, eroticism, and vengeance. She is compelled not by a devil inside her, or in Clay, but by animal drives (as if in a horned head), warped by the desires of human mimesis and myth, which create existential awareness, lack of being, and avenging racial egos.

That turning point, like others in the film, involves the sacrificial remixing of cultural memes through the characters' left, executive and right, devil's advocate brains, as well as limbic animal natures. Clay not only denies that his love for Lula will be a lie, he also wants the "whole story" of their future in her erotic fantasy game—in the mythic and mimetic theatre of her mind mixing with his (28). This may imply that he hopes for children with her, breaking through historical and racial barriers to achieve nature's primal goal. But Lula rebels at this—or at any narrative of their love continuing forever, romantically or through progeny. "How could things go on like that forever?" In the film, as in the play's stage directions, Lula pulls things out of the bag in her lap and tosses them over her shoulder onto the train car floor, as if expelling the future fruits of her womb with Clay. She then blames Clay for his future infidelity—although, according to Buss, that is an inevitable drive in the male body and brain. "But you mix it up. Look out the window, all the time. Turning pages. Change change. Till, shit, I don't know you."

Lula finds an orange at the bottom of her bag and bites into its skin. Then she peels it, comparing Clay to "Jewish poets from Yonkers, who leave their mothers looking for other mothers..." (28). While dropping the peels on Clay and tossing them further into the subway car, she suggests that Jewish artists handle the wounds of their ethnic history with humor and the erotic celebration of life: "poems [that] are always funny, and all about sex." Clay relates this to "the movies." But Lula questions whether he, as a black artist, can mix the memes of trauma in that positive way: "things work on you till you hate them" (29). Eating her orange and raising Clay's wrist, she teases him about being an "escaped nigger"—with others in the car now watching him. "'Cause you crawled through the wire and made tracks to my side," she says, eliding concentration camp and plantation imagery. Clay plays her game by joking, too, with his racial memes. "Plantations were big open whitewashed places like heaven, and everybody on 'em was grooved to be there" (29–30). But when he says, "And that's how the blues was born," Lula raises the stakes. She stands and dances, repeating Clay's line as a song of mockery and swinging her hips, thus connecting others in the car to their memetic, racial, erotic, and murderous game.

In the film version, Lula hits a white man with her hips, as he stands at a nearby pole, then screams at him, "Why, you son of a bitch. Get out of my way." As she turns her body back toward Clay, the bag on her arm swings around and another black man touches his hand to his face, as if nicked by Lula's fruit-bearing purse. She squeezes juice from the orange in her hand onto an elderly lady with glasses, who puts up her arms defensively. Lula then (as in the play) implores Clay to "rub bellies" with her, while rotating her hips in the aisle (30). But he stays seated and tries to get her down, reminding her about the "mirror" of a choral Other around their performance, expecting "Snow White" to be "the fairest one of all." Yet she continues to dance hysterically, mocking his blues, belly rub, and cultural identity. She even stands on the seats and rocks her crotch against a pole, like a nude dancer in a club, saying: "let's do the thing. Uhh. Uhh. Clay!" (31). She increases her insults, calling Clay "full of white man's words" and challenging him to "scream at these people" (31). She also adds a line to the stageplay, "Don't sit there dying the way they want you to die, baby," as she intensifies her taunting, maieutic dance. She sits with another black man in the subway car and teases them both about being "Uncle Thomas Woolly-Head" (32). When Clay rises and grabs the dancing Lula, dragging her back to his seat, a white man pulls him off of her, but Clay slugs him.

It is then that Clay's abject semiotic identity—as whitewashed black man—erupts to challenge the Western symbolic order, through Lula's *chora* of erotic, racial mockery (Kristeva). Limbic passions of lust, fear, panic, and rage fuel Clay's right-brain revolution of violent poetic imagery and physical language against the left-brain social Other within and around him. He screams at Lula to "shut the hell up" and slaps her face (33). He says he could murder her by squeezing her "tiny ugly throat." He says he could tear the *Times* out of the hands of an elderly white man on the other side of the car—and then does it. With the blades of a ceiling fan turning behind his head, Clay states: "if I murdered you, then other white people would begin to understand me" (35). But when Clay sits again, the film shows the elderly white man reading his *Times* untorn, suggesting either a continuity error or that the violence in this drama may be a fantasy, yet it has a real potential to erupt beyond the train car and screen.

Clay admits, when seated, that he would rather be a fool and insane, safe with his words and "clean, hard thoughts," like the "mirrors" of his people (35–36). But he tells Lula, while buttoning his collar and tightening his tie, to warn her father that the mirroring of "Western rationalism" by the "blues people," assimilating to the white fantasy of a triumphant "missionary heart," will someday result in the murder of whites by blacks "with very rational explanations" (36). Then, after Clay stands to get off the train, Lula stabs him. They sink to their knees together. When she pulls out the knife, he falls on top of her, as if in a post-coital hold. She orders the others in the car to get the black corpse off her. Four white men pick Clay up and carry him through the aisle, past another seated black man staring vacantly into space. The film cuts Lula's final lines: instead of the chorus throwing Clay's body off the train, as Lula commands in the play, the movie focuses on the corpse approaching the audience, its head growing larger to fill the screen—as if showing the memes of Clay's black skin and brain, heading into a future *chora*.

After more shots of the subway and empty platforms, Lula sits in a train car by herself. She writes in a small notebook; a black conductor walks by; and Lula moves forward in the car to stand seductively near yet another black man, reading a book in his seat. When she bites into an apple, they gaze at each other, both smiling. Thus, *Dutchman* suggests a ritual repetition of Lula's murderous mating game. She kills Clay and perhaps other black men by acting out her racist lust, fear, and rage—mirroring her fantasy of their sexual and deadly desires. Yet, Clay also acts out the rage behind his poetry and that of other black artists, showing how the friction between rationalist and blues memes burns within him, trapping him in left-brain self-criticism and right-brain vengeance, even as he chooses not to perform his violent fantasies against others.[11]

---

[11] Cf. Kumar and also Rebhorn. See also Löfgren 443, on the "self-consuming nature of ... [Baraka's] nationalistic phase."

Humans evolved by dominating and transforming nature, within and around them, reconstructing their environments as differing cultural worlds. As human social groups grew, from tribes to nations, religions, and racial identities, expanding across the globe and colonizing one another, they gained strength in stereotyping others as dangerous, devilish enemies. Such a desire to have "shared enemies" involves a fundamental insecurity: attempting to purge the evil within individuals and groups by projecting it onto the other (Volkan 19, 30–32,118–20). This is shown in *Dutchman* through the specific legacy of black and white, male and female otherness, in the 1960s and beyond. Sexual liberation and black power transform the drives of genetic reproduction and competitive survival into a mating and mixing of memes that use the bodies of Lula and Clay to propagate, even while sacrificing these characters as fantasy lovers and mortal enemies. But the film (and its original drama) also provokes the audience to continue evolving toward a greater awareness of the hatred and violence produced by our cultural warping of limbic animal drives, through the right-brain's devilish anxieties and the left's competitive controls. Thus, the development of human rights today requires not only better laws, but also a further evolution of the brain (in the gene–meme battle of replication and expansion) beyond brutal identity competitions toward respect for others' survival and reproduction. This involves sharing resources across the human family, rather than controlling others as racial enemies, sex objects, or terrorist threats. If we can realize our common hybrid heritage, as one species out of Africa, evolving and mixing our black, white, and other cultural ideals—to make new memes for our descendents—then *Dutchman* does not show an endlessly repeated tragedy, but encourages change in its past and future audiences.[12]

Works Cited

Baraka, Amiri. [LeRoi Jones.] *Dutchman and The Slave*. New York: Morrow, 1964.
——. *Home: Social Essays*. New York: Morrow, 1966.
Bergesen, Eric, and William W. Demastes. "The Limits of African-American Political Realism: Baraka's *Dutchman* and Wilson's *Ma Rainey's Black Bottom*." *Realism and the American Dramatic Tradition*. Ed. William W. Demastes. Tuscaloosa: University of Alabama Press, 1996. 218–34.
Blackmore, Susan. *The Meme Machine*. Oxford: Oxford University Press, 1999.
Buss, David M. *The Evolution of Desire*. New York: Basic, 1994.
Clericuzio, Alessandro. "Labyrinths of Language and Race in L. Jones's *Dutchman* and D. H. Hwang's *Bondage*." *America Today*. Ed. Giglioa Nocera. Siracusa, Italy: Grafia, 2003. 116–23.

---

[12] When I presented earlier versions of this essay at conferences in 2006, it seemed improbable that the US would have a black President in a few years. But now that has changed.

Dawkins, Richard. *The Extended Phenotype*. Oxford: Oxford University Press, 1999.

Diamond, Jared. *Guns, Germs, and Steel*. New York: Norton, 1997.

——. *Why Is Sex Fun?* New York: Basic, 1997.

Doane, Mary Ann. *The Desire to Desire: The Woman's Film of the 1940s*. Bloomington: Indiana University Press, 1987.

Donald, Merlin. *A Mind So Rare: The Evolution of Human Consciousness*. New York: Norton, 2001.

Gazzaniga, Michael S. and Joseph E. LeDoux. *The Integrated Mind*. New York: Plenum, 1978.

Gradie, Margaret I. Review of *The Journey of Man*. By Spencer Wells. *American Journal of Human Biology* 17 (2005): 522–23.

Harpendin, Henry. Review of *The Journey of Man*. By Spencer Wells. *Quarterly Review of Biology* 78.3 (Sept. 2003): 357–58.

Jablonski, Nina G., and George Chaplin. "The Evolution of Human Skin Coloration." *Journal of Human Evolution* 39.1 (July 2000): 57–106.

Kirchwenger, Gina. "Black and White." *Discover* 22.2 (Feb. 2001): 32–33.

Kristeva, Julia. *Revolution in Poetic Language*. New York: Columbia University Press, 1984.

Kumar, Nita N. "The Logic of Retribution: Amiri Baraka's 'Dutchman.'" *African American Review* 37.2–3 (summer 2003): 271–79.

Lacan, Jacques. *Écrits: A Selection*. Trans. Bruce Fink. New York: Norton, 2002.

LeDoux, Joseph. *Synaptic Self*. New York: Penguin, 2003.

Löfgren, Lotta M. "Clay and Clara: *Dutchman*, Kennedy's *The Owl Answers*, and the Black Arts Movement." *Modern Drama* 46.3 (fall 2003): 424–49.

Miller, Geoffrey. *The Mating Mind*. New York: Doubleday, 2000.

Mulvey, Laura. "Visual Pleasure and Narrative Cinema." 1975. *Narrative, Apparatus, Ideology*. Ed. Philip Rosen. New York: Columbia University Press, 1986. 198–209.

Newberg, Andrew, Eugene d'Aquili, and Vince Rause. *Why God Won't Go Away: Brain Science and the Biology of Belief*. New York: Ballantine, 2002.

Panksepp, Jaak. *Affective Neuroscience: The Foundations of Human and Animal Emotions*. Oxford: Oxford University Press, 1998.

Piggford, George. "Looking into Black Skulls: Amiri Baraka's *Dutchman* and the Psychology of Race." *Modern Drama* (spring 1997) 40.1: 74–85.

Pizzato, Mark. *Ghosts of Theatre and Cinema in the Brain*. New York: Palgrave, 2006.

——. *Theatres of Human Sacrifice: From Ancient Ritual to Screen Violence*. Albany: SUNY Press, 2005.

Ramachandran, V. S., and Sandra Blakeslee. *Phantoms in the Brain: Probing the Mysteries of the Human Mind*. New York: William Morrow, 1998.

Rebhorn, Matthew. "Flaying Dutchman: Masochism, Minstrelsy, and the Gender Politics of Amiri Baraka's *Dutchman*." *Callaloo* 26.3 (2003): 796–812.

Solms, Mark, and Oliver Turnbull. *The Brain and the Inner World*. New York: Other Press, 2002.

Tate, Greg. "How We Talk About Race." *American Theatre*. 17.5 (May-June 2000): 44–46.

Volkan, Vamik D. *The Need to Have Enemies and Allies*. North Vale, New Jersey: Jacob Aronson, 1988.

Wells, Spencer. *The Journey of Man*. Princeton: Princeton UP, 2002.

Chapter 3

DeLillo, Performance, and the Denial of Death

Jon D. Rossini

To ask for truth in theatre is contradictory, a repudiation of its essence. Consequently, death, a subject for which true statements are, a priori, inadmissible, is the subject most perfectly suited to the form of theatre.

Howard Barker, Death, The One and the Art of Theatre (4)

DELFINA: What is the word that describes the condition of a man who advances
               bravely toward his own grueling truth?
TEDDY: What is the word?
DELFINA: Perishability.

Don DeLillo, Valparaiso (103)

Howard Barker's 2005 theoretical manifesto, *Death, The One and the Art of Theatre*, argues for a distinction between "theatre" and "the art of the theatre," the former reflecting most current practice and the latter referencing a less inhabited terrain designed to lend "anxiety to the few" (1). Barker's primary project is castigating theater's shift from a focus on death to "political indoctrination and social therapy" (2). His resistance to the sociological project of theater reflects his personal aesthetics and functions to create a theoretical space for his own work. Yet, his concern with the fading "art of the theatre" is conceptually linked not only to Antonin Artaud's claims regarding theater and the plague, but also to Herbert Blau's concern with the contemporary loss of theatrical power articulated in *Take Up the Bodies: Theater at the Vanishing Point* (1982). Due to its "widespread adulteration in the social body," Blau wants practitioners to "reappropriate" the power of theater (11). In *Blooded Thought*, also published in 1982, he anticipates Barker's focus on the importance of death to the practice of theater: "the body's specific gravity is always there, subject to time, astride of a grave" (133). He carries this focus on death even further, claiming "it is the actor's mortality which is the acted subject, for he is right there dying in front of your eyes" (134). Blau thus emphasizes the centrality of human mortality to both the practice of acting and the audience's experience of theater.

This intimate relationship between theater and death is also present in the work of Don DeLillo, a writer best known for his novels such as *White Noise*, *Mao II*, and *Underworld*. As an alternative, or perhaps an answer, to Barker and Blau,

DeLillo uses the theater itself and performance elements in his novels as sites for negotiating both the denial and the acceptance of death, demonstrating in these spaces strategies for living with the human dread of mortality. DeLillo's novel, *White Noise* (1985), explores possible human strategies for surviving the constant psychic and environmental presence of mortality through both action and denial. But three other texts more clearly articulate possible transformational strategies for dealing with our mortality. DeLillo's play, *The Day Room* (first produced in 1986), presents death as a philosophical problem that haunts the human animal, offering conversation and theatrical performance as potential solutions. *The Day Room* is closely related to *White Noise* in the sense that death is manifest more as psychological dread than as a physical experience. A pair of later works, the play *Valparaiso* (1999) and the novella *The Body Artist* (2001), place death and the reaction to it center stage in a manner that moves beyond the philosophical concerns of DeLillo's work in the mid-1980s, to a more sustained and literal performance of death and its aftermath. In this shift from death as environmental and psychological dread to death as a lived experience, DeLillo returns a level of materiality to a discourse on death often abstracted in postmodern thinking. As a way of rethinking the denial of death, DeLillo offers the creative activity of performance not only as an alternative to dread, but also as a potential way of reforging our relationship with mortality.

DeLillo's first produced play, *The Day Room*, attempts to systematically articulate an alternative to the fear of death through the performance of language. This alternative manifests through the idealization and practice of conversation as a means of propelling action, "keep[ing] the world turning" (47)—as well as the literal practice of acting on the theatrical stage. *White Noise* and *The Day Room* have been paired briefly in other DeLillo criticism. But only Toby Silverman Zinman has provided a sustained analysis of the play in relation to the novel, a logical connection given the overlapping intellectual and cultural investments of the works, as well as the proximity of their creation. Partially authorizing this genre-pairing investigation, DeLillo himself acknowledges a complementary relationship between the novel and the theater. In an interview with Jody McAuliffe, DeLillo compares the creative processes: "[f]or me, each form, play and novel, is an antidote to the other" (McAuliffe 174). The term "antidote" shows a contrast between the personal experience of novelistic creation and the collective activity of theatrical creation. But it also indicates that the two genres accomplish very different cultural work, something DeLillo explicitly incorporates in his creative explorations. Unlike the dread of *White Noise*, which is contained within its covers and the readers' memories, a performance uses live experience to question the limits and security of knowledge, and offers the possibility of art bleeding into and transforming the real.

The Day Room consists of two interlocking acts. According to Judith Pastore:

> [Its] plot is extremely simple. Act One takes place in a hospital, part of which
> has an Arno Klein psychiatric wing. Two patients are visited by another patient,

two doctors and two nurses, all of whom turn out to be actually residents of the psychiatric wing. Act Two has the same cast in the day room of the psychiatric wing decorated to look like a motel room. The major characters are looking for a play put on by the Arno Klein troop. (434)

What Pastore's description eliminates in its attempt at simplicity is that "the same cast" in Act Two is never completely locatable as the same individuals from Act One. At the end of Act Two, we return to the opening image of the play, a man doing tai chi in a hospital room, suggesting that both acts are equally "staged" by those who inhabit the day room. This circularity heightens the difficulty of placing both the actors and their location, putting into question the fundamental nature of what is being witnessed by the theatrical audience and the actors on stage.

However, even as DeLillo recognizes his tendency to create theatrical worlds that are not easy to fix in place, he argues that this is a function of the genre: "the curious thing about my plays is they are not nearly as established in the world around me as my novels are. And that, in my own limited sort of outlook on theater, is an aspect of theater itself. It's not about the force of reality so much as the mysteries of identity and existence" (quoted in McAuliffe 179). Ironically, because of this very lack of establishment, there always seems to be a potential for the theatrical world to pass beyond the boundaries of the stage into the real world. In his interview with Mervyn Rothstein about working on the production of *The Day Room*, DeLillo described an experience of being in the world of the play.

> When we did this play in Cambridge, at Robert Brustein's American Repertory Theatre, I was taking a walk one morning and I heard someone call my name, and there was the director looking out a window. And within the course of the next two strides I saw a cast member crossing the street with her arms full of dry cleaning. There was no one else in sight. I had the feeling that the play had spilled out into the streets. For that one moment the world of the play had become the world itself—and this is like no other feeling I've had working on novels.[1] (Rothstein 22)

DeLillo's "feeling," enabled by the power of theater that transforms a Cambridge street into the interstitial liminality of a stage, is evoked by the powerful visual experience of a writer seeing his characters literally moving through the world.

Importantly, this event occurred during the production of a play deeply invested in questioning the possibility of theatrical limits through a series of interlocking sets designed to preserve the mystery of location and retain a fundamental ambiguity regarding the nature of the characters in the drama. However, this very metatheatricality leads naturally to an investment in an individual's relationship

---

[1]   In addition to this meditation in an interview, DeLillo also provided another extended account of theatrical defamiliarization from the same production in his brief essay on the play, "The Door Inside *The Day Room* (Notes Toward a Definitive Meditation)," in which he reports on his experience of seeing the crew building the set for the first act of his play.

with death through self-performance, of acting as a means of negotiating the
looming presence of death. DeLillo is very explicit about this in his description
of the play:

> it's about acting, in a peculiar way, not acting as a craft, but acting as a model
> of human identity.... It seemed natural to me beginning a play that theater
> itself would be one of the subjects I was interested in. And I began to sense a
> connection, almost a metaphysical connection, between the craft of acting and
> the fear we all have of dying. It seemed to me that actors are a kind of model
> for the ways in which we hide from the knowledge we inevitably possess of our
> final extinction. (Rothstein 21)

Here actors become exemplars of the practice of denial. But in the play itself, it
is clear that actors take on this role precisely because of their proximity to death.
While placing one's self close to death is dangerous, there is an undercurrent of
the potential acceptance of mortality tied into the practice of acting itself. Actors
place their bodies under scrutiny on stage, acutely reminding the audience of the
physical decay of the body. The actor's body is one that is supposed to die as Jolene
reminds us in *The Day Room*: "Young, old, ancient, budding, decrepit. Dying is
what we're all about" (90). This creates a paradox of acceptance and denial as
actors hide in characters to avoid the reality of death while simultaneously placing
their mortality on display. In this way, denial of death for an actor becomes not a
paralyzing or limiting strategy, but a way of having an entirely new experience,
just as the self must be denied in some forms of acting in order to fully inhabit a
character.

The relationship between acting and the knowledge of one's own mortality
is not new with DeLillo. Bruce Wilshire's *Role Playing and Identity*, published
the same year as Blau's works, provides a phenomenology of theater intent on
recuperating the possibility of a truly authentic experience of the self. For Wilshire,
as for DeLillo, theater serves as a fundamental metaphor for understanding human
subjectivity. Wilshire's approach intersects with DeLillo's central tenet about
the nature of theater—that theater and performance may sustain a fundamental
conversation about death—but differs in his sense of the possibilities. In his
chapter "The Limits of Theatrical Metaphors," Wilshire describes the problematic
limits of conceiving life as a sustained performance both on and off the stage. He
believes "that a person who 'performs' his death so that he vaguely believes that he
outlives it is the most wretched person imaginable, for he has failed to appropriate
his own greatest power and pleasure as a self, which is just to come home to
himself as he is" (266–67). Wilshire insists that the possibility of performance as a
means of establishing a distance between the self and the reality of death creates a
divided subjectivity. He thus asserts an existentialist argument for the recognition
of an authentic self. In doing so, Wilshire returns to the possibility of a modernist
self-conception that privileges authenticity—even as that appears impossible to
attain.

DeLillo's "phenomenology of acting," on the other hand, establishes a clear positive relationship between performance, denial, and the presence of death. While Wilshire sees the denial of death as a dehumanizing fiction emerging from a failed literal or symbolic performance, DeLillo argues that this is a necessary everyday life practice that can be learned from and by acting. Here he appears to argue in support of Ernest Becker's final claim in *The Denial of Death* that the primary means of dealing with mortality is to give a gift back to creation. In DeLillo's play the gift is the acting, the performance. Denial is a creative act, manifested as the performance of the Arno Klein troupe—which enables a real transformation for those who have witnessed the event within the world of the play and a potential transformation for audience members also witnessing the performance. This transformation functions as a theatrical response to the philosophical and critical concerns of both Blau and Wilshire, employing a sustained performance of "insanity" as a way of understanding our relationship to death.

Unfortunately, many reviewers of the 1987 Manhattan Theater Club production saw little or nothing new in *The Day Room*, referencing the plays of Pirandello, Beckett, and Orton for comparison. Frank Rich called DeLillo's play: "at best the kind of literary stage event that can respectfully be catalogued as 'interesting'— especially if one adds 'interesting' to the evening's many other euphemisms for death." Rich expands: "In Act II, *The Day Room* takes us to a motel that might not actually be a motel where we meet actors who might not actually be actors who are going to perform a play that might not actually be a play for madmen who might not actually be mad." The repetition of "might not" emphasizes Rich's frustration with what he sees as a tired exploration of the interplay between illusion and reality. However, in insisting on the question of what is real, Rich fixates on the wrong problem. The play is not only asking questions about theatrical illusion, it insists on the possibility of multiple realities that occur, in DeLillo's words, "sometimes simultaneously." "I didn't have illusion and reality in mind. ... I guess I'm interested in the way the play forms a kind of unending circular structure—it bends back on itself. This has greater significance to me than any sense of what is real and what isn't. To me, it's all real, but it's happening in different levels" (quoted in Rothstein 23). The experiences of the characters in the play indicate the presence of multiple explanations for the world as it exists and also seem to offer the possibility to the audience that the effects of the play might extend beyond the stage.

The putative locations of the play, a hospital room and a motel room, have their own strong associations for DeLillo as well as his characters. The ability to carry on a conversation, central to the premise of language-driven text-based theater in the modern tradition of psychological realism, is also central to the practice of the patients in the hospital. In speaking to Wyatt, the man who shares his room, Budge, the central figure of Act One, insists on the "setting" as something carefully put into place to imagine the possibility of conversation, a lost art that must be hunted for, much like the Arno Klein troupe in the second act. According to Budge, "[i]n hospitals, people are polite. They call each other mister, doctor. There's an element of formality. It's conducive to good talk" (7). But, according to Wyatt, the very politeness that allows this conversation to occur emerges because "[w]e sense the presence of death.... The hush of death. On airplanes, in hospitals" (7). Importantly, conversation is only enabled by an interchange with the psychiatric patients from "the other side," who are constantly being escorted back out as their identities as inhabitants of the day room are exposed. Before she is exposed, Nurse Walker informs Wyatt that the real disease is "[k]nowing that you're going to die" (19). Patients in the hospital are constantly aware of the possibility of death, but simultaneously shielded from it. "There's a procedure for getting [a] corpse down to the morgue. It is doubly or triply wrapped.... It looks like something else completely.... So patients won't be frightened and depressed" (17). This ritual of concealment parallels the practice of actors as they present themselves, concealing themselves within a character.

At the same time, the other side, the day room, seems closely linked to death through the presence of acting and actors within its space. Nurse Baker, the character most articulate about the condition of the day room in the other wing tells the audience (before she too is taken away):

> In the day room, a speck of dust is charged with danger.... People say things out of nowhere. The smallest word is packed with danger.... They dress up. Just like you see. They steal uniforms from the laundry and pretend they're us. Sometimes they don't even sneak out. They stay in the day room, dressed up like all *kinds* of people. (26)

The space of the day room provides, along with the basic act of "dressing up," the semiotic intensity of theatrical space. The danger Nurse Baker describes is never specified, but it appears to emerge from the intimacy with death manifested by the practice of acting that is going on in the day room (both the fictional stage space and the play itself). Here, the possibility of separating the space of performance from everyday life within the world of the play becomes difficult. Death itself haunts a space that has been fully colonized by the theater just as it haunts the space of the hospital. The only thing that keeps death away is communication, as suggested by the return of one of the patients, Grass, who ends the act by moving toward a chair in order to continue talking with Budge, thus reestablishing the importance of conversation as a means of propelling the play forward and resisting the knowledge of death.

The second act's motel room is established as a theatrical set within the very same day room Nurse Baker describes. For the Desk Clerk, one of the two characters who sets up and takes down the set, a motel is "built so you would have a place to deposit your stains in secret" (96). Of course, that same observation could be made in a metaphorical sense about a psychiatric ward. Just like the semiprivate hospital room of the first act, the semiprivate space of a day room— not easily accessible but nonetheless shared by everyone in the ward—provides the possibility of a communal secret in performance. Things are known and not known at the same time, in the same way that cultural structures are developed to isolate those who are mad from those who are normal. This institutionalization of the insane functions as an explicit form of cultural denial, making the day room an ideal space to engage the practice of denial in any form.

Nurse Baker's alter ego in the second act, Jolene, is the only character who makes explicit the location of the Arno Klein performance.[2] "We go on tonight, an hour from now, in a hospital right here in town. The psychiatric wing. There's a room called the day room. They don't use it at night. We've arranged to borrow it, transform it, do our play, disappear. Now you know" (90). These lines come from the end of what DeLillo himself understands to be one of the central speeches in the play. In this speech Jolene clarifies a relationship between acting and death that seems to echo Blau's claim for the actor: "[d]ying is what we're all about" (*Day Room* 90). She talks of the danger of being an actor, an idea present from the beginning of the act when the Desk Clerk and the Maid who put together the set for the motel room discuss the Desk Clerk's upcoming trip to help an actor friend commit suicide. According to Jolene, "We're just like everyone else, only quicker to pick up a danger.... We can't meet death on our own terms. We have no terms.... Our only hope is other people" (90). This ability to "pick up" danger enables the formation of an actor, or indicates the existence of one. Since the day room is a space of constant danger, a space where the possibility of death is viscerally present—like the hospital and the stage—it makes perfect sense that in this space actors come into being. But her speech also introduces the power of an audience to shift this experience of denial in a different direction—that of hope.

This communal experience is not a naïve claim, but one DeLillo is hoping to manifest paradoxically through the multiple levels of reality in his play. Jolene abruptly exits the stage, following her visit to Lynette and Gary, the couple searching for the Arno Klein troupe. Then another character, Freddie, who has seen a performance and is willing to describe it, references Jolene's alter ego— Nurse Baker, the "black nurse... [f]rom the other wing" (92). In response to some confusion from the other players not only about the nurse but also about the other wing, he says, "[h]ave I remembered something we were all supposed to forget? Don't they know there's more than one wing. There's another and another and another and another.... It's hard to know who shares our secrets" (92–93). Freddie's uncertainty about the status of his knowledge in this particular moment seems to lead to fear or frustration as he begins threatening to shut the whole thing down: "I can stop things cold with a well-constructed sentence" (93). This suggests that he can strip away the fantasy of the staging of the motel play through an acknowledgement of the shared space of the day room. But even this would not free the actors from the space of the stage. In the end he chooses not to, yet it is unclear what his motivation is. And thus, the audience is left questioning their own level of knowledge regarding the world of the play. What secrets do we share?

---

[2]   She is played by the same actor, though whether she is the same person within the world of the play is one of the suspended questions.

What insanities do we share? Is there another wing, since the first act seems to suggest that? Are we remembering things we were supposed to forget?

By the close of the play we have returned to the hospital and "realized" that it, too, is within the space of the day room. In DeLillo's own explanation of this circularity, he talks about both literal and figurative returns. The normative answer to the practice of denial is that these actors are patients spending their time in the day room acting out the same events over and over under the direction of Arno Klein. (Klein appears as a character in the play and also retains meaning as the institutional naming of their space within the first act—the Arno Klein wing.) Forgetting the right things and sharing the right secrets becomes a means of working through life. The play suggests that we are all mad, all in the day room, and all potentially attempting to share the secret of forgetting the reality of death. As Zinman writes following an analysis of Jolene's speech, "It is clear by now that we have been in the day room all along, that the characters who are looking for the Arno Klein Group are looking for themselves, that all the world's a loony bin and men and women merely inmates in it" (81). This paraphrase of Shakespeare broadens out into the larger claim that "madness is merely a name for the condition of being human on this planet near the end of the millennium" (Zinman 81). Zinman's claim suggests that we are not merely discussing levels of reality and illusion, but a necessary structuring of interpersonal relationships based on the knowledge of mortality, one fully articulated only in the liminal space of theater.

In describing his life, Freddie tells Lynette and Gary:

> Before Amsterdam I was an ordinary man. I spoke to people in a normal tongue. I did the ordinary things.... There's none of that now. I took a bath every day, naked, a man with a history, ordinary Fred. That seems so faraway. There were edges and separations.... A spoon was not a painting of a spoon. All that is lost to me now.... I talk to imaginary men, to ghosts on battlements. I accept it all. I believe it all. A mirage is water and the illusion of water.... Everything is true. Everything can and does and will happen.... (75)

Freddie has undergone a radical perceptual transformation after his exposure to Arno Klein's theater; he is unable to distinguish between a two-dimensional representation and the thing itself, or to separate the real object from the perceptual illusion. Able to grant a simultaneity to events and a sacred quality to the world, Freddie articulates himself as an actor who believes in the theater and who treats everyday life as a theatrical space. In doing so, he places himself closer to death not just by explicitly displaying his mortality but by giving up the "edges and separations" that structure reality. He is transformed into someone who can look death straight in the face, talk to "ghosts on battlements."

The normative reading of this anecdote is to see it as the mutterings of a madman, as a sign of pathology. In this reading, Freddie's transformed perception emerges from his entry into the cultural space where he is first exposed to institutionalized madness. The story of watching the Arno Klein group in Amsterdam functions as a kind of displacement for the real activity of accepting the institutionalized space of madness—the day room. However, this reading of Freddie's experience does not account for DeLillo's own description of Act Two as "an attempt to explain the first half of the play to myself; in a way it's the play about the play" (quoted in Rothstein 22). The question is not one of madness, whether Freddie's, the other players', or even the audience's. We too have witnessed the Arno Klein group, either in the first act, the second act, or both. We have all shared the experience of this piece of theater and thus can theoretically move beyond the either/or dichotomy and rethink the relationship between madness, death, and theater.[3] If a play and insanity are both secrets that we share in our attempts to displace death, then DeLillo leaves us here not just with an understanding of theater as a model of denial, but also with the possibility of a community in agreement.[4]

Of course, the question of subjectivity haunts all of DeLillo's cultural productions. Curtis Yehnert insists that DeLillo's model of subjectivity is not merely postmodern. According to Yehnert, the self-deception of DeLillo's fictional characters is epitomized by his understanding of theatrical acting. Yehnert quotes Jolene and DeLillo himself to show that self-deception is at the core of his characters, making them "nearly all actors" (363). If this is true, then the theater is in fact the paradigmatic space for understanding the subjectivity of DeLillo's characters. Yehnert also claims that "[t]he quest for self" in DeLillo's work "is not a search for the real and true, but for a relationship with uncertainty, silence, death" (363). While the second half of this formulation is valid, it does not preclude the possibility of searching "for the real and true," at least not within the explicit framework of theater and performance. The very shift away from the real through the theatrical model of a doubled body (actor and character but also the body playing two different roles) within a doubled space (day room and hospital, hospital and motel, stage and day room) helps remind the audience of the relationship between death and truth.

The play begins and ends with Budge, who is also Arno Klein, doing tai chi. This movement art suggests the ways in which repetition is not a simple thing, but a complex spiraling practice, a different mode of understanding perception and subjectivity. Through this practice we can see the other characters' actions as a repetitive spiral that makes clear the value of the performance itself—the

---

[3]   One logical space to explore this is the work of Antonin Artaud and his sense of reality as the pale shadow of theater. The ways in which Artaud's beliefs about performance and the work of theater were also reflected in a biographically realized cultural definition of insanity might fit in here as well.

[4]   A related issue about secrets emerges in *Engineer of Moonlight*, DeLillo's first play, when Eric says: "It's hard, growing up. You realize at a certain point that all your secrets are common knowledge. Everyone knows who you are" (35). The exposure of the secret, or an initiation into the understanding of a secret as communal property, becomes the pathway into adulthood.

journey that is taken. Since a spiral is a circular movement that also provides for development and growth, it helps explain how DeLillo can see the play both as circular and as containing its own self-commentary.

By the end of the work, the audience is forced to realize that they have seen the very play referred to in the second act: they have witnessed Arno Klein. The performance by the Arno Klein players becomes an example of this new relationship between death and truth. By resisting consumption, they create the possibility of transformation rather than commodification. They do this not only through performances in places where it is difficult or impossible to find them, but also because both the characters and the form of the play place into question the very status of performance. Ideally, their audience has been transformed, like Freddie, into a group of people who understand that illusion also has a material existence. In relation to the knowledge of death, there is a shift from the normative simplicity of denial to a space of complex communal understanding through the acceptance of multiple levels of reality, a change that can move beyond the space of theater itself.

In a later pair of works, the play *Valparaiso* and the novella *The Body Artist*, DeLillo moves away from a general environmental awareness of death toward the representation of a more materially present death. *Valparaiso* explicitly stages a series of self-performances through interviews in various media, all represented theatrically, and all implicitly invested in a sustained denial of the presence of death. The ostensible subject is an inexplicable error in travel that has the central protagonist, Michael Majeski, set off one day for Valparaiso, Indiana, and end up in Valparaiso, Chile. The improvised journey Michael creates allows him to come back to a place where "death maintains an incandescent distance" (52). Michael's journey is occasioned by his role as a substitute doctor going off to treat a patient with "an unnamed rare disease" (21), invoking the space of medicine haunting *The Day Room*'s first act. Following the manifestation of his instant celebrity and the over 140 interviews he performs in 4 days, most of them deliberate attempts at repetition, he quits his job to devote his full energies to the labor of recounting his miraculous day. Though the act of flying to the wrong place is the genesis of the work, the point of Michael's celebrity, and the sound bite that introduces the play to prospective readers and audiences, the frame of his attempted suicide captured on video foregrounds an eerie question about the way the media allows for a displacement of issues of mortality.

Partially a development of Delillo's idea of technology as a mediator for ideas about death, *Valparaiso* presents the media initially as helping sustain a problematic form of denial. Although there are a range of media in *Valparaiso*, the central role of television shifts away from the relatively humanized representation of that medium in *The Day Room*, where a live actor performs as the television, to a more technological presentation with the live performance of the taping of a television talk show. A dialogue with DeLillo's sense of place in other works also echoes throughout the plot, adding airplanes to hospitals and motels as charged spaces, reminiscent of Wyatt's claim from *The Day Room*: "The hush of death.

On airplanes, in hospitals" (7). Michael's experience of flying indeed clarifies that airplanes are spaces in which death is palpably present.

Valparaiso is more widely produced than *The Day Room* but seems destined for brief quotations rather than sustained analysis by DeLillo critics. This mode of analysis reflects one subject of the play itself, the media saturation that reduces everything to a sound bite in an interview. The framing of the play by projected images of Michael's attempted suicide indicates not only the omnipresence of death, but also the forms of denial instantiated by an attempt to escape the self through travel. The first act is dominated by various narrative performances, recreating the banal cultural importance of his convoluted literal and psychological flight. Ironically, the space of the interview, while partially one of repetition, also becomes a space of discovery in the second act when the nature of the initial projected image is made clear. Through probing questions in the sustained television appearance that subsumes the entire act, the audience learns for the first time that this is a video of Michael's suicide attempt, which occurred during his flight from Florida to Chile, with a plastic blanket bag secured over his head and around the neck by dental floss. The first image of this, "projected on the back wall and adjacent furniture" while his wife Livia rides her exercise bike, deliberately conceals Michael's face, sustaining the mystery of the power of his flight from the self (13).

For DeLillo, *Valparaiso* is in part a search for the self and in part a question of the emptiness and omnipresence of the media. Michael's search for self-knowledge is haunted by specters of death and violence—his own attempted suicide and the psychologically damaging injury to his son, events not fully understood until the second act. These events are minimized by the very act of interviewing, in which a presentation of Michael's story, his journey, allows them to be forgotten in the shared fascination of the story. It is as if the forces of technology have entered the space of *The Day Room* and displaced the conversations about death into something hovering on the edges of the narrative.

The play's first act is an almost continuous stream of interviews with people who have particular and insistent demands, ranging from the expectation of a seamless relationship between the real and the interview—"Everything is the interview" (25)—to a request that Michael present his story in the present tense. Through Michael's performance, however, the paradox of the interview process itself becomes visible. On the one hand he is completely committed to the form, and yet at the same time he is continuously misunderstanding it and being betrayed by it. When he is interviewed he thinks that he is creating a unique commodity, but the interviewers are searching for repetition, not an act of spontaneity that exposes the emptiness of his narrative. The act of interviewing consumes all of his time and energy, taking over the narrative of his life, and his self is shaped by the need to endlessly perform the epic failure of his journey. Yet, the fact that his search for identity is caught up in this process of interviews makes the interview the ultimate form of denial through language that propels Michael forward. Here, the extractive conversational paradigm of the interview replaces the civilized conversation of *The Day Room* as a defensive tactic in the quest to evade the knowledge of death.

The interview structure seems designed to both recall and forget the emptiness of its own practice, but it cannot withstand sustained reflection. In Scene 7, the interviewer begins to reflect on her own experiences and the potential connection in the process: "And I wonder what he's thinking in his male-type mind. And what would happen if we stop talking" (46). The silence does not lead to the implied possible intimacy but to a question, "[t]hen what?" The interviewer observes that "[she] begin[s] to recognize the moment for what it is... the first faint sign of indifference in his eyes. Interview eyes. Soulless. Shifting" (47). This protected space is enabled, as we discover in the second act, by his attempted suicide.

For Anna Deavere Smith, character emerges in the moment where the self begins to articulate a counter narrative to that which is being presented in the interview.[5] But for DeLillo, the richness of the event lies precisely in the fundamental American belief of the necessity of submission to the act of becoming a media commodity: spectacularized and replicated. It is clear that there is immense personal and psychological loss involved in this packaging, but Michael buys into it because he invests in his journey as emblematic and as a story in and of itself. The media, however, understand that the story must continue toward a recognition of the fundamental denial at its heart. Michael's only escape in the first act is into narrative, which is not the liberating communal space of conversation in *The Day Room*, but the passive soporific space of the controlled flight. Michael's experience is one of accepting the power of the narrative (the flight itself) to direct his journey, even as he has willingly placed himself in this space of travel and display. This structure parallels an interview's voluntary process: not a presentation of self but a submission of the self to another for the sake of self-presentation. Not surprisingly, in the last interview of the act, Michael has reached the point where he is re-enacting, on command, the story he has told over and over again, moving him beyond language toward physical action.

This sense of performance is heightened in the second act of *Valparaiso* through the fictional frame of a television talk show filmed in "a living room set... identical in appearance to the living room of Act One" (61). The host of the talk show, Delfina Treadwell, is an oracular reflection of mediatized identity, her performance a commentary on postmodernity and technology.[6] Treadwell is the first interviewer to explicitly inform the audience that Michael's son Andy was

---

[5] In her introduction to *Fires in the Mirror*, Smith talks about the development of her technique of using interviews as scripts for performance: "I staged many of these interviews, looking for the moment in the interview when the celebrity was struggling with the interviewer to free his or her identity from the perception that the interviewer had" (xxix).

[6] See for example Duvall's "Introduction". Interestingly, Treadwell is also the last name of the old woman who dies of dread after being lost in a mall for a few days in *White Noise*.

"[s]eriously injured. And psychologically damaged as well" (74). Michael, driving drunk with his son not wearing a seat belt, caused an accident that seems to be the implicit catalyst for his journey. Though there were hints of guilt in the first act, an empty room and a child temporarily with his grandparents, the media elided this story in pursuit of the repetitious sound bite.

As the talk show continues, we learn that not only is Livia pregnant with someone else's child, but that Michael "is a man so deep in self-estrangement he conceals his own actions from himself" (87). These problems emerge not from "the guilt of a damaged child or troubled marriage... [n]ot even the heaving mediocrity of life," but from "[w]ho he is," according to Delfina and her assistant Teddy (89). This act of exposure clarifies Michael's articulated distance from himself and suggests that the celebration of his journey emerges from the failure of his intended suicide. Delfina not only exposes his suicide attempt, getting him to narrate the process, she appears to understand his true desire to die as the ultimate end of his quest to escape himself. She kindly assists him in the process, becoming responsible for both the reality and the emptiness of his death through the act of televising it as well as providing a narrative and physical assistance. She ensures its documentation, but in doing so makes it consumable like every other television tragedy. Yet, she also ensures that he does not give in to routine and in to the system as he did before on the airplane. (In his narrative he explains that turbulence followed by the captain's voice calling him back to his seat was enough to derail his suicide project.) Instead of dental floss Michael and Delfina use a microphone cord to strangle him, suggesting the power of the media in this death, while Delfina insists on tracing his "last living thought" (104). The last thing he sees, the last thing he hears, is a memory of a gate agent telling him that he is not following his itinerary. This comment would function as a metaphorically satisfying response verging on cliché except for the fact that this last line he "hears" is actually spoken by Delfina: "Why are you going to Chicago if your itinerary says Miami?" (106).

Michael's actual death onstage provokes almost no reaction from the onstage audience: "*Livia is motionless, staring straight ahead. Teddy browses in a magazine*" (106). But Delfina's final commentary nevertheless attempts to understand the ways in which death is mediated through technology.

> (*To camera*) Someone dies, remotely known to you, but how real and deep the loss? Who is he? An image aloft in the flashing air. Not even that. A set of image-forming units, sand-grain size, that shape a face on-screen. How can it be? A life so unfleshed takes up intimate space. Someone spun of lightwaves and repetitious sounds. How is it possible? This odd soak of gloom heavy in your chest. (*To audience*) We live in the air as well as the skin. And there is something in these grids of information that strikes the common heart as magic. (106)

Her performance is notable not only for the evocation of the emotional investment in televised reality, but also for the clear distinction between two different modes of address: the camera and the audience. Michael's suicide becomes a meta-commentary on the power of representation in relation to death—on the spaces between narrative, performance, and the media. As LeClair argues regarding *White Noise*, "[t]he effect of televised death is, like consumerism, anesthetizing" (*Loop* 217). Part of the implication is that death must be witnessed, must be live, must be televised. And yet, the irony is that unlike the fundamental ethical horror of the snuff film—real death transformed into representation—this event is in fact never real.

Valparaiso involves a live performance about mediation. As a way of eliding the power of the media, the saturation of this event is limited to the physical parameters of the stage space. By staging Delfina's commentary not as a speech in a prose narrative but as a dramatic monologue, DeLillo questions the very terms of both technology and death. The live studio audience is also a theater audience, operating in a mode of reception that acknowledges both the facticity and the fiction of Michael's death, depending upon how carefully they are negotiating the dual role of talk show and theater audience. Ironically, in talking about the power of "grids of information" and "lightwaves," Delfina is describing a spectacle that the theater audience has witnessed without the mediation of television. For her argument to succeed, we would have to be in the space of the implied television audience, not in the live studio audience. We would need to be physically detached from Michael's death, rather than in the real position of an emotionally involved live spectator to his theatrical demise.

Michael's death is unsurprising in 20/20 hindsight and functions as the logical extension of a spiritual pilgrimage to the wrong place, a continual denial of death that allows one to function within a community of souls imbued with the condition of perishability. As witnesses to this theatrical death, however, we also know that the body onstage is in fact acting and not dead. This doubled "performance" of death adds another layer to Wilshire's concern with the failure that emerges from "performing" death. Michael's first suicide attempt suggests Wilshire's position, the danger inherent in a man's decision to perform his own death in order to outlive it. However, the second moves beyond it, suggesting that an understanding of death must happen on multiple levels of signification and echoing DeLillo's deep investment in the multiple layers of reality in *The Day Room*.

DeLillo here achieves a reclamation of theater as a privileged space to engage with death, recovering what Barker would call the "art of the theatre." By using theater instead of narrative, DeLillo enables a different kind of epiphany for his audience at the close of the performance. At the same time, he remains inconclusive by ending not with the positive statement of Delfina Treadwell, but with a return of the chorus of Air Reliance flight attendants who have functioned as commercial interludes and as a sign of the corporate and institutional passivity enabled by the structure of air travel. Their last performance is an idiosyncratic safety demonstration. The chorus is halted ultimately in mid-gesture, indicating the continued presence of the pacifying systemic features that aid our denial. However, this incomplete gesture leaves open the possibility that our experience of Michael's pilgrimage has provided a moment of escape and resistance.

Though Michael is an ambivalent figure at best, he shows us that anyone can become an actor and can transform denial. His problematic status enables the transference of empathy, an understanding of our communal process of denying death through acting that allows the audience, both the television audience of the play and, ideally, the real audience in the theater, to communally escape this denial.

As an alternative to the witnessing of a performance of death, DeLillo crafts the modernist novella *The Body Artist*. In *The Body Artist*, DeLillo charts the transformation of the titular character, Lauren Hartke, following the suicide of her husband, Rey Robles, a film director. This death in the novella, unlike in *Valparaiso*, occurs in the first quarter of the story, a death still not fully present but mediated by second-hand reports and newspaper obituaries, by printed language rather than televised images. The rest of the novella focuses on Lauren's process of grieving, which also becomes the creation of a new piece of body art entitled *Body Time*. Here, DeLillo's modernist language points away from the technologically mediated and disassociated bodily experiences of postmodernism so visible in *Valparaiso*.

In an early interview, Michael Majeski describes himself as "cut off from everything around me. And from myself as well" (*Valparaiso* 15). In response to the interviewer's magic "as if" question, he responds: "Some stranger had crept inside, like surreptitiously, to eat my airline food. Or someone had been superimposed on me, a person with my outline and shoe size but slyly and fundamentally different" (16). While for Michael the sense of bodily displacement and substitution is a feeling, for Lauren it is her goal as she crafts a performance piece to help her "organize time until she could live again" (*Body Artist* 39). All of her narrated experiences are gathered for this piece, but unlike the previous works discussed here, television is completely absent. The only media is print and although Lauren speaks on the phone and listens to "the anonymous robotic voice of a telephone answering machine delivering a standard announcement" (108), her only other contact with technology is through the internet, where she primarily watches web camera images of a desolate road in Kotka, Finland. This image is presented as a video for her performance at the end of the novella, a performance whose only presence for the reader is in the shape of an interview/review of the work, not a narrative description.

The printed interview situates Lauren's work implicitly against the performances in *The Day Room* and *Valparaiso*. "The piece... sneaked into town for three nights, unadvertised except by word of mouth, and drew eager audiences whose intensity did not always maintain itself for the duration of the show" (*Body Artist* 106). According to Mariella Chapman, author of the imbedded review, "[s]he is acting, always in the process of becoming another or exploring some root identity" (107). This self-exploration seems antithetical to the practice of hiding, except that she "tries to shake off the body—hers anyway" (106). This review appears to invoke the historical and conceptual division between the illusory quality of theater and the putative embodied reality of performance art. DeLillo does not traffic in this debate, but spends his time thinking carefully about embodied knowledge as potentially privileged. The question remains, however, whether the act of grieving and performing comes to a greater understanding of the self or leaves it behind. "Hartke's piece begins with an ancient Japanese woman on a bare stage, gesturing in the stylized manner of Noh drama, and it ends seventy-five minutes later with a naked man, emaciated and aphasic, trying desperately to tell us something" (107).

This final figure is an embodiment of a presence, a sound that haunted the couple in their rented house even before Rey's death. Left alone in the large house after his death, Lauren isolates herself from others, eventually discovering the source of the noise, someone she calls Mr. Tuttle after a former teacher. He may be a ghostly visitor, some kind of apparition, an odd waif, or perhaps the product of her imagination as a way of filling in the loneliness during her space of grief. The figure is deliberately obscure, operating in a temporality beyond the linear.[7] The only clear material manifestations of Mr. Tuttle witnessed by someone other than Lauren are in the performance of *Body Time*, so it is never clear if he has a material existence beyond her creative imagination. However, his form of subjectivity, even if imaginative, provides a crucial alternative to the narrative of Michael in *Valparaiso*, suggesting that a changing relationship to time and linear experience in performance is a way of moving beyond our denial of perishability. At the close of the novella, after implicitly suggesting her own creation of Mr. Tuttle, though once again remaining elusive, Lauren seems to move back into a comfortable relationship with herself. "She threw the window open. She didn't know why she did this. Then she knew. She wanted to feel the sea tang on her face and the flow of time in her body, to tell her who she was" (126).

The linear movement of time becomes a means of self-definition for Lauren, bringing her back from a space of trauma and grief that left her without a defined self. This definitional quality of linear time is also present in a similar manner in *Valparaiso*. The sense of time, of a life marked by time, is echoed in the seconds and tenths of seconds that play in the video projection of Michael's suicide, a sense of clock time that is suspended in the space of *The Day Room* as theatrical time takes over, suggesting possibilities other than forward flow. Time and its acceptance thus becomes a way of thinking differently about the process of perishability. Since performance takes place not only in space, but also in time, this shift highlights the increasing attention in DeLillo's work to the power of performance as an engagement with death. Even though Lauren's performance may not always be of herself, it becomes clear that performance as a response to death involves a practiced and disciplined attention to the body, whether or not it is the self. Thus, performance and the space of theater enable DeLillo to shift the

---

[7]   Cf. Di Prete, who makes a compelling argument for the novella's articulation of the temporal experience and vocabulary of trauma through the description of Mr. Tuttle's experience of time.

terms of denial itself, making it a generative, creative art that offers a different way of engaging with the knowledge of our own mortality.

Works Cited

Barker, Howard. *Death, The One and the Art of Theatre*. New York: Routledge, 2005.

Becker, Ernest. *The Denial of Death*. New York: The Free Press, 1973.

Blau, Herbert. *Blooded Thought: Occasions of Theatre*. New York: Performing Arts Journal Publications, 1982.

——. *Take Up the Bodies: Theater at the Vanishing Point*. Urbana: University of Illinois Press, 1982.

DeLillo, Don. *The Body Artist*. New York: Scribner, 2001.

——. *The Day Room*. New York: Alfred A. Knopf, 1987.

——. "The Door Inside *The Day Room* (Notes Toward a Definitive Meditation)." *The Lively ART: A Treasury of Criticism, Commentary, Observation, and Insight from Twenty Years of the American Repertory Theatre*. Ed. Arthur Holmberg. Chicago: Ivan R. Dee, 1999. 87–88.

——. *The Engineer of Moonlight*. *Cornell Review* 5 (Winter 1979): 21–47.

——. *Valparaiso: A Play*. New York: Touchstone, 1999.

——. *White Noise*. New York: Penguin 1985.

DePietro, Thomas, ed. *Conversations with Don DeLillo*. Jackson: University Press of Mississippi, 2005.

Di Prete, Laura. *"Foreign Bodies": Trauma, Corporeality, and Textuality in Contemporary American Culture*. New York: Routledge, 2006.

Duvall, John N. "Introduction: from Valparaiso to Jerusalem: DeLillo and the Moment of Canonization." *Modern Fiction Studies* 45:3 (1999): 559–68.

LeClair, Tom. *In the Loop: Don DeLillo and the Systems Novel*. Urbana: University of Illinois Press, 1987.

——. "An Interview with Don DeLillo." DePietro 3–15.

McAuliffe, Jody. "Interview with Don DeLillo." DePietro 173–180.

Pastore, Judith Laurence. "Pirandello's Influence on American Writers: Don DeLillo's *The Day Room*." *Italian Culture* 8 (1990): 431–47.

Rich, Frank. "Theater: Don DeLillo's 'Day Room'." *New York Times* 21 December 1987.

Rothstein, Mervyn. "A Novelist Faces His Themes On New Ground." DePietro 20–24.

Smith, Anna Deavere. *Fires in the Mirror: Crown Heights, Brooklyn and Other Identities*. New York: Anchor Books, 1993.

Wilshire, Bruce W. *Role Playing and Identity: The Limits of Theatre as Metaphor*. Bloomington: Indiana University Press, 1982.

Yehnert, Curtis A. "'Like Some Endless Sky Waking Inside': Subjectivity in Don DeLillo." *Critique* 42:4 (Summer 2001): 357–66.

Zinman, Toby Silverman. "Gone Fission: The Holocaustic Wit of Don DeLillo."
     Modern Drama 34:1 (Mar 1991): 74–87.

Chapter 4

Dust to Dust and the Spaces in Between: *Six Feet Under, The Gate's Ajar,* and the Meaning of Death in American Christian Theology

Alasdair Spark and Elizabeth Stuart

The pilot episode of *Six Feet Under* was shown on the Home Box Office network in the USA on June 3, 2001. Created by Alan Ball, the screenwriter for *American Beauty*, it focused on the death of Los Angeles funeral director, Nathaniel Fisher, Sr., and the effect of his demise upon his sons, daughter and widow, all of whom in different and various ways could be said to represent post-feminist, post-gay liberation, post-sexual revolution, postmodern America. A success, the series concluded in August 2005 after five seasons and 63 episodes. Though evidently concerned with death and the funeral business, the episodes revealed the struggles of each member of the Fisher family in the aftermath of the death of the patriarch (who continues to appear to them individually). This initially suggested that *Six Feet Under* was going to be about life after patriarchy and how identities might be negotiated in a cultural space where patriarchy might be dead but still haunting its victims. As Dana Heller has noted, the dead in *Six Feet Under* pass across the consciousness of the Fisher Family as a multi-cultural rainbow of races, genders, sexualities, and classes, exposing and at the same time undermining the white, middle-class Fisher family and the particular fantasy of American national identity which they represent (82). However, a few months after the first season had finished, the United States found itself under terrorist attack and haunted by almost three thousand dead in New York, Washington, and a field in Pennsylvania. Suddenly, *Six Feet Under* was about more than the death of patriarchy; it was also about the death of security and about death itself. One of the final episodes deals explicitly with the Iraq War and the death by suicide of a severely disabled veteran ("Static," episode 62).

Death rips apart human constructions of reality and plunges the living into a fissure, a liminal space, an awareness of their own betweenness. In this way, "normality" is suspended and the usual rules of life cease to apply. Such a space is necessarily uncomfortable, but it does offer an opportunity to speak the unspeakable and confront that which is repressed. Alan Ball has noted that the dead function as a sort of "Shirley Valentine"[1] type of wall upon which the central characters in *Six Feet Under* project their concerns and engage in dialogue with themselves. "[W]hen death has touched your life in such a frighteningly intimate way, your entire world becomes surreal" (quoted in Heller 82.) The Fishers make this surreal world of the dead seem everyday. David, the Fisher who spends the most time with the dead, has the complexion and stiffness of an embalmed body. "I look like you," one corpse quips at him. He embodies the surreal, liminal state. (David also struggles with first accepting his homosexuality and then negotiating his gay identity. This provides one of the binding themes of the program.) His brother Nate, who literally ran away from death and the surreal funeral home location that was his childhood, is pulled back to it and the funeral business by his father's death. He then becomes seriously ill, loses his wife Lisa and finally dies. He thus becomes a ghostly presence, as his father had predicted when Nate first encountered him in his postmortem state in the morgue: "And you thought you'd escape. Well, guess what? Nobody escapes" (Pilot episode 1). Down in the basement, in the body preparation room, the Fishers seek to control death, to stitch together the wounds and stave off its decay. But even as they work against death, the dead force them to confront things they would rather deny, not the least of those being mortality. At home in their funeral home, the Fishers are unable to leave the liminal space of the dead. So the narratives of their lives hold up to western culture in general, and North American culture in particular, a deconstruction of the codes and constructions by which we regulate ourselves and others while living.

In as much as *Six Feet Under* might be concerned with the death of patriarchy, the death of security and the exposition and deconstruction of North American ignorance and fear of the processes of death and funeral practice, it focuses on a very specific segment of life after death, the time and space between death and the funeral. This is mapped out in the opening sequence of each program as a succession of images mixed together: pictures of the funeral director's clinical process conveying the human tragedy of death (for example, in clasped hands, rent apart) as a body is accompanied from hospital gurney to grave. The audience is confronted by the surreal nature of death in these opening sequences by Thomas Newman's haunting music, as the stark images are accompanied by a vivacious, light-hearted theme. Every so often a sharp clanging sound seems to convey the terrible suddenness and/or finality of death with the sound of a knife slitting something open or apart. At the very beginning of the title sequence a shimmering human form stands at the end of the corridor watching as the gurney on which the corpse rests shudders into movement. It is possible to read this shimmering figure as the dead person watching their own body being taken away for disposal to the funeral home. Interestingly, only Nathaniel Fisher, Sr., continues to appear after his burial. All the other dead are seen to disappear with their interment. In itself this reflects the beliefs of many religious traditions—including Spiritualism,

---

[1]   In Willy Russell's play *Shirley Valentine* (1986), the eponymous character talks to the wall in her kitchen and to a rock on a Greek beach to investigate her inner life.

Hinduism, ancient Judaism, and some Native American traditions—that the dead stay close to their bodies until the funeral rites when the living and the already dead assist them in passing into the next life. (This is particularly evident in "Everyone's Waiting," the final episode, where Ruth sees Nate in her last moments and David sees his former lover, Keith.) But it also neatly suggests the existence of an afterlife while at the same time avoiding the representation of what the content of that existence may be.

Within its liminal spaces, *Six Feet Under* constructs the dead as utterly vulnerable. Of the 77 deaths depicted in the program, only 13 could be classified as deaths by natural causes. Eleven murders and 8 suicides are reported. One man is mauled to death by a cougar ("Ecotone," episode 60). Another is executed by lethal injection ("Twilight," episode 38). Another is killed by a falling lunch box ("Someone Else's Eyes," episode 22). And another is chopped to pieces in a dough mixer ("The Foot," episode 3). Death is depicted as a violent, messy, and random event—sometimes so tragic as to be absurdly comical. As such, death mocks our attempts to construct daily meaning and long-term security around ourselves. The modern "natural" death in old age is displaced in this program by a thoroughly postmodern death: the surprise of our own mortality (post-AIDS and post-9/11). The program shows the vulnerability of the human body, lying broken, burned, burst open, and naked on the Fishers' preparation table. It is finally consigned to the hands of the strangers on whom the dead are dependent for the navigation of the liminal space into an unknown beyond. Paradoxically, though, vulnerability is also the source of strength. The dead are beyond the confines of the smugly secure construction of the western subject. This is conveyed in the pilot through the advertisements for various funeral products which punctuate the episode, their humour lying in their absurdity. But the dead are past the comforts and constructions which capitalism seeks to bring to death and they mock the Fishers' efforts to reconstruct them. The dead do not care any longer about personal hygiene. So in their freedom, lying in the cool dark of the mortuary, they offer the Fishers a new horizon from which to review their own lives.

David Fisher's struggles to come to terms with his sexuality are conducted almost entirely in a dialogue with the dead. In the fourth episode of season one, "Familia," a deceased Latino gang member called Paco, murdered by a rival gang, engages in conversation with David while his chest is being stitched together, ribbing him about his profession and sexuality. Later, he challenges David's acceptance of homophobic abuse and encourages him to stand up for himself both as a gay man and as an independent funeral director. "Don't be a pussy," he advises when David's mother begins to ask questions about his relationship with his lover Keith. Citing Christian Scripture, he compares David's denial of his own sexuality, and his impatience with Keith's resistance to homophobia, to Peter's denial of Christ. Paco encourages David to understand that masculinity and Christianity can involve resistance to homophobia even as he forces him to acknowledge his own gayness through light-hearted abuse. "Let go of me, you fucking fag," he barks at David as they clasp hands in the final moments of the funeral. His last words to

David as he follows his own coffin are "Don't be a bitch" ("Familia," episode 4). In this surreal, queer space of death no one has to follow society's scripts any longer and a gangster can become the voice of God and liberalism.

Later in the first season, in the episode "A Private Life," David has to deal with a victim of a vicious homophobic attack. The deceased, Marcus Foster, again confronts David with his doubts over the compatibility of his sexuality and his faith. From the slab, Marcus tackles David using a standard Christian fundamentalist discourse: being gay is not what God intended; it is a choice. Marcus propels David into adopting a counter position; thus David persuades himself out of his own internalized homophobia. The rawest moment in this episode is when Marcus, his ghostly face still battered and covered in blood, says to David, "no matter how nice you fix me up, I'm going to Hell... 'cause you're going there too" ("A Private Life," episode 12) His words are mirrored at his funeral on placards held by Christian protestors (as they were at the funeral of Matthew Shepard, the gay student murdered at the University of Wyoming at Laramie in 1998). But they are violently resisted by David who falls to his knees at the end of the episode, pleading with God to help him: "Take this pain away. Please fill this loneliness with your love. Help me, God. Please help me." David's prodigal brother, Nate, is also baited by the dead. In a third season episode, "The Trap," he is forced to face his ambivalent feelings about his relationship with his wife, Lisa, by the ghost of a man who had been missing for twenty-five years, after leaving his family one day to buy a newspaper and never returning, and who now challenges Nate to do the same ("The Trap," episode 31). However, this time he stays.

Thus, in *Six Feet Under*, in accordance with the beliefs of many religious traditions, the dead are at their most disturbing and dangerous in the liminal time between death and the funeral. They nag the living, challenging, mocking, and saying the unsayable, "I'll say whatever I goddamn please," Paco responds when David objects to him, calling him a "born bitch" during his funeral ("Familia," episode 4). The Fishers may be able to control the corpse—stitching, cleaning, dressing and making up the body—but evidently they cannot contain the spirit/soul. And yet, as already noted, what sustains their continued existence and where the dead go when the Fishers despatch them are not examined in the program. This is not to say that religion is ignored. David's faith is as central to his identity as his sexuality, and the tension between the two is one of the dominant themes of the first season. Christian, Buddhist, Jewish, and Humanist funerals are depicted. But no religious underpinning is offered for the appearance and disappearance of the dead. In the obituary of the final season's last episode, "Everyone's Waiting," the deaths of the Fishers as much as eighty years in the future are recorded. Thus, the audience is caught up more intensely than ever in the transcendence of reality and yet still no theology of a life beyond the funeral is offered.

In one of the most powerful sequences of the first episode in season three, "Perfect Circles," Nate is first shown as having died on the operating table. He then has a conversation with his father about consciousness and parallel universes. The conversation ends with Nate opening his coffin. A blinding light streams out of it that eventually blanks out the screen and the '2002' from Nate's obituary. Nate is not dead after all but his conversation with his father is the closest the program comes to offering a description or explanation of a life after death. Consciousness may reside in and be shaped by subatomic particles that move backwards and forwards in time and are in all places at once ("Perfect Circles," episode 27). The existence of worlds beyond (and in parallel with) our own is acknowledged but no religious explanation is offered for them.

The origins of this vision of a death without an afterlife can be found in an earlier American response to the facts of death. The Fisher family business has its beginnings in response to the American Civil War (1861–65), which disrupted the set pattern of domestic, familial death. The very large loss of life (to disease and famine as much as to battle) required the development of methods for transporting the dead and techniques for preservation. Specialist firms followed the troops to war and began to advertise their services to families in advance of battle. The development of the funeral director business then advanced apace after the Civil War under the influence of a new theology of life after death, evoked principally by one novelist, Elizabeth Stuart Phelps. Her *Gate's Ajar* series (1868–1901) preached the continuity of life after death. It thus encouraged the desire now typical of American families and provided by American morticians—to preserve the body from decay in a state that reflects life rather than one that recognizes death.

In many ways Elizabeth Stuart Phelps's novels had a similar impact in post-Civil War western culture as *Six Feet Under* has had in our post-9/11 age. *The Gate's Ajar* was first published in 1868 and sold 80,000 copies in America and 100,000 in Britain (Kelly 7). Only Harriet Beecher Stowe's *Uncle Tom's Cabin* outsold it in nineteenth-century America. It was a publishing phenomenon, was translated into several languages, and spawned an industry of goods, including funeral songs, a cigar, a collar, and a tippet (Ward 113). It inspired a whole new genre of writing about the afterlife and was satirized by Mark Twain (Suderman). Phelps herself followed the novel up with more on the same theme: *Beyond the Gates* in 1883, *The Gates Between* in 1887, and *Within the Gates* in 1901. The original novel was inspired by Phelps's dissatisfaction with the theology of life after death taught at Andover Seminary in the face of the Civil War. Phelps, the daughter and granddaughter of prominent Congregationalist theologians, grew up in the seminary. Though officially barred from study there because of her gender, she managed to attend classes with the famous theologian Professor Park. It was in his classroom that she first became fully aware of the limits of the theology she was being taught. The Civil War broke out in 1861 and in such a heavily masculine place as Andover the effects were immediate and devastating. Phelps recalled the sound of drums resounding through the window of her theology class and the lecturer falling silent. "Silence helps the drum-beat, which lifts its cry to Heaven unimpeded and the awful questions which it asks, what system of theology can answer?" (Ward 72). Certainly not the Calvinistic theology of "Brimstone Hill," as Andover was known (Kelly 27).

Phelps herself lost to the war a young man to whom she had "a deep attachment," Samuel Hopkins Thompson. The Civil War and the failure of the theology of her father to deal with death in a way that she and other women found satisfying and comforting prompted Phelps to begin writing *The Gate's Ajar* in 1864 when she was just 20. (She had already had a short story published at 13.) Looking back on her motivations thirty years later she wrote:

> wished to say something that would comfort some few... of the women whose misery crowded the land. The smoke of their torment ascended, and the sky was blackened by it.... For it came to seem to me, as I pondered these things in my own heart, that even the best and kindest forms of our prevailing beliefs had nothing to say to an afflicted woman that could help her much. Creeds and commentaries and sermons were made by men. What tenderest of men knows how to comfort his own daughter when her heart is broken? What can the doctrines do for the desolated by death? They were chains of rusty iron, eating into raw hearts. (Ward 97–98)

Phelps then was motivated to write out of a profound sense of the failure of Christian theology to speak with any authenticity *to women* (that is to say to those who grieved) at a time of crisis and by a conviction that this was at least partly due to the fact that the dominant theology of her time and context reflected the experience of men.

The extraordinary success of the novel suggests that she hit a nerve. In order to understand the appeal of *The Gate's Ajar*, one must understand something of the shifting patterns of understandings of life after death in Christian doctrine and culture. Colleen McDannell and Bernhard Lang point to two dominant models that seem to have alternated in Christian history: 1) the theocentric which emphasizes the discontinuity between this life and the next and which tends to present a non-social, static image of heaven in which the soul is lost in adoration of God; and 2) the anthropocentric which emphasizes the continuity between the present and next life and presents a social image of heaven in which human relationships still matter. The "modern heaven," as it emerged in the eighteenth and nineteenth centuries, was ultra-anthropocentric and the social matrix of the Church was replaced with the married couple or the family. Thus, Emanuel Swedenborg's (1688–1722) vision of a materialist and social heaven, in which there is change and progress towards an angelic existence, is also a busy one and a sexual one. True loves (not necessarily married on earth) will be united and indeed it is this perpetual passion that will be the essential source of eternal happiness.

Lang argues that Swedenborg created a rational heaven for a rational age that was only too ready to dispense with "unreasonable" Christian belief in the resurrection of the body. It was in the process of jettisoning the ancient Christian belief that all desire has its *telos* in God for the modern belief that all desire has its *telos* in heterosexual relationships. Swedenborg's visions may have been dismissed by Kant as "eight volumes quarto full of nonsense" (101).

But his influence was vast on new faith structures such as spiritualism and Mormonism and on mainstream Christian theologians. For instance, Charles Kingsley, the Christian socialist, novelist, and chaplain to Queen Victoria, believed in the eternity of marriage and one of his drawings depicts a couple with wings engaged in sexual intercourse. Susan Chitty has said that, for Kingsley, heaven "would consist of one perpetual copulation in a literal physical sense" (17). Less graphically, William Blake in one of his sketches, "The Meeting of a Family in Heaven" (1808), had already domesticated heaven by depicting it as a nuclear family reunion, with parents and children locked in an embrace surrounded by protecting angels. It was this vision that Elizabeth Stuart Phelps developed against the reformed theocentric view of heaven, which she encountered all around her, but which gave no consolation to women affected by the Civil War.

The two central characters in *The Gate's Ajar* are female. Mary Cabot is the narrator who is thrown into despair by the death of her brother Royal in battle. Dr. Bland, her minister, and Deacon Quirk only add to her pain by preaching a theocentric view of heaven in which human relationships are severed. Mary muses, "If I were to go there it could do me no good for I should not see Roy. Or if I should see him standing up among the grand, white angels, he would not be the old dear Roy. I should grow so tired of singing! Should long and fret for one little talk...." (10). Wracked with grief for her brother and for her beliefs, Mary absents herself from communion and refuses to conspire with the spiritual platitudes of resignation and God's will that come from the clergy. For this she is branded as rebellious, doubts are cast on her brother's redemption and she faces the constant repetition of a theocentric understanding of the afterlife in which human relationships are absolutely severed.

Into her despair comes Mary's maternal aunt, Winifred Forceythe. (Note the thoroughly female alliance.) A thirty-five-year-old widow, she can empathize with Mary's pain and with her distress at her church teachings. "She put her other arm around me with a quick movement, as if she would shield me from Deacon Quirk and Dr Bland" (52). Aunt Winifred preaches against Dr. Bland through the evidence of her own consolation and through her theologizing. A widow of a clergyman and well read in theologians past and contemporary (Augustine, Luther, Taylor, Hamilton, Robertson, Butler, and Chalmers), whose wisdom she drops into conversations, Winifred sets out gently but resolutely to deconstruct the theocentric heaven of Bland and Quirk. She accuses Bland and Quirk of constructing a cold, abstract heaven inappropriate for a warm relational humanity or indeed for a God who became human (109). She argues that, in rejecting the materialism of the Roman Catholic Church, Christians of their sort have "nearly stranded ourselves on the opposite shore," which involves a forgetting of Christ's humanity and the implications of it for a life beyond this one (110).

In response to Dr. Bland's assertion that the "glory of God is the primary consideration," Winifred replies: "But the glory of God *involves* these lesser glories, as a sidereal system, though a splendid whole, exists by the multiplied differing of one start from another" (109). She accuses them of failing to appreciate the symbolic value of the Book of Revelation:

> Can't people tell picture from substance, a metaphor from its meaning? That book of Revelation is precisely what it professes to be,—a vision, a symbol. A symbol of something, to be sure, and rich with pleasant hopes, but still symbol.... It never occurs to them, that, if one picture is literal, another must be. If we are to walk golden streets, how can we stand on a sea of glass? How can we "sit on thrones"? How can untold millions of us "lie in Abraham's bosom"? (77–78)

As long as the Bible, common sense, and reason do not forbid a particular conjecture, Aunt Winifred is happy to advance it as a probability nearly amounting to certainty (87). Thus, she is heavily dependent on Butler's theory of analogy and Platonic notions of the ideal. She constructs a thoroughly relational and domestic heaven from biblical references, reason, and experience. She argues that since this life is a preparation for the next, God would not have created love between people simply to sever it at death (74).

Winifred has a thoroughly relational view of the human person; to be human is to be in relationship with others. Therefore, to go into the next life stripped of those relationships would be to go shorn of one's individuality (86). She notes that Mary did not love Christ less once Lazarus was raised (53). So why should loving a human being diminish or detract from love of God? Her favorite biblical passage is the Transfiguration because it seems to confirm individuality, continuity, and relationship—and the kind of supernatural embodiment that is necessary for social intercourse (75). Winifred reflects the then common belief that the soul passes immediately into heaven with some kind of embodiment that may change at a future resurrection (113).

Although she explicitly denies being a Swedenborgian, Winifred acknowledges that she used to be influenced by him and in private admits to Mary that "Swedenborg is suggestive, even if you can't accept what seem to the uninitiated to be his natural impossibilities" (171). She finds his vision of celestial cities compatible with biblical revelation and subscribes, without acknowledging it, to his theory of the angelicization of human beings after death and the possibility that some return to earth as God's messengers (89–92). She finds it frustrating that biblical commentators will not allow her to translate certain passages to justify her belief. (She specifically names "Stuart"—Phelps's actual grandfather.) But this does not stop her, because for Winifred experience is the ultimate authority.

Winifred's adoption of a Swedenborgian position on angels also enables her to postulate the existence of marriage in heaven. "Christ expressly goes on [from having denied marriage in heaven] to state, that we shall be *as* the angels in heaven. How do we know what heavenly unions of heart with heart exist among the angels?" (166). Her Platonism allows her to postulate heaven as an ideal form of earthly life in which relationships are restored, domesticity reigns, and little girls are given pianos rather than harps (144–45). With regard to hell, Winifred does not seek to deny its existence; she can only conclude that we will not love those who hate God and hence there will be no pain at a separation (167). It is Christ rather than God who features in Winifred's heaven. She imagines him inhabiting heaven in human form as a friend to its denizens (200–201). And it is on Jesus's humanity that Winifred's ultimate hope rests, "He knows exactly what we are, for he has been one of us; exactly what we hope and fear and crave, for he has hoped and feared and craved, not the less humanly, but only more intensely" (203). As "our great Type, no less in death and after than before it," he demonstrates the reality of the continuous personality and the maintenance of relationships (204).

In the end even Dr. Bland comes round to Winifred's thinking but only after himself experiencing the torture of losing his wife in a horrendous accident. "No Greek and Hebrew 'original,' no polished dogma, no link in his stereotyped logic, not one of his eloquent sermons on the future state, came to his relief" (217). He experienced their "cold steel" and could only cry out against "the blank heaven of his belief." The only form of comfort comes in the shape of Aunt Winifred before whom he stands "like a man and like a minister, hardly ready to come with all the learning of his schools and commentators and sit at the feet of a woman" (218). The final triumph of this female theology based upon analogy, conjecture, and intuition over male orthodoxy is symbolized by Bland throwing his sermon on heaven onto the fire (220). Having capitulated to Winifred's theology Bland becomes more human and Mary "more ready to be taught by him than ever before" (223). Then, having triumphed over Bland, Winifred develops breast cancer. She dies taking a message to Roy and greeting her long departed husband with her last earthly words.

As this suggests, Aunt Winifred was in many respects a prototypical feminist theologian. Well versed in contemporary scholarship, she privileges women's ways of knowing, particularly relational knowing, and women's experiences as well as women's needs, against a rational, non-relational theology. Acknowledging no boundaries to her sources and grounded in a Christology that stresses the humanity of Christ, she constructs a theology for a specific time and place. In responding to the needs of women, this ultimately satisfies the deepest longings of men as well, as the conversion of Dr. Bland to Aunt Winfred's ways of thinking demonstrates, and as the popular response to the novel confirmed. As Aunt Winifred defeated the theological establishment, so did Elizabeth Stuart Phelps herself. The reaction to her book from theologians was predictably outraged and dismissive. She who had spent her formative years on the outskirts of the theological establishment at Andover took some delight in the fact that the religious papers "waged war across that girl's notions of the life to come.... Heresy was her crime, and atrocity her name. She had outraged the church. She had blasphemed its sanctities...." (Ward 118–19). Obviously influenced by the classical liberal theology of Schleiermacher and Coleridge that emerged out of the Romantic Movement, Phelps produced a piece of theological reflection in novel form that exposed the inadequacy of contemporary American Protestant theology in the face of war, death, and bereavement.

Sales of her novels demonstrate that Phelps spoke to the spiritual crisis of her generation in a manner that her father and other contemporary theologians could not. According to Helen Sootin Smith, writing in the introduction to the 1964 edition of *The Gate's Ajar*, Phelps spoke to "thousands of semi-educated readers" to whom neither transcendentalism nor Unitarianism appealed. A contemporary suggested that the novel's success lay in the breaking of the taboo on speculation about the afterlife, which dominated American Christianity at that time (Spring 567). Like Emily Dickinson (who may have been an influence upon her) Phelps took on the "tyrannical Father-God of New England orthodoxy" and his cold heaven (St. Armand 56), replacing him with "the mother God who serves her children" (McDannell and Lang 272). Phelps took women's experience seriously, perhaps too seriously, and gave it ultimate value. It did not merely point towards the truth but was the truth. As Stansell notes, "to comfort the women she gave them the hope of a women's heaven, a paradise ordered on the small scale of a woman's life: gardens, furniture, New England cottages, children, and sitting room pianos" (244). The horizon was extended, but only so far. Aunt Winifred conjures up a heaven that is inhabited by happy, self-indulgent, self-satisfied people, who are busy loving, working, and playing with other white, Anglo-Saxon Protestant Americans, most of them friends of the narrator. There are a few, if any, poor people there; it is filled as the churches of the time were with the upper and middle classes of society (Suderman 99).

It was this that led Mark Twain to describe her vision as "a mean little ten-cent heaven about the size of Rhode Island," while others spoke of "a celestial retirement village" or said: "Boston tea-drinkers, here is your paradise at last" (McDannell and Lang 273–74).

Ann Douglas offers a searing critique of Phelps's work in the context of her analysis of the "feminisation" of American culture in the nineteenth century. She locates *The Gate's Ajar* within the consolation literature of the period, as a form of protest against "the competitive, aggressive, non-familial society" America was becoming under capitalism, which saw women and clergy confined to the domestic sphere, but as guardians of American culture that promptly proceeded to feminize and in particular to maternalize (200–226). What heaven awaits Phoebe, Mary's servant, remains unclear. But given that Winifred believes that this life is a "great school-house" for the next and that talents picked up here will be fully extended there, a downstairs afterlife might be expected. Douglas chiefly laments this process in which theology was lost to religiosity, literature, and "feeling," because sentimentalism was no opponent to capitalism.

Yet, despite the undoubted crassness of Phelps's vision of the afterlife, it was a form of protest literature within its context. Even while it was implicated in that context—perhaps being most offensive in its unthinking glorification of materialism—it was also a resistance to the marginalization of women in the growth of the capitalist order. It was thus a defiance of the assumption that "masculine" virtues and the public stage of competition would have the last word. It shares with

Six Feet Under a desire to transcend the rational and enter into a space beyond reason, even though if it does not quite manage it.

Like Phelps, the creators of *Six Feet Under* must deal with death and the dead at a time when dominant religious discourses fail to satisfy, despite a cultural compulsion to look into the face of death and feel insecure about living. In the process of doing so, they too have cast a large question mark over hetero-patriarchal normativity and dominant religious orthodoxies. However, while Phelps dared to move beyond the liminal and the surreal into the realm of the dead, Alan Ball and the scriptwriters of *Six Feet Under* avoid this precisely. Even God is absent from the world of the dead in *Six Feet Under*. In this it reflects the postmodern phenomenon of the re-enchantment of the world following the death of metanarratives and the Enlightenment project. Postmodernism has opened up a rationalized western culture to Otherness, to spaces of transcendence, magic and mystery, a space teeming with angels, faeries, and the like. But in contrast to the pre-modern western world, this Otherness is a parade. It has no foundation, no anchor, no consistency and no ultimate explanation. It is possible these days to believe in angels without adhering to any of the belief systems from which angels emerge. It is just as possible to believe in life after death and in ghosts without rooting that belief in any religious narrative. (Evident, for example, in the rise of TV psychic mediums such as John Edwards.)

Six Feet Under demonstrates that in a postmodern cultural context it is easy for the dead to re-emerge from the shadows of modernism and claim back their place in our consciousness. *Six Feet Under* recognizes this by challenging the modern tendency to disguise death by hiding it in hospitals, hospices, and industrial crematoria or the parallel tendency (surely inspired by Phelps and the other creators of the modern heaven) to embalm, stitch up, and make-up the dead for satisfactory viewing by the living, presenting them as comfortable, happy, complete, and even looking domesticated and alive. By presenting death as random, messy, and difficult in the series—and presenting the dead as being with us still, laconic and disconnected—death is rendered mysterious once again, even as unveiled in its gory, painful detail. Each episode begins with an end that parodies and deconstructs the modern construction of history. The dead have not fallen off the end of the conveyor belt of life, they are somehow still present. However, as befits a good postmodern sensibility, death is mysterious, but not religious. We are presented with a series of micronarratives (most episodes begin paradoxically with an obituary) but no metanarrative, not even in the finale of the series. The corpse of the week is never situated within a larger story or related to other dead persons.

Six Feet Under also portrays the curious disconnection between Christianity, death, and the afterlife under these same contemporary postmodern conditions. As the Radical Orthodoxy school of Christian theology has pointed out, it has yet to recover from a disenchantment that took place under modernity and that some believe resulted in the contraction of Christian discourse to the mundane (Smith). At the same time, in order to secure its place in the academy, theology ceased to speak of the supernatural or surreal in any realistic manner. Instead of considering life after death, theology threw itself into theologizing about life before death. The dead and life after death are not subjects of much interest to contemporary theologians. Sex and sexuality, on the other hand, seem to be much more available as topics for contemporary theological disputation, almost to the point of obsession. This shift in Christian discourse is illustrated in *Six Feet Under* by the fact that the Church appears principally as an actor in the drama of David's sexuality. It is sidelined in death, rendered shadowy and virtually invisible, unmentionable and silent, even in the overtly religious culture of the United States in which church attendance remains high and disputes about Church and state remain lively. As *Six Feet Under* indicates, the Church appears to have largely forfeited its role as the midwife of the liminal space of death, as assisting both the living and the dead through this space of betweenness. Often, the Church seems speechless in its presence.

All of this matters because, like Phelps's novels, *Six Feet Under* proved popular. It was one of the most acclaimed TV series of recent years, winning forty-two awards during its five seasons. At least part of the explanation for its success must lie in how it dealt with death and the dead in an unapologetic, unhesitating and unflinching manner. It met a cultural yearning (repressed though it may be) for a confrontation with the inevitable and for a search for meaning within death. In one sense the timing was fortuitous, since these desires could only have increased after 9/11, an event which made death, funerals, memorials, and other observances front page and prime-time news. From 2003 onwards, the coffins coming home from Iraq have kept such issues current. In some ways it might be seen as a diversion, since *Six Feet Under* offers a vision of a life beyond not just death but beyond patriarchy, beyond contemporary constructions of gender, race, and sexuality. Yet, it thus fulfills one of the traditional roles of religion in providing an eschatological platform from which we may review, critique, and seek to transform our lives. In this, the non-specific genre of the program (drama? comedy? tragedy?) proved a valuable asset. If tragedy and comedy are the twin components of all religion, they are held together perfectly in the program from the moment the theme music begins to the closing credits. To laugh in the face of death is to seek to deprive it of its ultimate power over our lives. In dealing with death so openly and so comically, *Six Feet Under* worked to deny the grim reality which otherwise it displayed so often. In doing so, it spoke the very words that religion now finds the hardest to articulate—words against death—but without the promise of a describable, discernable hereafter (Davies 1–22).

Phelps's understanding of death or heaven contained no mystery. It was simply an extension of this life underpinned by the Christian metanarrative. Though a form of protest literature, it offered the comfort of a fissure repaired, of normality resumed, values reasserted, and relationships restored. In effect, it was the comfort of the embalmed body restored to "life," clothed in its Sunday best, smiling serenely, and suggesting an experience of happiness unavailable to the living. The dead in *Six Feet Under* are different. While subject to the embalming process by the Fishers (though Nate is resistant to it and buries his own wife out in the desert unembalmed and un-coffined), the dead critique the process and refuse to play the part which religion has created for them. Walking and talking with their final human contacts, they refuse to slip peacefully and immediately either into the eternal adoration of a theocentric heaven or into Phelps's family reunion in the sky. Their refusal suggests an afterlife thoroughly other than that—too other to depict in fact. They make demands of the living. They require attention. They create and need drama. They suggest that life goes on, but they will not (or cannot) tell us where, how, or why. In *Six Feet Under*, death is made deeply mysterious again. For, as 9/11 and the events which followed it have reminded us, nothing and nobody deconstructs our metanarratives like death and the dead.

Works Cited

Chitty, Susan. *The Beast and the Monk: A Life of Charles Kingsley*. London: Hodder and Stoughton, 1975.

Davies, Douglas. *Death, Ritual and Belief*. London: Continuum 2002.

Douglas, Ann. *The Feminization of American Culture*. New York: Knopf, 1977.

Heller, Dana. "Buried Lives: Gothic Democracy in *Six Feet Under*" in *Reading Six Feet Under: TV to Die For*. Ed. Kim Akass and Janet McCabe. London: I.B.Taurus.

Kant, Immanuel E. *Dreams of a Spirit-Seer*. New York: McMillan, 1900.

Kelly, Lori Duin. *The Life and Works of Elizabeth Stuart Phelps, Victorian Feminist Writer*. Troy: Whitston, 1983.

Lang, Bernhard. "The Sexual Life of the Saints: Towards An Anthropology of Christian Heaven." *Religion* 17 (1987): 149–71.

McDannell, Colleen, and Bernhard Lang. *Heaven: A History*. New Haven: Yale University Press, 1988.

Phelps, Elizabeth Stuart. *The Gate's Ajar*. Boston and New York: Houghton, 1868.

St. Armand, Barton Levi. "Paradise Deferred: The Image of Heaven in the Work of Emily Dickinson and Elizabeth Stuart Phelps." *American Quarterly* 29 (1977): 55–78.

Smith, Helen Sootin, "Introduction" to Elizabeth Stuart Phelps, *The Gate's Ajar*. Cambridge: The Belknap Press, 1964.

Smith, James K.L., *Introducing Radical Orthodoxy: Mapping a Post-secular Theology*. London: Authentic Media, 2005.

Spring, Elizabeth T. "Elizabeth Stuart Phelps" in *Our Famous Women: An Authorised Record of their Lives and Deeds*. Hardford: A.D. Worthington, 1883: 561.

Stansell, Christine. "Elizabeth Stuart Phelps: A Study in Female Rebellion." *The Massachusetts Review* 13 (1972): 239–56.

Suderman, Elmer F. "Elizabeth Stuart Phelps and *The Gate's Ajar* Novels." *Journal of Popular Culture* 3 (1961): 92–106.
Ward, Elizabeth Stuart Phelps. *Chapters from a Life*. New York: Arno, 1896.

PART II
Tracing Ghosts

Chapter 5

Thornton Wilder's "Eternal Present": Ghosting and the Grave Body in Act III of *Our Town*

Anne Fletcher

Thornton Wilder's exploration of ontology through theatre—his admixture of verb tenses, his hyperbole about humankind in relation to the universe, his creation of both a literal and a metaphysical landscape in situating his characters, and his prizing of the simple actions of daily life—find their most successful expression in the "American classic" *Our Town*. And it is within *Our Town*'s graveyard scene that Wilder's thoughts on the corporeal and the spiritual are best interpreted. Drawing on the playwright's insistence that the stage operates in the "eternal present," I will examine the performance of the grave bodies as ghosts in *Our Town*. I will also consider how Wilder's representation of the dead points to the possible instilling in his audience of a desire to attain "presence" in life. For, if there is a message to be gleaned from *Our Town*, I contend that it lies in the Zen notion of "presentism," as Emily espouses in "living every every minute" (Wilder 110). Utilizing precepts of Buddhism,[1] while touching on New Time Theory and acting theory, I will gloss the final act of *Our Town*, focusing on the various representations of the dead in it and Wilder's purposeful juxtaposition of them: from the inherently optimistic Mrs Soames to the dower Simon Stimpson who committed suicide, to the sage Mrs Gibbs who admonishes her newly-dead daughter-in-law to refrain from testing a return to the living and to continue with the process of "letting go." Through an examination of the degree to which each grave body, as a ghost, has abandoned the physical world and looks toward the eternal, and how each is portrayed onstage by the living actor in "real" time, I assert that Wilder's schema parallels Buddhist thought with regard to living, dying, and letting go. Wilder's means to that end include his deployment of states of being, notions of knowing and remembering, and a non-linear view of time.

In my analysis, especially with regard to acting Wilder's "eternal present," I will refer to Southern Illinois University Carbondale's 2005 production of the play.

---

[1]   With its integration of meditative practice with tasks of daily life, Zen is perhaps the most popular school of Buddhism in the West, and may well be the most applicable to *Our Town*. For the purposes of this study, however, rather than apply precepts of a particular practice, I have elected to employ terminology from an array of Buddhist epistemologies.

This particular production is crucial to my arguments, not simply because I was involved with its dramaturgy, but because the director, Lori Merrill-Fink practices insight meditation. Also, Hilary Chandler, the actress playing Mrs Gibbs, is even more studied in Buddhist practice than I and utilized concepts to which I refer in this article in her performance. Two other cast members were privy as well to my coupling of Buddhist theory, play analysis, and critical theories. I was careful, however, after discussions with Merrill-Fink and Chandler, to refrain from interjecting my theories into the rehearsal process, as we all agreed that the acting problems inherent in playing a state of being, as will be discussed shortly, are not easily navigated by undergraduate actors.

In Act III of *Our Town*, Wilder weaves a complex expression of time, place, and action. Through his deployment of what might be termed "deep" time, simultaneity of time (and action), or non-linear time—akin to that purported by New Time theorists, non-Western notions of "presentism," and "witnessing"—in addition to his presentational stage conventions, Wilder highlights a philosophical confrontation between the living and the dead as well as offering an internal debate among the dead as to the meaning of life. The intricacy of this layering of time, corporeality, and action is compounded in the play's production, as the theory and practice of acting and performance reverberate and rebound off the performance text. For in *Our Town*'s final scene we see *live* actors *in the present* portraying: 1) live characters in a present state of bereavement; 2) a newly deceased character onstage in the form of a ghost, attending her own funeral while her physical body is ostensibly present onstage in its coffin—a position to which I will refer as "the in-between"; 3) the more "experienced" or longer dead; 4) live characters in the present; and 5) live characters enacting a scene from the past, with a "dead" character returning to her twelfth birthday in the costume of a young girl, but in the physical body of an adult woman. Wilder's tinkering with temporality problematizes the traditional acting practice of "immediacy" or "being in the moment." By contrasting the peace and knowledge of the dead with the carelessness of the living, Wilder challenges reader, audience member, and actor with the difficult task of striving for "presence."

Also at play concerning time in *Our Town* is a self-referential version of Marvin Carlson's "ghosting"[2] and a canonical reverberation similar to that cited by Harry Elam in his recent work on August Wilson.[3] By this I mean that traces from Wilder's earlier pieces appear in this play almost *verbatim* and significant moments from within the play itself inform later moments. Traces of the historical past and of the fictive past of Grover's Corners haunt the play as well. Time, then—time as present, time as past, time as static, time as active, time as repetitive

---

[2]   Carlson explores the "ghosts" of past theatrical productions that inform the spectator's reception of productions in the present. See also Pizzato.

[3]   Elam describes the ways in which the plays in Wilson's canon reverberate off each other, reference other African-American plays, and relate to African-American history and culture in resounding and often surprising ways.

and/or ritualistic, time as memory, and time as eternal and infinite—operates variously throughout the play, culminating with the interactions of the living, the dead, the in-between and the eternal in Act III.

Before examining Act III, it is profitable for us to investigate Wilder's notion of "positionality" and to consider how the playwright utilizes simultaneity, syntax, and stage semiotics to create a cosmology within the world of the entire play. Wilder creates a powerful yet subtle belief system that subverts typically Western notions of time as it situates itself in a prototypical New England setting. Wilder's metaphysics do not spring *a priori*, nor are they confined to the world of this particular play or the cosmology depicted in *Our Town*. Throughout most of Wilder's career—in his novels, short plays, and full-length plays alike—the author struggled to articulate his beliefs about the relationship of life and the living to the dead and the hereafter.

Three earlier one-act plays serve as direct antecedents for *Our Town*, as do at least two novels, *The Woman of Andros* (1930) and *Heaven's My Destiny* (1935), in their treatment of characters who are given the opportunity to return from the dead. The Alcestis myth was Wilder's lifelong obsession (Blank 16). In *Thornton Wilder*, Rex Burbank acknowledges "The Long Christmas Dinner," "Pullman Car Hiawatha," and "The Happy Journey to Trenton and Camden" as "works in which he [Wilder] tries for the first time to affirm the presence of universal religious and moral values in the everyday lives of Americans" (66). Burbank also credits "Pullman Car" as Wilder's attempt at "combining all levels of time and space and relating the life of the mind to the life of the universe" (71). Wilder scholars aver that this one-act is the closest of Wilder's plays to *Our Town* in terms of theme(s). In "Pullman Car" we see Wilder's experimentation with positionality, contextualizing the present action in terms of the past. The three early pieces, published together in 1931, point to Wilder's desire to "make the opaque matters of everyday transparent" (Burbank 67), and to utilize a fairly objective depiction of daily rituals to point toward discoveries about life. Through his deployment of theatricalism and minimal staging techniques, Wilder could relate the daily to the eternal and within the worlds of the plays articulate a metaphysical construct.

On the other hand, Wilder's novels prove problematic in their explication of his message and warrant mention here by way of comparison to techniques he later utilized with the grave bodies in *Our Town* and with regard to the implications derived from the live bodies portraying them onstage. Wilder's successful treatment of metaphysical subject matter onstage contrasts with his clumsy and didactic expression of the same in narrative form. Malcolm Goldstein assesses the novel *The Woman of Andros*:

> For the most part the book presents a philosophical discourse without the action necessary to sustain it; we are taken into the thoughts of the characters for a direct revelation of their anxieties, but denied the satisfaction of observing these anxieties expressed through action. (Goldstein 68)

I maintain that *Our Town* still troubles the relationship between stasis and action, but that Wilder deliberately utilizes this to build to his contrast between the living, the dead, and the "in between" in Act III. In *Our Town*, Wilder lends action to his philosophical discourse. The intertextuality of Wilder's works is a "bonus" for readers and audience members familiar with his other writing. But knowledge of Wilder's complete canon is not a prerequisite for appreciating the belief system presented and debated in *Our Town*.

In *Our Town*, the ubiquitous character of the Stage Manager wanders throughout the play. His omniscient presence pervades the play's action. As the playwright's *raisonneur*, he embodies the residents' and, by extension, our own pasts, presents, and futures. The Stage Manager is, as Peter Arnott spoke of the Greek Chorus, both "in" and "out" of the play's action. The script is peppered with the Stage Manager's witticisms and musings. The play's action demands that he step in and perform certain roles: soda fountain proprietor and minister. Even the Stage Manager's *absence* is marked. For when he exits the stage we are drawn into the play's action in the present tense and are exposed to its representational elements, namely the realistic behavior of the characters in their relationships, the topicality of their conversations, their desires, and the tactics they use to attain them. This couching of the representational within a presentational framework, this balance between the two, assists us in accepting both the theatricality and the believability of the graveyard scene.

The syntax of the Stage Manager's lines offers us a window into Wilder's concept of the stage as existing in what he dubbed the "eternal present." For the Stage Manager utilizes verb tenses that carry us across time not only within the confines of the play's action, but backward to a time before the play begins, forward beyond the scope of the play's action, and even into time as experienced by the dead. Wilder himself proclaimed "the notion of time as immutable and consecutive action" (quoted in Bryer 33), as merely one option in a multiplicity of modes of expression. "In *Our Town*," Wilder said, "time was scrambled, liberated." For example, time is conflated in the Stage Manager's forecasting: "First automobile's *goin'* to come along in about five years," followed immediately by a switch in verb tense, "*belonged* to Banker Cartwright," and reverting to the present, "*Lives* up in the big white house" (Wilder, *Our Town* 7, emphasis mine). Shortly after this speech, the Stage Manager tells us that "Doc Gibbs *died* in 1930" (9). Another significant instance—and one that will be recalled in Act III—is when the Stage Manager speaks of Joe Crowell's demise. In Act I (May 7, 1901), Joe has just spoken with Doc Gibbs and the Stage Manager interjects:

> Want to tell you something about that boy, Joe Crowell there. Joe was awful bright—graduated from high school here, head of his class. So he got a scholarship to Massachusetts Tech. Graduated head of his class there, too. It was all wrote up in the Boston paper at the time. Goin' to be a great engineer, Joe was. But the war broke out and he died in France—All that education for nothing. (11)

Throughout the play, then, the Stage Manager operates among different planes of time and different planes of consciousness. Actors and audience members are cognizant of the present date of the production (and the Stage Manager states it). But the play opens in 1901, flashing forward and backward at designated moments, as the script reverberates off and subtly displays the time of its composition (1938, pre-World War II America). Wilder's toying with time is intricately crafted. He subverts chronology, the expected mode and indeed the arc of the play's story of George and Emily, not only by flashing forward and backward, but by interrupting one action with another and then abruptly halting the action he inserted. Examples of this tactic are the move from the wedding to the soda fountain scene, its subsequent truncation, and the Stage Manager's thanking Mrs Gibbs and Mrs Webb as he shoos them off the stage and moves on with other action. As Wilder himself proclaimed, "Time is something we create... not something we submit to...." (Haberman 58).

To emphasize the value Wilder places on the rituals, habits, and small details of everyday life in this deceptively simple little play, he contextualizes Grover's Corners and its population. The most stunning instance of this positionality is Rebecca's often cited recollection of the address on Jane Crofut's letter from her minister:

REBECCA: It said: Jane Crofut; The Crofut Farm; Grover's Corners; Sutton County; New Hampshire; United States of America.

GEORGE: What's funny about that?

REBECCA: But listen, it's not finished: the United States of America; Continent of North America; Western Hemisphere; the Earth; the Solar System; the Universe; the Mind of God.... (48)

Later in the play we learn that Rebecca left Grover's Corners and moved to Ohio; Mrs Gibbs died there when she traveled to visit Rebecca. Much later in Act III, we also return to the metaphysics Wilder established with the address above as we witness life and death positioned against the universe and the Mind of God.

There are other examples throughout the play, as Wilder deftly sets Grover's Corners in relation to specific geographic locales, near and far, as well as in time. The play vacillates between giving us the sense that Grover's Corners is the center of the universe, its inhabitants unique, and the notion that even if the town stands in for all American small towns, it is banal and its citizens insignificant. In Act II, just before the drugstore scene, Emily declares, "Grover's Corners isn't a very important place when you think of all—New Hampshire" (71). She pauses, to draw her comparison, for the scope of Emily's physical world is small. This oscillation between specificity and generality is established at the opening of the play. In the Stage Manager's first monologue not only are we immediately introduced to *Our Town*'s theatricality and presentational style of production, but the Stage Manager specifically names the particular production's director and actors, "produced and directed by A... (or: produced by A...; directed by B...). In it you will see Miss C...;

Miss D...; Miss E...." (5–6). This gesture of naming the actors not only establishes the play's metatheatrical quality, but it complicates the audience's reception of the characters these actors will play. At other times throughout the piece, the Stage Manager directs the actors and fully acknowledges the artifice of the stage. Wilder's deliberate distancing of performer from role, and hence from audience, has implications for the graveyard scene in Act III and for the Stage Manager's final speech of the play.

The Stage Manager identifies Grover's Corners in terms of longitude and latitude and the town's proximity to Massachusetts. Wilder's ghosting of the past as informing the present onstage, through his manipulation of time and place and his positioning of Grover's Corners vis-à-vis the town's heritage and its people's ancestry, appears again when the ancestors witness George and Emily's wedding. Wilder's framing device—the omniscient Stage Manager's speeches and his mention of the cemetery with its "earliest tombstones" that "say 1670–1680" (8) — does not serve simply as a trite organizational crutch. These speeches, along with other devices, legitimatize and contextualize the lived experience of Grover's Corners. Professor Willard's appearance, with his attendant social standing as a professor and his "factual" account of the town's sitting "on the old Pleistocene granite" as "some of the oldest land in the world," functions in much the same way (23).

The Stage Manager's speech on the burying of the cornerstone for the new bank looks forward to the future: "for people to dig up... a thousand years from now...." (35). He comments on the technological advance that will preserve the "reading matter with a glue—a silicate glue—that'll make it keep a thousand—two thousand years." Again, he places Grover's Corners on a time continuum as he alludes to Babylon and ancient Greece and Rome. The metatheatrical quality of *Our Town* surfaces also when the Stage Manager includes a copy of the script in the time capsule, "So—people a thousand years from now—this is the way we were... in our growing up and in our marrying and in our dying." According to Wilder's own writings about this play, he was "searching for a new form in which there will be a perpetual counterpoint between the detailed episodes of daily life—the meal, the chat, the courtship and the funeral—and the ever-present references to geological time and a distant future for the millions of people who have repeated these moments" (quoted in Bryer 33). This reverberation of the past against the present and future—through remembrance and repetition—adds immediacy to the cemetery site rather than the scene's action. As we will see, the scene is often purposefully static and Wilder employs "states of being" in it rather than a series of action verbs.

The passage of time remains important throughout the play and the Stage Manager is its primary purveyor. At the top of Act II he tells us that three years have passed, emphasizing and defining the time span through phrases like "a thousand sun rises" and "a thousand days" (49), explaining how much and yet how little can happen over the course of a three year period. It is here that he enumerates the themes of the play's three acts: "Daily Life," "Love and Marriage," and "another act coming after this: I reckon you can guess what that's about" (50). At the opening of Act III the Stage Manager informs us that another nine years have passed. But, the linearity of time and its passage is not Wilder's primary concern. Just as he offers the trellises "for those who think they have to have scenery" (7), he begins each act by having the Stage Manager place the play's action chronologically to keep his audience acclimated. The play's action then progresses chronologically, but time is as mutable as it is in Greek tragedy. Wilder allows the Stage Manager to conflate time and at the beginning of Act III to place the activities in Grover's Corners—and by extension all human activity—as timeless,"on the whole, things don't change much around here..." (88). Again, Wilder balances the mundane and the vital, pointing to how the inhabitants of this small New England town stand in for all humanity, emphasizing the repetition of the cycle of life with its attendant daily rituals and important ceremonies such as birth, marriage, and ultimately death and funerals.

Just before he stands in as the minister who performs George and Emily's wedding ceremony, the Stage Manager offers one of the most effective of Wilder's ghostings: "And don't forget all the other witnesses at this wedding,—the ancestors. Millions of them." Wilder himself acknowledged how he deliberately utilized the words "hundreds," "thousands," and "millions" to emphasize the repeated rituals of life in *Our Town* (xii). As time blurs a-chronologically, as rituals are recognized and enacted inter-generationally, as humankind is situated against the universe and all eternity in *Our Town*, Wilder expresses the Buddhist precept of the "universal One"—the idea that we are all part and parcel of a greater world that moves on and across time in perpetuity and ultimately in peace.

In the wedding scene, both Emily and George panic and wish to remain as they are, in essence to stop time. Emily exclaims, "Why can't I stay for a while just as I am?" (81). At this point in their lives George and Emily are motivated by their fear of their future. Their desire to remain unchanged is not evocative of a newly found appreciation of life in the moment. Due to the fact that much human behavior is fear-based and rooted in projection onto the future or dwelling on the past, Buddhist mythology is filled with parables about facing one's fear. Meditation is the Buddhist's primary aid in alleviating the pains and sorrows that arise when fear reigns and when focus is placed on the past or future rather than on the lived present. For now, Wilder allows the young couple's trust in each other to resolve their temporary terror, as Emily asks George to love her, "I mean for ever. Do you hear? For ever and ever" (82). The notion of eternity permeates the play and is of primary concern in Act III when time, place, action, and even corporeality are called into question along with prescriptions for living and processes for dying. The Stage Manager summarizes: "everybody knows in their bones that *something* is eternal...." (90). Wilder's depiction of the dead in Act III points toward what that "something" might be.

In Act III Wilder recalls individual images he utilized in the earlier acts and puts them to work in combination. Some of the most poignant and potent of these images are the celestial ones that have subtly shone through the entire play.

As the Stage Manager describes the hilltop cemetery with "lots of sky, lots of clouds,—often lots of sun and moon and stars" (88), we recall a young Emily commenting on the "terrible" moonlight. Or we remember the Stage Manager's opening monologue when he described the sunrise and noted, "The morning star always gets wonderful bright the minute before it has to go,—doesn't it?" (6). Yet, when he muses about the eternal, the Stage Manager points to humanity and not to the stars: "And it ain't houses, and it ain't earth, and it ain't even the stars... that something has to do with human beings" (89–90). Dead human beings, according to the Stage Manager, wait for their eternal part. As they wait, "the earth part of 'em burns away, burns out..." (90)—like a meteor as shooting star. Earlier in the play, the ladies walking home from choir practice stop in their tracks and, according to Wilder's stage directions, are "silent for a moment, gazing up at the moon" (41). Little Rebecca likewise muses that "the moon's getting nearer and nearer and there'll be a big 'splosion," wondering if the moon is also "shining on South America, Canada and half the whole world?" (45). But for the grave bodies in the cemetery, the stars bear greater significance than they do for the living, and the play ends with the Stage Manager's allusion to the entire galaxy. In the graveyard scene, Mrs Gibbs focuses on a distant star and encourages Emily to do the same. As actress Hilary commented about her portrayal of Mrs Gibbs at SUIC in fall, 2005: "For me, it was all about stillness." It is Chandler's comment that helps us enter into a discussion of the performance of the grave bodies themselves, to examine them in relation to their counterparts in the realm of the living, and to the cosmos.

At the act's opening, Wilder prepares us for the deep structure of Act III, which combines multiple levels of time, Buddhist-like contemplation, and celestial imagery to prompt a sense of stillness and acceptance in actor, character, and audience. We enter a scene of deceptive simplicity which becomes increasingly more complex. Only at the play's end do we recall that *Our Town* embodies stillness and simplicity. Wilder's stage directions note that the audience has witnessed the stagehands re-setting the stage for the cemetery scene. Rows of chairs have been placed to represent graves and cemetery markers. At the end of the intermission, actors take their places, seated in these chairs; one is left empty, of course, for Emily. Wilder is careful to warn his reader that, "The dead do not turn their heads or their eyes to right or left, but they sit in quiet without stiffness. When they speak their tone is matter-of-fact, without sentimentality or, above all, without lugubriousness" (87). The grave bodies' lack of "stiffness" and their "matter of fact" tone point subtly to two crucial elements of Buddhist practice: the notion of simply "being" and the attainment of "balance."

Once again we can draw a significant comparison between Wilder's *Our Town* and the practice of meditation. For the products of both give the appearance of ease and effortlessness but are in truth founded on skill and practice. The "first pillar" of meditation is concentration: focusing without straining, which creates a state of openness and receptivity.

> The state of concentration we develop in meditation practice is tranquil, at ease, relaxed, open, yielding, gentle and soft. *We let things be*; we don't try to hold on to experiences. This state is also alert.... It's awake, present, and deeply connected with what's going on. *This is the balance we work with* ... (Salzberg and Goldstein 15, emphasis mine)

In their workbook on insight meditation, Sharon Salzberg and Joseph Goldstein expound on the tightrope metaphor often used in explaining this balance: "your most important balance is to be at ease, not too tight, not too lax. The same is true of meditation. You simply stay as balanced as you can" (18). The aim in the practice of meditation is to be fully present with what is, with life on life's terms. This goal is paralleled by Wilder both thematically (in his message about appreciating daily life) and practically in his expression of time onstage—its enactment in the moment, and yet its connection with all eternity. Meditation is referred to as "non-doing" (18), a concept related to the acting problems in Act III.

In keeping with Wilder's intentions, the SIUC production's director Merrill-Fink admonished her cast of "grave bodies" to "speak to each other as if you were still alive" and "ignore all stage directions about disembodied voices." Before the dead begin to speak, the Stage Manager delivers a lengthy monologue in which he introduces the grave bodies, reminding us of who the secondary characters were earlier in the play. But he also explicates the dying process or, more specifically, the departure of the dead from worldly confines, constrictions, and concerns:

> the dead don't stay interested in us living people for very long. Gradually, gradually, they lose hold of the earth... and the ambitions they had... and the pleasures they had... and the things they suffered... and the people they loved. (90)

Here the Stage Manager expresses the Buddhist principle of "letting go"—a concept not unique to Buddhism, but executed perhaps most purely by its practitioners. According to Buddhist doctrine, it is advisable to recognize that with every breath we die a little. Daily meditation is practiced so we will be prepared for the moment of physical death and ultimately let go with ease and freedom, in peace. Buddhist practice involves recognizing how little we control in life and thus relaxing into a state of powerlessness and acceptance, a state in which we no longer grasp for unattainable goals. Buddhism is not a giving up; it is a way of coping with the negativity and pain that unwarranted striving perpetuates. Buddhists attempt to live life without "likes" and "dislikes" or at least to acknowledge ambitions, pleasures, and desires for what they are. In Act III of *Our Town*, through his interpretation of the processes of dying, Wilder advocates a state of being akin to that purported in Buddhist thought.

The Stage Manager explains to the audience the differences between the dead and us. In his fictive account of a place where the living, the newly dead, and the dead might meet, he thus delineates the grieving process.

> Some of the things they're going to say maybe'll hurt your feelings—but that's
> the way it is: mother 'n daughter... husband 'n wife... enemy 'n enemy... money
> 'n miser... all those terribly important things kind of grow pale around here. And
> what's left when your memory's gone, and your identity, Mrs Smith? (90)

As he transitions from one section of the speech to the next, the Stage Manager
once again breaks the fourth wall, this time insinuating himself into the realm of
the audience by interrogating a figurative "Mrs Smith." In this way he extends
Wilder's notion of memory and identity to the audience, including us all in the
process of "letting go," reminding us that each of us will pass the way of the
grave bodies someday. Not only does Wilder challenge our notion of memory,
but he takes on the frightening concept of identity. A common meditative practice
involves practitioners asking themselves, "Who am I?" They continue to probe
with additional queries, such as "Am I my job?" and "Am I my body?" or "Would
I still 'be' without my head? Without my arms? Without my legs?"—until they
reach a state of knowing that there is something that would still "be," but it is not
based on mind, intellect, or physicality.

Likewise, the Stage Manager's speech at the opening of Act III is notable for
embodying Wilder's treatment of death, the afterlife, and eternity, or what Wilder
named "the All, the Everywhere and the Always" (quoted in Burbank 66). It also
illustrates his technique of reprising thematic concerns and images, culminating
in an extended scene fraught with expressions of awareness and degrees of being,
levels of being that have every bit as much to do with the processes of acting the
scene as they do with living life, and with dying well. For example, the word
"know" is utilized by Wilder no fewer than twenty-five times in Act III of *Our
Town*. "Understand" and "realize" appear four times each; "remember" and
"forget" (or "forgotten") a total of eight times. The notion of memory is implicit
throughout the scene, beginning with the Stage Manager's linking it to "identity"
as the act opens. Remembrance, remembering with reverence, what we remember,
and what we forget are vital concepts in an examination of Act III.

Wilder's use of transitive verbs rather than active verbs, however, complicates
the actors' jobs in performing their grave body roles in the cemetery scene. Beyond
the implication that the actors must play a negative intention or a state of being,
they also must tackle the nearly impossible task of playing a dead object onstage.
Wilder has created difficulties for his actors by loading the scene with levels of
being (or becoming) as opposed to actions. He has positioned the bulk of the cast
in chairs, limiting their physical movements and forcing them to be still, although
not inanimate. The Stage Manager and Emily do move about, and Dr and Mrs
Webb re-enact the scene of Emily's twelfth birthday, into which Emily steps as
well. Joe Stoddard and Sam Craig appear as living characters who speak, yet the
funeral procession is mimed in silence. Even Dr Gibbs and George, as the living
at their wives' graves, utter no lines and their movements are limited. With regard
to this lack of physical movement in the scene (and recalling Hilary Chandler's
comment on playing the grave body of Mrs Gibbs), I argue that the force and

presence of stillness, if we allow ourselves to surrender to it, can be far greater than the might of movement.

Earlier in his career, Wilder wrestled with the metatheatrical depiction of action in his plays, and with expunging didacticism from his novels. Influenced to a large degree by Gertrude Stein[4] and dissatisfied with his early novels (except for *The Bridge of San Luis Rey*), Wilder worked toward developing his own theory of drama. In "Some Thoughts on Playwriting," he commented on stage time and theatricality. He ultimately preferred drama to narrative fiction because the theatre audience sees "pure existing" (96) and stage action takes place, regardless of the characters' use of verb tenses, in the "perpetual present" (83). As Burbank notes, "Wilder achieves thereby on stage a present that encompasses all time—the action becomes an 'Act in Eternity'" (89). However, while noble and successful overall, this notion of the past within the present, and of all time being present onstage, makes the playability of the drama problematic. In his analysis of *Our Town*, Burbank continues, "The conflict is basically inner, between consciousness and unconsciousness or between awareness and appreciation of life and insensibility and self-perception" (90). Thus, it is difficult for an actor to play inner conflict. Actors usually perform actions, not states of being.

Yet Wilder's non-representational staging technique is part and parcel of his dramatic theory. It was his intention for theatricalism to serve as the underpinning of his philosophical musings on the efficacy of the theatre and on the very nature of being. To Wilder, European realism and the well-made play form encouraged determinism and patriarchy, with realism existing only in the past tense. He sought to create something different in the American theatre, something immediate, and he believed the most productive route to this end was through theatricalism and simplified stage semiotics. As Christopher Wheatley asserts, Wilder's theatre "occurring in the present tense should escape determinism and authority by *presenting being in action*" (144). To Wilder, "it is precisely the glory of the stage that it is always 'now' there."

The reconciliation of "being" and "action" becomes the central problem in staging Act III of *Our Town*. Ac*tion* and ac*ting* are, of course, closely related. Hence, actors utilize action verbs as they execute tactics in the interest of achieving objectives; their objectives embody the pursuit of whatever their characters want. Director and acting theorist Robert Cohen even categorizes all tactics as falling under the rubrics of "to threaten" or "to induce" (70). The conundrum of Act III becomes the problem of effectively presenting being in action.

Wilder's syntax in *Our Town* offers clues as to how that problem might be reconciled by director and actors. Wheatley describes the play as "a series of gerunds, 'growing,' 'living,' 'marrying,' dying,'" and posits that these verbs become

---

[4] Gertrude Stein's thoughts on being an American, America in terms of time, place and action, cogent language, and humankind versus eternity all influenced Wilder during their long friendship. It is significant that their friendship blossomed prior to his penning of *Our Town*.

"nouns through enactment. The residents of Grover's Corners are not identified by a past... but by their actions in the stage's eternal present" (151). Gerunds, too, are arguably less effective than action verbs in terms of acting choices. This lovely notion of "the stage's eternal present" is successful in production only in so far as theatrical production (as opposed to film) involves the corporeality of the actor in relation to the immediacy and proximity of the audience. The essence of this audience/stage dialectic lies at the crux of Wilder's "eternal present" and relates to another of his suggestions in "Thoughts on Playwrighting," his notion of the "group mind" or collective conscious.[5] It is through the liveness of actor and audience that empathy is produced. Because of *Our Town*'s ultimate subject matter (death and the afterlife), Wilder's ghosting achieves a grandness that may well surpass all other American dramatic literature.

Thus, spectators bring to the experience of Act III all of their personal "baggage" concerning memory, death, and dying—their own ghostings. They identify primarily with Emily as she comes to the realization that she failed to appreciate and live life fully. But the audience also identifies tangentially with each of the secondary characters and their philosophies. They and their ancestors merge with the audience's heritage as time and action converge, putting character, actor, and audience all on the same plane of experience or being. This conflation of experience allows the audience to take part fully in the lived experience of Act III and to fully identify with the grave bodies on a moment-to-moment basis. As a result, Wilder and the actors who perform the cemetery scene succeed in presenting states of being. I contend that it is the multiplicity of levels of being-ness and knowing-ness, brought together in a shared, lived experience with the audience that allows for this ghosting to succeed onstage.

Because of the simultaneity of several levels of time (and of consciousness), coupled with the disjuncture of time when Wilder interjects the flashback scene, Act III is a complex scene to analyze. To do so, with emphasis on the grave bodies, we must disentangle the layers of time and parse the scene. The Stage Manager's wonderful line about "layers and layers" is apt with regard to Wilder's deep structure and appropriate in evaluating his expression of what it means to be dead. An apt analogy often used by Buddhist practitioners regarding layers of being is that of the onion: as its layers are peeled, one after the other, there is nothing but being at the center.

The town's cemetery is peopled with a variety of characters: those with whom the audience became familiar earlier in the play and several "extras," named and unnamed, who are brought in here, at the end of the play. Among the dead, there are twelve speaking parts. We learn, through his conversation with the undertaker, Joe Stoddard, that Sam Craig's parents are buried there, too, and Old Farmer McCarty as well. Some have been dead longer than others. Together and individually the

---

[5]   In "Some Thoughts on Playwrighting," Wilder addresses the celebratory, festival quality of the theatre experience. He notes that "the pretense, the fiction on stage would fall to pieces and absurdity without the support accorded to it by a crowd...." (90).

grave bodies, to varying degrees, illustrate the process of dying, the phenomenon of being dead, and the possibility of eternal life.

Apart from Emily, the principles in the scene are Mrs Gibbs, Simon Stimson, and Mrs Soames. In life, Mrs Gibbs was kind to Stimson and in death she continues to tolerate his persistent pessimism. Mrs Soames functions in much the same way she did earlier at the wedding: she interjects pithy comments and muses over what life was like. Mrs Soames and Stimson seem to remember a great deal more than Mrs Gibbs, indicating, as we will see according to Wilder's continuum of the dying process, that they have not been dead as long. (According to Joe Stoddard, Mrs Gibbs died "two-three years ago.") Sometimes with Mrs Gibbs as their mediator, Mrs Soames recalls happy memories of life while Stimson ruminates over the darker side of existence.

> MRS SOAMES: Childbirth. *Almost with a laugh.* I'd forgotten all about that. My, wasn't life awful—*With a sigh.* And wonderful.
> SIMON STIMSON: *With a sideways glance.* Wonderful, was it? (95)

Occasionally, lines are also attributed simply to "The Dead" and are apparently spoken in unison, chorus-like.

The living include Joe Stoddard, Sam Craig, Dr Gibbs, George Gibbs, the Webbs, and the four unidentified pallbearers. Those who live in the past are Dr and Mrs Webb, Howie Newsome, and the Constable. The Stage Manager moves freely among the dead, the living, the in-between, and those occupying the lives past in the birthday scene, marking his presence as eternal, at least within the world of the play. In Buddhist philosophy, at the time of death we move into an in-between state known as the "bardo" and we are offered a guide. Likewise, the Stage Manager might be considered Emily's guide in Wilder's play.

It has been raining, and the mourners constitute a mass of umbrellas; the pallbearers carry Emily's coffin. They mime this; the space occupied by the imaginary coffin is obscured from view.

> *Pause. Suddenly Emily appears from among the umbrellas. She is wearing a white dress. Her hair is down her back and is tied by a white ribbon like a little girl. She comes slowly, gazing wonderingly at the dead, a little dazed. She stops halfway and smiles faintly. After looking at the mourners for a moment, she walks slowly to the chair beside Mrs Gibbs and sits down.* (96)

As the newest arrival to the cemetery, Emily vacillates between her desire to remain in the world of the living and an almost instinctual pull to settle in among the dead. She is simultaneously nervous and in awe. Emily exists in a time and place of the in-between, bardo-like. She is disconcerted by her status as grave body and still clings to aspects of her corporeal existence, utilizing multiple verb tenses, like the Stage Manager in the past. "But, Mother Gibbs. How can I ever *forget* that life? It's all I *know*. It's all I *had*" (97, emphasis mine).

Mother Gibbs encourages Emily to talk less, to "Just rest yourself" and to "Just wait and be patient" (99). Emily is dismayed that Mrs Gibbs has forgotten her legacy and seems uninterested in the details of George and Emily's farm, the drinking fountain for their livestock, and their Ford. She glances almost furtively at the funeral party and bemoans the fact that "It won't be the same to George without me" (98). But Emily senses that she will eventually become accustomed to life among the dead. She describes the distancing process between her and the living that has already begun: "I feel as though I knew them last thousands of years ago." Yet, she still attempts to link the living with the dead when she recognizes Mr Carter: "Oh, Mr Carter, my little boy is spending the day at your house." "Is he?" asks Mr Carter, absently. The dead no longer grasp at the remains of their lives; they have already let go. But Emily is still torn. She recognizes some of the frailties of the human condition and asks Mrs Gibbs, "Live people don't understand, do they?" Emily also exclaims, "Mother Gibbs, when does this feeling go away? Of being... *one of them*? How long does it...?" (98–99). Dr Gibbs brings leftover flowers from Emily's funeral to his wife's grave. Emily struggles with her emotions, but the longer-dead Mrs Gibbs does not even look up at her husband kneeling before her grave, reminding us that she has moved beyond the earthly qualities of grasping or desire.

Emily, still clinging to aspects of the life she knew, imagines herself back on the farm and decides she will return to life. Before the flashback to Emily's twelfth birthday begins, the Stage Manager warns her, "You not only live it; but you watch yourself living it..... And as you watch it, you see the thing that they— down there—never know. You see the future. You know what's going to happen afterwards" (101). This notion of watching, or more specifically witnessing, is multifaceted indeed and compounds the acting problems inherent in playing this scene. "Witnessing" is another Buddhist concept and the Stage Manager's idea of watching yourself is framed in Buddhist terms. Witnessing is not necessarily judging, it is simply observing and it can occur in the meditative state or as a detached and rather disembodied feeling while awake. In Buddhism, however, witnessing has nothing to do with seeing the future, for all Buddhist practice transpires in the present. Witnessing is not an action and Buddhist theory is simply one lens through which to view *Our Town*. Asking actors to "play Buddhism" would be a fruitless endeavor indeed.

The actress playing Emily has already had to deal with the complexity of quickly changing objectives while she was seated in the cemetery—desiring to reactivate the living and at the same time to sit quietly with the dead. Presumably, she has found tactics and active verbs with which to work the scene. Now she must adapt to her situation as a performer playing a newly dead twenty-six-year-old character in the fictive present, then returning to fourteen years earlier in a fictive past. She is challenged to accomplish this acting feat without anticipating, without resorting to preciousness or posturing, and with the illusion of the first time, at the same time incorporating the Stage Manager's admonition that she watch herself and that she be mindful of the story's end. Wilder is at his most masterful in the flashback scene, for here he strategically allows dramaturgy, acting theory and technique, philosophy and metaphysics, and the shared experience of actor and audience to converge in touching and remarkable ways. It is in this section of Act III that we see Wilder's most effective execution of ghosting, figurative and literal, with Emily's return to life. For, with the ghosts of our communal and individual pasts as lived experiences in the mind, we watch the ghost character of Emily participate in a past experience with the newfound knowledge that no one in the scene lived the moment fully the first time.

Before Emily leaves the graveyard, however, Mrs Gibbs tries to dissuade her. As the speaking grave body most detached from the living, Mrs Gibbs defines the nature and purpose of being dead, "When you've been here longer you'll see that our life here is to forget all that, and think only of what's ahead, and be ready for what's ahead. When you've been here longer you'll understand" (101). Wilder never explains "what's ahead," but Mrs Gibbs's thought takes as its referent the Stage Manager's idea that the dead are "weaned away from earth" and await "the eternal part in them." Waiting is as difficult a "non-action" as any state of being an actor might play. A student of Zen Buddhism, Hilary Chandler (playing Mrs Gibbs) achieved an active stillness by focusing on the distant star. Despite the confines of a simple wooden chair, she used that star, somewhere out over the auditorium, as an object of meditation coupled with the notion that there is, for Mrs Gibbs, something "ahead." This approach enabled Chandler's performance to achieve an active stillness. Thus, for the duration of Act III, she evoked her experience of "presence" in a Buddhist sense and Wheatley's concept of "being in action."

The actress playing Emily, however, is further challenged as she enters the realm of the flashback scene. This scene is bound to the previously mentioned notion of remembering and forgetting (Bryer 33). Donald Haberman gives an eloquent explication of why Emily's return works so beautifully in *Our Town* and explains Wilder's unique expression of the past and memory.

> Wilder has... created his own time separate from that time of the audience.... He has presented in recognizable sequence birth, marriage, and death.... But the sequence—particularly its end in death—gives the events a special poignancy, and the events achieve a meaning beyond the sequence.... The repeated shifts in time are reminders that all parts of life's sequence are in operation for any number of people at any time. It is the force of memory that is always the present time. This memory, juggling all the events at once... keeps the action in the eternal now on the stage. Wilder offers memory as the real thing... a greater value than the actual experience. (58–59)

Here, Haberman explains how Wilder deliberately toys with time. But Wilder's use of time also relates to today's "New Time Theory," in which time exists without present, past, and future tenses (Craig, *Time* and *Tenseless*; Oaklander; and Oaklander and Smith). Eastern thought has long expressed time as a continuum, with the notion of reincarnation and the potential for numerous re-entries. The metaphysics of reincarnation involves the idea that we each possess an eternal spirit that returns, uniting with a new family and a new set of life circumstances until we learn the lessons we are intended to learn. But Wilder creates a unique framework in which time, experience, ritual, and memory combine with microcosmic and macrocosmic world views to express a philosophy that advocates balance—one that encourages appreciating the moment and accepting life (and death) on life's terms—a philosophy akin to, although not a replication of Buddhism.

The Stage Manager reminds Emily of forgotten details from the day: that it had been snowing, that her father had been away. Emily acknowledges the old white fence she had forgotten and the postcard album that was her birthday gift from George. The first pain she encounters as she relives that day from fourteen years ago is when she spots Howie Newsome on his familiar milk route, realizing that although she is immersed in the past and seeing him, he is really dead. She cries out in reaction to this strange simultaneity of time. Next, she encounters Joe Crowell, whom we know died in World War II. Then she observes her mother at work in the kitchen, going through the very same daily rituals she pursued for some forty years.

Helpful toward the playing of this scene (and others) is acting teacher Uta Hagen's reworking of her "moment of real life" exercise first expressed in *Respect for Acting*. Over the course of several decades, Hagen came to acknowledge the inability for the actor to remain "in the moment" for, as Emily says, "every, every minute." Hagen adjusted her exercise to take into account the idea that, as focused as one might be, the human mind is always looking toward the future.[6] In *A Challenge to the Actor*, Hagen created an acting exercise that accommodates simultaneity. In acting parlance, Hagen does not encourage "anticipation." What she allows for is the notion that "given circumstances" impending in the script can affect the present moment onstage (123–28). Thus, not only the actress playing Emily, but the character of Emily, like the person watching a sad movie for the second time, returns to life with the knowledge of what is to come. She knows the end of the story; she tries (as the character) to relish the moment, but is confronted with the lack of observation and appreciation that emanates from the characters in the living. It is this clash of sensibilities that affects the audience so intensely and gives rise to feelings of empathy, sadness, and regret.

The scene between Emily and her mother is perhaps the most troublesome in the play from a performance standpoint. Mrs Webb's nonchalance must contrast with Emily's anguish as she "can't look at everything hard enough" (107). Emily has become, as the Stage Manager intimated she would, both participant and witness. She is cognizant of how her life story will play out, resulting in her eventual trip up the hill, to her grave. She pleads with her mother, "Oh, Mama,

---

6   In the spring of 1992 I was privileged to attend a workshop conducted by Uta Hagen at the Lyric Stage in Boston. It was here that I was introduced to her more recent thoughts on "expectations" and performing one minute of real life.

just look at me one minute as though you really saw me," employing a variety of verb tenses, "I'm dead... I married George Gibbs .. Wally's dead, too,... don't you remember? But just for a moment now we're all together..." (109). How could Mrs Webb remember? For her, these milestones in life have not yet been passed. Again, we see the notion of a continuum of time, a sort of moving sidewalk onto which individuals might step at any given moment.

But there are hints in the text that on occasion certain characters do appreciate moments while they live them. Chandler and the actor playing Doc Gibbs identified some of these moments in which their characters relished existence, in the form of the simple pleasures of life, and they took the time to bracket these moments in performance. These included Dr Gibbs's enjoyment of his cup of coffee and the moment when Dr and Mrs Gibbs stand outside in the night air amidst the heliotropes. These distinctive choices enhanced the actors' portrayal of the couple in the SIUC production of *Our Town*.

Emily's farewell to Grover's Corners is more than an exercise in sensory recall (although it is a fine opportunity to utilize that technique). In her short enumeration of sentient beings and tangible items, to which she says good-bye, the actress playing Emily executes what is "immediacy" or "here and now" or "being in the moment" or "relishing" in the nomenclature of acting, and the character exhibits the practices of "mindfulness," "presentism," and "witnessing" in the Buddhist lexicon. When Emily returns to her seat among the grave bodies, she does so with a keener understanding of what it meant to be alive and with less reluctance to let go of her corporeality.

In his angry outburst about the living, another grave body, Simon Stimson, expresses the flipside of a Buddhist principle when he criticizes the living as being "always at the mercy of one self-centered passion, or another" (111). Buddhist practitioners aspire to rid themselves of all desires or attachments. Buddhism recognizes that at the very least humankind is plagued by "likes" and "dislikes" and at the very worst these preferences are magnified into passions and hatreds. Buddhists desire not to attain a placid state, but rather to live fully, without being judgmental, in each moment. Perhaps Simon Stimson has not been dead long enough to evolve into a place of forgiveness, compassion or, at a minimum, of letting go. We see, though, that Mrs Gibbs has. She reminds Stimson "that ain't the whole truth" and quickly moves on to advising Emily to look at the star. "Another Man Among the Dead" comments: "A star's mighty good company" (112). "A Man From Among the Dead" follows up with how his son "knew the stars" and "used to say it took millions of years for that speck of light to get to earth... millions of years." Thus, near the play's close, Wilder has returned to where we began, with the image of the morning star and with the positioning of the grave bodies in relation to the universe and across millions of years.

Twice near the end of Act III, Wilder employs distancing effects. The first is the convention of Emily returning to her chair, pointing up the fact that there is an actress playing the character of the newly dead Emily in her past. The second is the Stage Manager's last major stage direction, when he draws the curtain on the grave bodies and the cemetery scene. Here again, Wilder draws attention to the self-consciousness of the stage action, recalling the metatheatrical construct with which he began the play. Within the play's imaginary world, the sky is clearing as the Stage Manager delivers his last speech. One last time Wilder alludes to the stars, the galaxy, and implicitly to the Mind of God. This time he relates the energy exerted by the star to that of humankind, the audience. "There are the stars—doing their old, old, crisscross journeys in the sky.... Only this one is straining away.... The strain's so bad that every sixteen hours everybody lies down and gets a rest . You get a good rest, too...." (113–14). Thus, in the play's final lines, Wilder adroitly fuses stage time and presence with audience time and presence. His notion of existence as a continuum of simultaneity rather than chronology, his prizing of daily ritual, and his positioning of human beings with their finite lives set against eternity—all this coalesces in the cemetery with its ghostly grave bodies and the audience as witnesses.

Works Cited

Arnott, Peter D. *Lecture Notes: Seminar in Greek Staging*. Tufts University Press, 1987.

Blank, Martin. *Critical Essays on Thornton Wilder*. New York: Hall, 1996.

Bryer, Jackson R. *Conversations with Thornton Wilder*. Jackson: University of Mississippi Press, 1992.

Burbank, Rex. *Thornton Wilder*. New York: Twayne, 1961.

Carlson, Marvin. *The Haunted Stage: The Theatre as Memory Machine*. Ann Arbor: University of Michigan Press, 2001.

Chandler, Hilary. *Interview with Author*. 12/12/2005.

Cohen, Robert. *Acting Power*. Palo Alto, California: Mayfield, 1978.

Craig, William Lane. *Time and Eternity: Exploring God's Relationship to Time*. Wheaton, IL: Crossway, 2001.

——. *The Tenseless Theory of Time: A Critical Examination*. New York: Springer, 2000.

Elam, Harry. *The Past as Present in the Drama of August Wilson*. Ann Arbor: University of Michigan Press, 2004.

Goldstein, Malcolm. *The Art of Thornton Wilder*. Lincoln: University of Nebraska Press, 1965.

Haberman, Donald. *The Plays of Thornton Wilder: A Critical Study*. Middletown, Connecticut: Wesleyan University Press, 1967.

Hagen, Uta. *A Challenge for the Actor*. New York: Scribner's, 1991.

Merrill-Fink, Lori. Rehearsal for SIUC Production of *Our Town*. Southern Illinois University Carbondale: 9/19/2005.

Oaklander, L. Nathan. *The Ontology of Time*. Amherst, NY: Prometheus, 2004.

Oaklander, L. Nathan, and Quentin Smith. *The New Theory of Time*. New Haven: Yale University Press, 1994.

Pizzato, Mark. "Nietzschean Neurotheatre: Apollinian and Dionysian Spirits in the Brain Matters of *Our Town*" in *Nietzsche and the Rebirth of the Tragic*. Ed. Mary Ann Frese Witt. Madison, NJ: Fairleigh Dickinson University Press, 2007. 186–218.

Salzberg, Sharon, and Joseph Goldstein. *Insight Meditation: Workbook*. Boulder: Sounds True, 2001.

Wheatley, Christopher. "Thornton Wilder, the Real, and Theatrical Realism" In *Realism and the American Dramatic Tradition*. Ed. William W. Demastes. Tuscaloosa: University of Alabama Press, 1996.

Wilder, Thornton. *Our Town. 3 Plays*. New York: Perennial Classics, 1998.

Wilder, Thornton. "Some Thoughts on Playwrighting" in *The Intent of the Artist*. Ed. Augusto Centeno. Princeton: Princeton University Press, 1941.

Chapter 6

When Ghosts Dream: Immigrant Desire in Lan Samantha Chang's *Hunger*

Belinda Kong

What does it mean for a ghost to dream, and to dream in a non-native country? For Lan Samantha Chang, this question seems tied to another: what does it mean for a ghost to hunger, and to hunger for something that is possible only in the space of the other? In her 1998 novella, *Hunger*, Chang poses these questions to us via her ghost narrator, Min. In a voice of quiet intimacy, Min begins her parabolic tale of the Asian-American immigrant experience with the line, "I often dream about the restaurant where I met Tian" (11). Tellingly, Min's retrospections do not open with an account of immigration, either on the shore of the old country or on that of the new. Instead, they open with her first encounter with her future husband, and in a place of hunger, of want and consumption. We intuit that Chang is marking here the inaugural point of Asian-America, whose future will be brought into being not by an emigrant parent's oceanic journey or by a child's triumphant birth in America, but from the inner geography of immigrant desire. On Chang's terms, hyphenated self-consciousness is born in the instant when Min registers a belated insight, when she acknowledges an already taken-in wisp of the foreign: "I drew one cold, sweet breath of air and truly understood that I had arrived in America" (12). Min's spectral dreaming in America, which is also a form of remembering, thus recollects the past even as it suggests the future, as both unfold in the space of insatiable hunger and ongoing inhalation.

Asian-American Female Gothic

Before probing the dreams of ghosts, we can more fully grasp Chang's engagements if we situate her text within several contexts in Asian-American literature. The first is the Asian-American female Gothic tradition. Despite our critical tendency to emphasize its social-realist dimensions, Asian-American writing has persistently shown a fascination with the Gothic. Particularly in its explorations of the uncanny, the Gothic offers resonant figural analogs to themes of cultural and racial otherness. For instance, if we take as symbolic markers Maxine Hong Kingston's *The Woman Warrior* and lê thi diem thúy's *The Gangster We Are All Looking For*, two exemplary *bildungsroman*s that frame the last quarter century of Asian-American women's writing, we will observe an increased intensity in

Gothic appropriations as well as an expansion in the representational boundaries of Asian-American identity. Both Kingston and lê invoke the tropes of the ghost and the double. But while Kingston aligns the truly haunting and ghostly with Chineseness and the double with Chinese-Americanness, lê re-integrates the two tropes into one figure, that of a spectral twin-like brother who drowns in Vietnam. From Kingston's earlier Gothic economy to lê's more recent one, we can see a dramatic redefinition of Asian-Americanness whereby cultural identity and alterity are reapportioned, with the uncanny sliding from the Asian side of the hyphen into the hyphen itself. That is to say, in our latter-day phase of Asian-American literature, identity is no longer articulated exclusively via nativity in America, nor America via an othering of Asia. We now read the Asian-American hyphen backward as much as forward (Kong).

Still, for lê, the Asian double stays spectralized in Asia. Although the twin-like brother is given a narrative afterlife to parallel the girl-protagonist's in America, his story is told only elliptically through hers, and then only as a failed traversal opposite her completed one. Within this Asian-American female lineage, Chang presents a Gothicizing of the hyphen in another direction. The ghost and the double are divorced once more in *Hunger*. As in *Woman Warrior*, an immigrant mother inhabits the role of the ghost, while her two American-born daughters incarnate the doubles. However, instead of casting the child as her protagonist, Chang boldly reverses a basic convention of the Asian-American *bildungsroman* by narrating through the posthumous voice of the immigrant parent. The doubles motif remains attached to American nativity and the ghost to immigrant parenthood, but the usual hierarchy of existential substance between Asia and America is leveled. Turning inside out Kingston's model of a "solid America" enmeshed in the "invisible world" of emigrant talk-stories (Kingston 5), Chang positions us in the place of the spectral narrator. Through Min's eyes, we too come to perceive America as a phantom otherworld in perpetual twilight, a muted but unreceded realm of memory that "flickers up... dim and silent, never changing" (11), illuminated fleetingly through fragmented images of an "arched shadow" or a "pale sidewalk" (75). In effect, America as much as Asia becomes the site of alterity. What Chang allows us to ask concerns the future of Asian-Americans. If our reality is conceived as already ghostly, if we see ourselves as narrating from the uncanny time of the past but in the place of the American present, what comes after?

For an answer, we may pause on Min's reason for lingering in America. In the instant of her death, as her body is ravaged by cancer, Min makes what is perhaps her strongest resolution in the story: "My body was being left behind. The room dimmed, the sounds of traffic ceased. The world's winds took hold of me. The earth began to rush below, and I who had once dreamed of leaving Brooklyn—I decided I would not let go.... I held on. I will not leave" (106). Unlike her husband, whose ghostly spirit she imagines taking flight eagerly to "retrace the route he so many years earlier traveled" and "plunging over the bright Pacific" to return at last to his ancestral home in China (96), Min chooses to continue her spectral afterlife in New York. If her life in America has hitherto been defined by fears, and her few desires by the fantasy to escape back to her mother's ghost in Taiwan, it is only in her own afterlife that Min begins to hope and dream *forward*: "I am waiting; every day I wait in hope that this will come to pass. More than anything, I want my daughters to meet again" (114). Significantly, this re-orientation from past to future hinges on her two daughters, on that other form of afterlife anchored in biology and blood. Chang thereby implies that it is by way of the American-born generation that the immigrant can gain an American grounding, albeit posthumously. Min's holding on and not letting go means, in turn, that the diasporic reunion of a fractured Chinese-America will only take place in America, not Asia.

We can read this shifting of ghostly alliance as Chang's attempt to redefine the figure of the Asian immigrant. The tendency within Asian-American literature to foreignize the immigrant parent, to forge an Asian-American identity out of an alienation of the emigrant generation, is so pervasive that I will cite just one particularly relevant example: Amy Tan's Suyuan Woo in *The Joy Luck Club*. In addition to being the sole missing maternal narrator in Tan's text, Suyuan interests us here because of her phantom status: having died of a "cerebral aneurysm" on the main narrative's first page (5), her apparition reappears in the book's final paragraph, as the composite image of her three daughters in a photograph taken in her native Shanghai: "Her same eyes, her same mouth, open in surprise to see, at last, her long-cherished wish" (332). On Tan's handling, the immigrant mother's specter materializes only in Asia, just as her wish for her daughters' reunion is achieved only in China. An inescapable Asianness shrouds the immigrant parent even after death.

Chang's Min may express a similar wish as Tan's Suyuan to reunite her estranged daughters, but rather than clinging tenaciously to exilic nostalgia or projecting a necessary "homecoming" for the next generation in Asia, Min is a character capable of transformed desires and transplanted loyalties. By the novella's end, especially after Tian's death, we are made aware of Min's growing identification with America:

> I quit working at the restaurant and found a job at a shoe store off Atlantic Avenue, close to home, and I stayed there without incident for two years. I discovered, to my surprise, that by listening to and speaking with my daughters, I had learned enough English to answer almost all of the customers' questions. As a matter of fact, whole days went by when I did not speak a word of Mandarin. (97)

Chang gives us here a subtle portrait of the transmutations in immigrant affinities. In this widowed stage of her life, Min comes to think of the Atlantic rather than the Pacific (a geography almost synonymous with Asia) as "closer to home," so it is not by coincidence that this period also witnesses her belated discovery of her already considerable knowledge of English. This insight indicates that she has long been linguistically and culturally Americanized, much longer than she or anyone else realizes, and that her earlier sense of self as a predominantly Chinese-identified and Mandarin-speaking immigrant has yielded to a more acculturated one. Her geographical attachments are now unambiguous: "I had no desire to live anywhere else" (97). Hence her decision upon her death to remain in America as a ghostly guardian, to act at once as memory-keeper of Chinese-America's inaugural past and as hopeful witness to Chinese-America's recollected future. This decision we might call, à la Kingston, an act of claiming Asian-America.

In this transfer of Min's allegiance from origin to diaspora, we discern Chang's effort at expanding the literary boundaries of Asian-American identity. Just as Min's spirit lies waiting for the opening of the kitchen window and the return of her runaway daughter, so the literary figure of the immigrant parent, Chang intimates, awaits the opening of the Asian-American hyphen to finally let it in. We may view Chang's use of the Gothic here as an aesthetic plea against ideological foreclosure and cultural finality, so that what comes after may retain the open potential of otherness, of that which exceeds what has been and what already is. Hovering on the hyphen's threshold, Min's specter reminds us that the formation of a diaspora is not a *fait accompli* but an ongoing process, and that Asian-America is not a closed body whose *telos* must be powered by the engine of its forked history. Asian-America's continual accretion of "outside" or "otherworldly" elements into its geographical situation means that the narratives of Asian-America's past cannot fully forecast the narratives of its present, nor the present its future. Chang alerts us to this unforeseeable surplus in Asian-American writing by filtering that most familiar and well-worn of Asian-American themes—the mother–daughter conflict—through the defamiliarizing eyes of the hitherto foreignized and now spectralized mother. This is what it means for her ghost to dream, and to dream in an adopted country.

When Chinese Mothers Speak

But what does it mean for a ghost to dream, not just in an other-land, but in an other-tongue? How does one translate the dreams of ghosts so that they may be at home not just in the new country but in its language? To address these questions, we can situate *Hunger* within a second context in Asian-American literature, the discourse of the Chinese immigrant mother.

As critics have pointed out, the preoccupation with matrilineage in Chinese-American women's writing is a longstanding one, stretching from early works such as Jade Snow Wong's *Fifth Chinese Daughter* and Chuang Hua's *Crossings* to Kingston's memoir and more recent fiction such as Tan's novels. This Chinese-American female tradition, especially in its post-*Woman Warrior* period, typically explores the American-born daughter's vexed relationship with an immigrant mother who is, as Sau-ling Cynthia Wong aptly puts it, "simultaneously tough and vulnerable" (178). Yet, beyond images of female strength and weakness, what has received less critical attention is the issue of narrative voice, that is, how the immigrant mother is made to speak in a text. This issue designates a specifically narratological problem because, more often than not, the Chinese mother functions as the symbolic locus not just of cultural but linguistic otherness. Whether solely or primarily Chinese-speaking, whether in possession of a smattering of pidgin English or wholly conversant in colorful Chinglish, the Chinese mother is often represented as one who resists linguistic assimilation and absorption, whether out of traditionalism or smugness, recalcitrance or rigidity. The result is a narratological shift whenever her voice emerges, a modification in the language or discursive mode of a text's English.

We can track this narratological bump around the Chinese mother via two opposing models. For an example of the first we may turn to Kingston's portraits of Brave Orchid and Moon Orchid in *Woman Warrior*. Although these two sisters play out antithetical poles of the female doubles motif of femme fatale versus fair maiden, woman warrior versus damsel in distress, Kingston's narratological personification of them is the same. Brave Orchid falls squarely under the category of the intractable and unassimilated maternal type. Even after having lived in the United States for decades, she still "could never learn English" (149). Since both women are characterized as mainly Chinese-speaking, the narratological dilemma arises as to how their voices should be transcribed or translated in the English text. Kingston's method recalls what V. N. Volosinov has termed *linear style*, the construction of reported speech with "clear-cut, external contours" but "whose own internal individuality is minimized" (120). With Kingston's use of linear style, we can readily identify the moments when Moon Orchid or Brave Orchid speaks. But the idiosyncrasies of their speech, the signature marks of their grammar, syntax, diction, and so on, down to the very language they employ, are manipulated and smoothed over to align with the text's dominant narrative mode. The result, as Volosinov indicates, is a general "stylistic homogeneity (in which the author and his characters all speak exactly the same language)" (120).

This homogenizing effect may be interpreted as an erasure of individuality or ethnic-linguistic difference, and indeed, in Volosinov's Marxist analysis, linear style exemplifies the coercive ideologies of medieval "authoritarian dogmatism" and enlightenment "rationalistic dogmatism" (123). Yet, in our late stage of the dialectical history of narratology, we can reread liner style as an anti-foreignizing aesthetic within the contemporary politics of multicultural English. With Kingston's usage especially, linear style confers upon immigrant characters their measure of belonging and authoritative presence in standardized English, which is also, as she is keenly aware, the language of power. The one means by which she allows herself to indulge in narratological irony and distancing is through free indirect discourse, as when, in their interior monologues, Brave Orchid mistakenly calls a Boy Scout a "cowboy" (114) or Moon Orchid fondly refers to her Asian-American nephews and nieces as "sweet wild animals" (134). On the whole, these narrative ripples do not so much disrupt the stylistic integrity of the text as they register linguistic confusion, mistranslated idioms, and perceptive eccentricities, albeit by accenting the Chinese mothers' cultural otherness.

Kingston's discursive gestures of othering can be appreciated as relatively confined if we juxtapose them against Amy Tan's and Gish Jen's model of immigrant ventriloquy. To be sure, Tan and Jen are very different writers; one is associated with euphoric essentialism, the other with satiric hybridity. Yet both take the alternative narratological route of what Volosinov calls *pictorial style*, the construction of reported speech as "individualized," with "all the linguistic peculiarities of its verbal implementation" preserved (121). In more current vocabulary, and in the context of immigrant representations, we sometimes call this a "faithful" or "authentic" rendering of, in Tan's famous phrase, "all the Englishes" in multicultural America. In fact, Tan admits to adopting pictorial style quite baldly. From her essay "Mother Tongue," we know that the quirky speech of her fictional Chinese mothers is drawn, in the spirit of linguistic accuracy and filial fidelity, from her own mother's real-life English, which she not only quotes from but underscores as "videotaped and then transcribed" (272–73). Hence we have, in *Joy Luck*, such putatively authentic immigrant English as Lindo's "You want to live like mess, what I can say?" (186), An-mei's "Why can you talk about this with a pscyhe-atric and not with mother?" (210), and Suyuan's "Maybe taste not too bad. But I can smell, dead taste, not firm" (234). These colorful expressions pepper not only the daughters' but also the mothers' narrations.

Contrary to Volosinov's claim for pictorial style's individualizing capacity, in Tan's hands, it has the opposite effect of homogenizing all four mothers into one narratological voice. Tan alternates between pictorial and linear styles, between the mothers' "broken" or "limited" English and their "internal language," what she imagines to be the immigrant's "translation of her Chinese if she could speak in perfect English," a language of "intent" and "passion" ("Mother Tongue" 279). Yet, her text ultimately grants the greatest degree of linguistic mobility and power not to the Chinese mothers or their Chinese-American daughters, but implicitly to the author herself. Sau-ling Cynthia Wong argues this point forcefully: if Tan's intention is to "do full justice to [the mothers'] native intelligence, and restore them to the dignity they deserve," then this "cause is decidedly not served well by such slight linguistic skewings" and "quaint, circumlocutious literal translations" that conjure up only too swiftly the "'comic,' pidginized 'Asian English' found in Anglo-American writing on Asians" (189). In Wong's view, Tan's narratological choice for her Chinese mothers is entirely complicit with mainstream orientalism.

More recently, but to wider critical approval, Gish Jen has amplified this ventriloquy model. In her short story "Who's Irish?" the Chinese mother is again marshaled as the centerpiece of linguistic difference, and the central narrative tension is again thematized as a mother–daughter cultural clash. This time, however, the immigrant mother becomes, as in *Hunger*, the story's sole narrator. Unlike *Joy Luck*, then, "Who's Irish?" is less structurally dialogical, though not altogether monological. In Jen's hands, the historically marginalized and pidgin-speaking immigrant comes to dismantle the authority of native speakers, as the Chinese mother's fierce conversational power over more linguistically conventional characters is repeatedly highlighted. At Thanksgiving dinner, for instance, hers is the dominant voice at the table, and one that is not adverse to delivering a most un-PC lecture on the causes of ethnic success and failure. "Why the Shea family have so much trouble?" she asks her American-born Irish in-laws (4). "They are white people, they speak English. When I come to this country, I have no money and do not speak English. But my husband and I own our restaurant before he die. Free and clear, no mortgage. Of course, I understand I am just lucky, come from a country where the food is popular all over the world. I understand it is not the Shea family's fault they come from a country where everything is boiled."

Yet, in spite of Jen's attempt at inverting the hierarchy of linguistic power, Wong's critique of Tan seems applicable here still—even if Jen bestows on her narrator the capacity for subversive mimicry: "I tell them, Confucius say a filial son knows what color his mother's hair is" (3). This Chinese mother, to be sure, has enough cultural savvy to know, and enough verbal facility to mock, fortune-cookie English, but her mimicry is not the same as Jen's ventriloquy. As with *Joy Luck*, the ultimate linguistic authority here lies not with the Chinese mother but with Jen herself. The ability to move between linguistic registers of standard and pidgin, high and low, native and immigrant is accorded only to the American-born author, whose power of ventriloquy is decidedly withheld from the hyperbolically Asianized narrator. In this narratological universe, the Chinese mother can at most mimic and challenge, but never acculturate or surpass. The point of her arrested development is marked precisely by that authorial trick of entering into the other's psyche on the other's own terms.

We may now return to *Hunger* and put Min into dialogue with her literary counterparts. Significantly, both she and Jen's narrator are working-class immigrant women, and both narrate their stories after the deaths of their husbands. Chang, however, rejects the pictorial style of ventriloquy, which would accentuate her own class privilege and linguistic authority over the Chinese mother once again in a tradition that is already too aloof. Instead, she writes Min's voice in linear style, so that the latter's internal language may be brought into harmony—literally brought into line—with the external one of her Asian-American daughters. We can say that Chang inherits Kingston's narratological method but without the touches of ironic distancing, that she fulfills with greater empathy Tan's avowed aim to restore interiority and eloquence to the Chinese mother, and that she counteracts Jen's exoticizing of immigrant English by claiming Asian-American status for it. Reversing Volosinov's political prioritizing of the pictorial, which after all echoes not a little of the ethnographic picturesque, Chang recuperates linear style as a non-foreignizing and more capaciously inclusive aesthetic. It is an aesthetic, couched unostentatiously in its own terms, that answers the immigrant desire for inclusion.

Hungering Trickster

Jen's and Chang's narrators share one other suggestive attribute: they are both associated with working in Chinese restaurants. In Asian-American literature, the Asian restaurant has been a highly charged symbolic site, often serving as a metaphor for American consumption of ethnic labor, the ghettoizing and debasement of Asian-American cultural production, and Asian-America's collusion in this consumer circuit via self-orientalizing panderings. Examples are abundant, but perhaps the most vigorous remains Frank Chin's play *The Year of the Dragon*, in which the protagonist, Chinatown tour guide Fred Eng, bitingly refers to the cultural industry of Chinese-American cuisine as "food pornography" (86).

Hunger may also be located within this lineage, as tapping into themes of cultural consumption and ethnic production, raising questions especially about the social *telos* of working-class minority labor. Indeed, class concerns have governed critical receptions of Chang's novella thus far. For instance, Lisa Marie Cacho, in her brief review of *Hunger*, reads it as exposing Asian-American ideological "compliance" with "culturally racist dominant narratives of Asians in order to achieve socioeconomic 'success'" (378). Similarly, Jonathan Freedman, in an article on the "discursive bleedings" between representations of Jewish- and Asian-Americans from the mid-nineteenth century onward, turns to Chang's work as offering a "counter-vision of upward mobility myths," as illustrating the self-destructive side to immigrant "assimilation" of the model minority myth via "the high-cultural path to ethnic success" (96–97). Both critics, in effect, translate the titular metaphor of hunger into class terms.

Instructive as these readings are, though, what we may want to keep in mind is that Chang does not depict compliance and assimilation as necessarily self-colonizing operations, if these words designate, in their most pared down form, the process of absorbing and altering, of letting the other enter into one's interior and changing one from inside out. We have already seen the enabling aspect of this process in Min's unintended incorporation of English. Clearly, Chang does not posit as the proper Asian-American ethos a simple resistance of "dominant narratives" or "upward mobility myths" as if these objects of desire violate some inner core of ethnic integrity. As Freedman rightly notes, Chang's vision is not "so much critical or affirmative as compassionate" (96). To extend this reading, I will suggest that Chang, perhaps out of an acute consciousness of the pejorative connotations around both "assimilation" and "consumption" in American discourses of racial politics, gives us instead a less familiar and overfilled figure of hunger: the Chinese trickster.

As Anne Birrell has fruitfully demonstrated, the trickster in Chinese mythology is distinguished by a number of motifs: the theft of a treasure of the gods, punishment by metamorphosis, and consequent regeneration or immortality. Among Birrell's numerous examples, we can isolate two primary ones. The first is Kun, the mythic demigod who tries to save the world from the flood by stealing God's self-renewing soil to dam the floodwater. For his theft, Kun is condemned to ritual execution, but rather than decomposing, his body remains incorrupt, and from his belly issues forth the great Yü, who succeeds where his father failed in controlling the flood (79–81). The second is Ch'ang O, the legendary lunar goddess who steals from her husband the elixir of immortality, a gift he had received from the Queen Mother of the West. While Ch'ang O escapes to the moon, punishment pursues her and she is metamorphosed into a toad, a creature whose sloughing off of its skin suggests the same regenerative cycle as the moon (144–45, 176). To Birrell's prototypes we may add a third: Monkey or Sun Wukong, from the folklore epic *Journey to the West* (1592), who devours not only the Heavenly Queen's peaches of immortality but also Lao Tzu's life-giving elixir, and who is subsequently entrapped by the Buddha under a mountain for five hundred years before he is released on a pilgrimage that will ultimately earn him new life in enlightened buddhahood. What all these tricksters have in common is a desire for that which only the gods possess, and by implication, a desire to attain godhood. Their thievery may be motivated by altruism, as with Kun, or by greed, as with Ch'ang O and Monkey, but they all take the treasures of others because of a self-perceived lack. Most importantly, we notice that the Chinese trickster is not a figure of straightforward villainy or heroism but a paradoxical one of transgressive daring and punished ambition, retribution and reward, representing at once the essence and excesses of a life force that continually reincarnates itself.

It is this paradox of trickster desire that Chang captures in the trope of hunger (which Ch'ang O and Monkey prefigure in their theft of food), and the character who most visibly embodies this hunger is Tian. Although Chang does not reveal this explicitly, Chinese readers will readily recognize that *tian* is Mandarin for heaven, that Tian is named after rulers and gods, as one who strives for divinity. Leaving Beijing as a young man with nothing but the gift of a violin from his German music tutor, swimming in darkness across the Taiwan Strait to board a refugee ship that would be the first step in his eventual journey to the West, Tian is the rebellious trickster par excellence. He can repudiate family, culture, and country but not an inner imperative. "Everyone," he tells Min, "has things they want to do in their lives. But sometimes there is only one thing—one thing that a person *must do*. More than what he is told to do, more than what he is trained to do. Even more what his family wants him to do. It is what he hungers for" (29).

In Min's final summing up of his life, she seems in agreement with the gods that Tian cannot "escape the punishment that invariably comes to people who dare to dream such flagrant and extravagant designs," who are driven by such "immensity of... hunger" (113). Even early on, Min evokes the trickster's terrifying excesses when she describes Tian's violin playing in language suggestive not just of predatory hunger but also thievery: "His bow struck the strings. It seemed to drop from above, the way a hawk will plunge with sudden swiftness to its victim.... I felt as if he had achieved these sounds through a feat of magic or theft" (20). Not by accident, then, does Chang engineer the episode of Tian's "fall" from socioeconomic grace, his being passed over at the music school for a promotion that would have granted him definitive access to the halls of middle-class America, after the very pattern of the trickster's theft. A silver tuning fork inadvertently falls into Min's coat pocket, and Tian, out of "a fierce recklessness," immediately appropriates it for himself and transfers it to his own pocket. "A gift from heaven," he justifies to Min, as he thrums "a perfect 'A'" with the instrument (24).

The "A" note of America here reverberates with his own name, as immigrant desire for national inclusion and trickster desire for heavenly power converge.

Tian's theft of the tuning fork, though executed without premeditation or design, is nonetheless thematically linked to another episode of intentional burglary in Min's childhood:

> Many years ago, when I lived in Taipei with my parents, we were visited by a thief. Like many island buildings of that time, our house had been designed after a Japanese dwelling, with light wood screens and fragile walls. The burglar entered easily, smashing his hand through the window and reaching in to unlock the door.
>
> He ignored my father's cheap radio. Through some uncanny instinct, he found almost every object that my parents had preserved from their lives on the mainland. The figured silk my mother had brought from Shanghai. One translucent and thin-edged rice bowl from my father's household. A string of carmine prayer beads that had been a present from my older aunt. (90)

This anonymous burglar is also rendered like a trickster, with an "uncanny instinct" for sniffing out the most valuable possessions, particularly objects that emanate an ancestral aura. As with Tian's thievery, we can certainly read this scene of "trickster wants so trickster takes" as a class allegory, as the defiant rebellion of the underprivileged who hunger for socioeconomic equality, racial progress, political inclusion, and so forth. The trickster is one who punches through barriers dividing the haves from the have-nots, his robbery but a rightful redistribution of material goods. But in this instance, the traffic of objects is narrated from the perspective, not of the unpossessing, but of the dispossessed.

On this other side of the hole dwell not the gods but the already dislocated and disinherited. As Chang subtly insinuates, Min's parents were among the many refugees who fled mainland China during the Sino-Japanese War to settle in Japan-occupied Taiwan. We are thus led to imagine how, in exile and under colonization, they nursed the few heirlooms that they, like Tian, had been able to carry away. The hole, a metaphor for social passage and material transfer from the trickster's point of view, becomes for Min's family a visual emblem and reminder, not just of tangible losses from a single burglary, but of a more basic and pervasive historical loss of cultural inheritance, a loss for which there is "no easy inventory." From their side of the uncanny, the trickster's hunger creates a hole of melancholia: "But we saw the hole, and we did not sleep. My mother stayed awake for hours.... For weeks afterward, she would reach for something and find it missing, and she would weep the helpless tears of one whose life has slid through aging hands" (90–91).

It would seem that trickster desire, fixated on its own lack or gap, cannot but fail to derive satisfaction from itself and must therefore puncture another's space so as to open up a corollary gap there. Tian expresses this unfillability of desire when he tells a pregnant Min after his grand recital, "I feel empty—the way I imagine a woman must feel after she has had a child" (26). Unlike Min's sense of maternal reproduction as fulfillment and continuation, her belief that "there could be nothing as precious as children and the thread of family blood" (29), Tian describes his musical production not as creative labor but as an aftermath of emptiness. Little wonder, then, that the metaphor of the hole, and the implied inheritance of loss, shadow Min even in America: "There was a hole in our house, like a great mouth, filled with love words and lost objects" (61). Indeed, Min appears to court and even initiate this fate. At the novella's start, drawn to Tian's "confident English" and tailored appearance, she performs an act of trickery herself. Like a fox fairy who seduces unsuspecting scholars in ghost tales, she steals his hat in the sure knowledge that she would "exchange it for the man who wore it" (12–14). For her "heavenly" theft, she, like other mythic tricksters, is punished (by an unhappy marriage and a cancerous death) and at the same time compensated (with the double immortality of a spectral afterlife and two daughters).

Still, Min presents us with a different model of desire from Tian's. Whereas he takes, and keeps, on the assumption of divine favor, without thought of ever relinquishing the accidental object, she steals in hopeful anticipation of an eventual exchange. Her trickery is thus premised not on another's deprivation or dispossession but on her own projected affinity and transformation. If Tian's trickster desire is structured on negativity, on an insatiable lack, and may be called a paradigm of the unincorporatable, hers is structured on a fulfillable wish and may be called a paradigm of the potential. The former is oriented toward the past and origin, the latter toward the future and diaspora. The former hungers; the latter dreams. In Chang's terms, it is the latter form of immigrant desire that extends the promise of a fuller Asian-American future.

Inheritance of Desire

Intriguingly, Min's very name intimates this paradigm of desire without lack, though this will be apparent only to a reader attuned to the traffic between languages in Chang's text. While Tian's name carries Chinese resonances alone (for he is the figure of nostalgia), Min's can be read more interlingually (she the figure of diasporic fertility). First, if we read intralingually in Mandarin, *min* may denote the people or masses, a meaning that certainly accentuates her loneliness and displacement from Chineseness, her sense of being "a member of a dying tribe" (97). More obliquely, we may see her name as missing the letter *g*, in which case *ming* will variously invoke the words for name, fate, and brightness or understanding. Further coupled with Tian's name, *tian ming* refers to heaven's will and echoes of *yuanfen*, the concept of romantic destiny Min's mother explains as "that apportionment of love which is destined for you in this world" (17). Conversely, *ming tian* refers to tomorrow and suggests the time of futurity.

Now, if we bring the Chinese connotations into play with the English text, we become aware of two other meanings. First, along temporal lines again, we hear

Min's name captured in her own sentiment about "the seductive and naive idea that there lay some hope of healing in mining the past" (82). Despite her disparaging tone, we know that Min as our retrospective narrator is also the primary figure of "mining." Thus, read bilingually, her name sounds out an interplay between past and future, memory and dream. Second, and this returns us to the notion of desire, Chang alerts us to that other definition of *mine* as singular possession. In an unmistakable scene, Min's two daughters, Anna and Ruth, fight over a necklace of plastic beads: "'That's mine!' Anna cried. I stopped in the middle of locking the door; the English words sounded so fierce and strange as she claimed them. 'No!' Ruth cried right back at her in English. 'Mine!'" (46–47). This argument over ownership of a parental gift marks the story's introduction of English into the Chinese-American home, for the daughters speak only English to each other from that day on. Chang dramatizes this linguistic induction as founded on a voicing of want and possession, which also happens to be a near-echo of the maternal name with its missing *e*, a name of incomplete possession on American terms. But if we add here the observation that *e* is the Mandarin *pinyin* for hunger, we come full circle to the interlingual implication of "Min" as desire without hunger. Moreover, unlike Anna's name, Min's is not a palindrome that ends where it begins; rather, it illustrates a forward motion, an advance from the *m* state of migrancy or immigration to the next one of *in*-ness.

Still, for all her potential for cultural absorption, and for all the utopian possibility of her paradigm of desire, Min remains a ghost with a stalled out wish by the novella's close. As a waiting phantom, she reminds us of the existential trope of *Waiting for Godot* and the postcolonial one of waiting for the Mahatma. Her Asian-American messiah, however, will be the runaway Ruth, and judgment day the time when her two daughters reunite. If Min inherits only a legacy of loss from her mother, Anna and Ruth by contrast inherit the two different threads of desire from their parents, one silently hopeful, the other insolently demanding. But in this next generation, the trickster's hunger undergoes a mutation. While Anna resembles Min and Ruth Tian in temperament, each evinces qualities of both parents, and both crave more from life than the stagnant enclosure of their parents' house. This desire for surplus recalls the trickster's, and appropriately, both Anna's and Ruth's names include elements of Tian's. "Anna" renders palindromic the second half of "Tian," and her Chinese name, Anyu, likewise replicates the tail end of his name. Though Ruth's Chinese name, Ruyu, is not translated in the text, we surmise that the most probable *ru* for a female name is the word for likeness, which contains the character for mouth, a square symbolizing a hole. And *yu*, as Chang tells us, stands for jade, the stone of emperors. Yet at the same time, both daughters' names mollify Tian's abyssal and anguished longing. *An* means tranquil or peaceful, while the other component of *ru* is the character for woman, and the other meaning of *ru* is *if*. Hence, the parent–child doubling is not a strict one, and both children resignify the father's infinite hunger for mobility and freedom in terms of the mother's satiable dreaming of possibility. Their corporeal afterlife of

Asian-American desire, unlike Min's ghostly one, merges the two paradigms of hunger and dream, thievery and loss.

Yet the daughters, too, do not enact a utopian present. Their English names have Hebrew roots and Biblical resonances, but only ironically, in negation, for neither is the progenitor of kings or prophets. Like Naomi and Stephen in Joy Kogawa's *Obasan*, Ruth and Anna represent the stunted generation of a multiply diasporized clan, the former fleeing to Europe and the latter locked in the old parental home, both barren of progeny. Together, they embody the threat of a tribal extinction that would once and for all end even spectral dreaming.

Anna, conceived without the knowledge of her father and delivered before he could arrive at the scene of her birth, and born a girl before her mother learns through acculturation to love her without the burden of inherited bias, may be considered prematurely American. In a heart-wrenching moment, faced with the disappointment of a daughter rather than a son, Min turns her head to the wall and leaves the newborn Anna unacknowledged in her birth (31). Ruth, on the other hand, resembles Tian's family in China and is the recipient of all his buried affection. But turned "sideways" in her mother's womb and pried out through a cesarean as if she were "undecided about entering the world" (42), she may be considered belatedly Chinese. Tellingly, Min utters Ruth's Chinese name for the first time only upon the latter's departure from home (90). It would seem that the sisters' separation, their opposite ways of missing the right time of nativity, measures the gap that needs to be closed before Asian-America can repossess its capacity for procreation and regenerating.

Perhaps it is not by accident, finally, that Chang names the sisters bilingually. The hermeneutics required to read their future will not be simply interlingual, as with Min, but will entail a fuller knowledge of the lineages of both languages, both cultures, even if it means we are borne beyond to a third language, a third source of prior incorporation. Is it not fitting, then, in a work that strives for interiorized transformation, that the diasporic reunion of heirs will occur, in the language of origin, when the runaway likeness returns to imperial peace, and in the language of adoption via its linguistic ancestry in the original diaspora, when fugitive mercy rejoins static grace?

Works Cited

Birrell, Anne. *Chinese Mythology: An Introduction*. Baltimore: Johns Hopkins University Press, 1993.

Cacho, Lisa Marie. Review of *Hunger*, by Lan Samantha Chang, and *The Barbarians Are Coming*, by David Wong Louie. *Journal of Asian American Studies* 3.3 (2000): 378–82.

Chang, Lan Samantha. *Hunger: A Novella and Stories*. New York: Penguin Books, 1998.

Chin, Frank. The Chickencoop Chinaman *and* The Year of the Dragon*: Two Plays*. Seattle: University of Washington Press, 1981.

Freedman, Jonathan. "Transgressions of a Model Minority." *Shofar: An Interdisciplinary Journal of Jewish Studies* 23.4 (2005): 69–97.

Jen, Gish. "Who's Irish?" *Who's Irish?: Stories*. New York: Vintage, 1999. 3–16.

Kingston, Maxine Hong. *The Woman Warrior: Memoirs of a Girlhood Among Ghosts*. New York: Vintage, 1976.

Kogawa, Joy. *Obasan*. New York: Anchor Books, 1981.

Kong, Belinda. "The Asian-American Hyphen Goes Gothic: Ghosts and Doubles in Maxine Hong Kingston and lê thi diem thúy." in *Asian Gothic: Essays on Literature, Film and Anime*. Ed. Andrew Hock Soon Ng. Jefferson, NC: McFarland, 2008. 123–39.

lê thi diem thúy. *The Gangster We Are All Looking For*. New York: Anchor Books, 2003.

Tan, Amy. *The Joy Luck Club*. New York: Ivy Books, 1989.

——. "Mother Tongue." 1990. *The Opposite of Fate: Memories of a Writing Life*. New York: Penguin, 2003. 271–79.

Volosinov, V. N. *Marxism and the Philosophy of Language*. Trans. Ladislav Matejka and I. R. Titunik. Cambridge, MA: Harvard University Press, 1986.

Wong, Sau-ling Cynthia. "'Sugar Sisterhood': Situating the Amy Tan Phenomenon" in *The Ethnic Canon: Histories, Institutions, and Interventions*. Ed. David Palumbo-Liu. Minneapolis: University of Minnesota Press, 1995. 174–210.

Wu Chengen. *The Journey to the West*. Trans. and ed. Anthony C. Yu. 4 vols. Chicago: University of Chicago Press, 1977.

Chapter 7

A Return to Memory, Possibility, and Life: The Spirit of Narrative in John Edgar Wideman's *The Cattle Killing*

Ian W. Wilson

In *The Cattle Killing* John Edgar Wideman melds some of the early history of Africans in America with chapters from the art history of England, the early independence of the United States, and a tragic period of South African history. Ghostliness, both on the part of the ghostly spirit that inhabits multiple female characters and in a metaphoric sense on the part of the protagonist, serves as a uniting metaphor to bring these elements together. Through the ghostliness, connections between times and places are made and a radical narrative structure can be justified. As Wideman samples various kinds of texts, he collapses stable notions of realistic and novelistic time, poses central questions for history and historiography, and insists on the fluid nature of identity and narration, all while maintaining both the importance of the act of storytelling and a skeptical stance vis-à-vis the effectiveness of this undertaking.

The Dance of the Spirit's Trail: The Restless Spirit of *The Cattle Killing*

The ghostliness of Wideman's text leads to some initial confusion. Keeping with African tradition and the text's own literary exigencies, an old African spirit haunts this novel, taking various forms over its course. Always a woman, always pulling the protagonist toward her, she seems always to be in danger. Inhabiting the bodies of multiple women throughout the novel—a visitor to the protagonist's religious gathering, a bald caretaker for a white child, a lady's maid, and the novel's primary narratee—the ghost lives in the present but carries with her the burden of the past and a skeptical view of the possibilities of the future. This spirit dominates the novel and necessitates many of its narrative strategies. If the spirit were not present, the narrative could very well have taken the form of a linear description of the life of the protagonist. As it exists, however, the spirit and its ontological status force the text into strategies of fluid narration, the sampling of a variety of texts and historical realities, and a drawing of parallels between distinct timelines, which forces their collapse. Above or behind all these strategies, however, stands the importance of the storytelling that the novel inscribes into its form and themes.

The narrative strands of this novel attach themselves to readers like tatters of cloth. Readers will never be able to completely rid themselves of it.

The Cattle Killing makes direct reference to African religion, introducing traditional African notions of the supernatural into its mix of materials. After the prologue but before the story begins, readers find direct connections between African theological models and the novel.

> Certain passionate African spirits—kin to the *ogbanji* who hide in a bewitched woman's womb, dooming her infants one after another to an early death unless the curse is lifted—are so strong and willful they refuse to die. They are not gods but achieve a kind of immortality through serial inhabitation of bodies, passing from one to another, using them up, discarding them, finding a new host. Occasionally, as one of these powerful spirits roams the earth, bodiless, seeking a new home, an unlucky soul will encounter the spirit, fall in love with it, follow the spirit forever, finding it, losing it in the dance of the spirit's trail through other people's lives. (15)

As we will see, this ghostly figure plays a constant role in the life of the protagonist, never allowing him to live without the past.[1]

Like the ogbanji this "passionate" spirit that dominates the novel repeatedly inhabits bodies. Anyone who happens to fall in love with one of its hosts is cursed to follow the trail of the ogbanji through many other lives. The protagonist encounters this spirit in four different guises: first as a lady in her Sunday best in a vision while he resides outside the small Pennsylvania town of Radnor, second as a starving and doomed African servant woman who has abandoned fever-ridden Philadelphia, third as the servant and amanuensis of a white Philadelphia woman, and fourth as the indistinct, ailing narratee of most of the novel. Though the protagonist seeks the spirit more or less purposefully, Wideman indicated in an interview that he fails to understand this spirit's true nature: "He makes the mistake of thinking that the bodies she tends to inhabit are really her. But the spirit is much more than the bodies" (Interview with Derek McGinty 191). He knows he seeks a woman and is struck by similarities between certain women he meets and by how much these women draw him to them. The book ends, however, without the protagonist understanding the spirit's true identity, an identity that exceeds the human and the physical. The protagonist's confusion recalls the Igbo belief that those who die unhappy deaths or are buried incorrectly fail to enter the world of the dead properly. They inhabit a realm between life and death, causing trouble among the living as a means of expressing their frustration (Gomez 133).

---

[1]   Such practice evokes Henry Louis Gates's argument in *The Signifying Monkey* that music, mythologies, philosophical and epistemic systems, and patterns of performative practice are likely to have been retained by African slaves in their lives in the Americas and then by successive generations (4). See also Herskovits for one of the foundational texts of the idea that African American culture preserves aspects of the African past. More recent studies include those by Genovese, Gomez, Pitts, Raboteau, and Stuckey.

Rather than beginning with the protagonist's first encounter with the spirit, I will begin with the reader's. During the yellow fever epidemic of 1793 in Philadelphia, this woman has left the city with a small, sickly and perhaps dead, very light-skinned child. The confusion she engenders in the protagonist briefly extends to a judgment of whether she is living or dead. He notes:

> For a moment it seemed the entire figure might be some kind of life-size doll propped against a tree. So little did she stir. Not a sound or nod or blink. Arms limp on either side of her body. Carved child quiet on her lap. Chin tucked against a bosom neither rising nor falling with the rhythm of breath.
>
> Though the vital force seemed unnaturally suspended, I never feared she was dead. Enchanted by a wizard's spell, perhaps, but not dead. The scent of her too fierce. Her skin too hot and wet. (39)

From the outset the narrative focuses on the ambiguous and liminal nature of the bodies the spirit inhabits: neither dead nor alive, they move through the narrative like ghosts. The protagonist, much taken by the strange woman, is also uncertain whether she is the child's mother or its caregiver (or both). After she walks into the lake with the child, drowning herself, he feels as though he has abandoned her and searches for her in one way or another for the rest of the book.

This is not the first time, however, that the narrator has encountered this being, whose reappearance makes clear her relationship to the world of spirits. Indeed, only through later reflection does he begin to make connections between the various women he has encountered, believing that an identical spirit possessed them. Once, after he has fallen into what seems like an epileptic seizure, a woman he does not recognize helps him. He continues his story:

> Was she a visitor. A dependent who'd recently joined one of the regular families. Or was she kin to the myriad others I see whether my eyes open or closed as I sit, dazed, drained by the effort of recovering my wits.
>
> Thusly I met her the first time. Thusly she returns. The more I've thought of it since, the more I wonder if she belonged, like those other presences crowding the arbor that day, to the world of special seeing.
>
> In the clearing I witnessed two roads crossing. One for people like us, who worshiped at St. Matthew's. The other a thoroughfare frequented by our ancestors, our generations yet to be born. One highway solid earth, the other air, the stuff of the invisible ether where angels float. Perhaps seeing the spirit road and those who traverse it meant I was on my way to join them. The falling fit my middle passage. But she crossed over instead. Tended me. And perhaps because she tarried a moment to cool my feverish brow, perhaps she was left behind. If not left behind, suspended between her world and ours. (76–77)

The sentences, "Thusly I met her for the first time. Thusly she returns," suggest that the spirit woman has always been a part of him, and that the searching he undergoes throughout the text is a central part of his being. Thus, he paradoxically meets this female spirit for the first time and recognizes her appearance as a return: a return not just of this very spirit or ghost, but also to a kind of collective memory.

The evocation of many crucial issues of the African diaspora—such as the middle passage, the mythic path walked by the ancestors, descendants running in both Africa and America at the same time, and the ancestor-spirits themselves— makes strong connections to African spirituality, as does the setting for this scene. The clearing, similar to the one in Toni Morrison's *Beloved*, is the site of special spiritual activities that include elements of traditional African religion. Such locations were common in the era of slavery as places for slaves to worship freely on their own terms, often after attending a traditional Christian religious service (Gomez 265–69).[2]

Upon his arrival in Philadelphia, the protagonist begins to hear stories, many conflicting, of the black woman who cared so much for her young white charges that she took one of these children out of the city to save it (52). The protagonist accepts the veracity of these stories, arguing, "My way of reckoning learned from the old African people, who said all stories are true. What mattered was that I had found her again" (53). He finds her, of course, not in the physical sense but "living" in the stories told about her. The protagonist lets the story of the woman stand on its own merits, which raises a critical point for the novel. It functions under the presumption that telling stories keeps people alive, both those who are characters in the stories and those listening to them. However, great melancholy inhabits the novel's pages as well, melancholy tied to doubts about the efficacy or sufficiency of these stories to succeed at either attempt at keeping people alive. On one of the novel's last pages, we read, "If someone is listening" (208). This skepticism about the power of stories in the midst of obsessive storytelling is perhaps a typical postmodern gesture.

The protagonist's encounters with Kate, the third manifestation of the spirit, are only very briefly mentioned, though Kate becomes arguably the most important meeting point between them. Kate often seems the best-drawn character of the four manifestations of the African spirit—the only one with a name, the only one who manages to tell her story—but she remains relatively shadowy in the novel. Readers never learn anything about her past, and the most important part of her story—the ending—remains completely unknown. It seems at times that Kate is the narratee to whom the protagonist tells his stories for most of the book. Yet Kate's situation and that of the narratee fail to match up. The text avoids making the distinction between Kate and the novel's main narratee too clear for the same reason: it makes the similarities evident. The women the protagonist encounters are very similar, since the same African spirit inhabits them.

---

2   Richard Allen (1760–1831), an important Philadelphia preacher, a founder of the African Methodist Episcopal church, and a religious reformer (on whose life much of Wideman's protagonist's experiences are based), also conducted such meetings for black Philadelphians as part of the Free African Society, though in an urban setting.

Ultimately the text provides a vital clue that proves that Kate cannot be the protagonist's main narratee. At a certain point—whether it is before or after she has given birth is unclear—the protagonist loses contact with Kate, though he has searched for clues about her location in the diary the blind Mrs. Thrush dictated to her (198–99). Kate is not only lost to the protagonist at this point in his story; she is so lost that he has no hope of reconnecting with her. As with the story of the spirit's first appearance and sudden vanishing, and the story of the silent African woman with the white child entering the lake, the protagonist mourns for his loss and searches for her in stories. But does not yet make the vital connection: just as he encountered the spirit before she appeared as Kate, he will encounter her again. In his final encounter with the spirit he still fails to realize that his efforts to maintain contact, to keep the woman alive, are both pointless and unnecessary. The spirit inhabiting the body will continue to live in another form, another body. His stories can also live on in other forms, told by others (just as he tells Liam's and Nongqawuse's stories) and perhaps even in written form.

The fourth and final incarnation of the spirit is a vital part of the novel's narrative conceit. The basic setup inside the frame created by the author-narrator, present during the novel's prologue, is that the protagonist tells his story and those of people he has met to a convalescing woman to aid in her recovery. Throughout the novel there are a number of instances where the protagonist and his narratee, this fourth manifestation of the spirit, speak. Never is the situation so clearly demarcated as at the novel's beginning. He seems to go to her every night to tell her a little bit more of his story. In the midst of his story of wandering in the wilderness, the protagonist is interrupted by a woman's comments:

> I'm thanking you for your story. But I think you must leave now. Is your story finished.
>
> At your pleasure, dear lady. Finished for tonight.
>
> Is there more, then. Are you teasing me, now.
>
> No, no. My tales are poor, untidy things. No beginnings or ends. Orphan tales whose sole virtue is you listen. Goodnight. May your dreams be pleasant....
>
> One morning you'll open your eyes and everything will have changed. God's best blessing and worst curse upon us. Change, always change.
>
> Not you, my dear friend. You must never change. Tell me you will return tomorrow. And the morrow, and the morrow.
>
> Yes. Of course. As long as there's breath in this body. (29)

The protagonist then creeps away from the woman, down from the loft where she lies, and past her relatives, who have been warned that his "curing" her ills—his storytelling—might last weeks (30).

The protagonist's goal is clear: he senses a relationship between this woman and the spirit he has been following for years, perhaps decades. His hope: "She'd be free to grow stronger, new, till she was ready to emerge from the mirror of the water, clamber naked onshore, changed as seasons and dreams changed the land" (31).

Again, the narrator makes the same mistake over and over: he hopes not for communion with the spirit, whom he loves, but for a return to health of one of the bodies the spirit inhabits. By the end of the novel readers may realize what the protagonist never does: the spirit seems to burn through bodies, hastening their death. The degree to which the spirit is caught—cursed—in a cycle of repetitive inhabitation of bodies is unclear, as it is unclear whether she is also cursed by love.

The protagonist seeks his lover through her many guises, all along failing to realize who she really is. The protagonist of *The Cattle Killing* even wonders whether his search might result in his becoming a ghost himself: "One day my body would desert me and I'd be a ghost rooted to nothing, roaming aimlessly forever unless my body returned" (144). Ghosts in *The Cattle Killing* are not to be feared, but they do possess certain powers and are charged with certain tasks. These tasks, I would suggest, include bringing the present into alignment with the past (and the future) and challenging those still alive to start to grasp the interconnectedness and unfinalizability that is present everywhere.

"My tales are poor, untidy things": Narrative Strategies in *The Cattle Killing*

Wideman's novel features an extremely complicated structure of narration, mixing levels of writing and storytelling, often slipping between a first- and third-person narration focusing on the same character, and equally as often shifting from dialogue into monologue/narration. As such this aspect of the novel suggests a polyphonic "signifyin(g)" narrative, to use Gates's term[3] The reader encounters something quite complex in the reading process, as can be seen in the following excerpt.

> She follows the procession when it turns off the main road, onto a footpath overgrown with the tall, dry grass of that season. Follows us into the thick woods, to our humble threshing ground. Watches Rowe lay me down.... Who are these African people, she asks herself....
>
> One of them places a rolled shawl under the prostrate man's head. They surround him, heads bowed. A murmuring like bees. What do they intend, hiding themselves away deep in this grove of trees.... Her people in a somber, concerned mood. Yet agitated, alarmed.

---

[3] In a conversation with writer William Henry Lewis about Wideman's complex use of narrators and narrative levels, Lewis noted that he admires the complexity but ultimately just lets Wideman's narrative happen, lets the levels merge and flow into one another almost effortlessly. In so far as Wideman achieves this depiction of flexible and permeable levels in his books, he achieves one of his overall goals for his fiction: to make connections between disparate times, disparate places, and disparate cultures.

No birdsong in the clearing. All nature hushed, expectant. She realizes that she, too, is holding her breath....

It's over quickly. The man shudders once. Rests quietly after his utterance. Fire on its way to do its work. Warn the people. A burning house glows orange behind dark hills. He settles back on his arms. They are talking to him....

Where she finds water he can't say. Can't account for the miracle of its coolness. But she surely does find it and surely wipes his forehead. (77–78)

In this portion alone there are a minimum of two narrators present and three dominant voices. It begins with narration by the protagonist: the "me" being laid down by Rowe in the third sentence of the excerpt. He has been the narrator for approximately six pages prior to this point, with a description of an apocalyptic vision immediately preceding the above passage. By following pronouns and possessive adjectives, we note a slippage of narration in the second paragraph. After moving into the woman's thoughts in the first paragraph with the words, "she asks herself," the next several paragraphs (not all of which are quoted above) remain with her, which is suggested by the use of the phrase "young man" to describe the narrator and the obvious outsider perspective at this meeting of local African-descended Christians. As the scene becomes not merely reflected on but partially narrated through her words, she becomes a sort of temporary narrator herself. Occasional comments by the impersonal third-person narrator punctuate her narration: "her people" uneasily observe the protagonist's convulsions; "she realizes" that she has become so intensely involved that she has been holding her breath. In the penultimate paragraph quoted above, the fragment, "Warn the people," implies the immediacy of the panicked thoughts of the protagonist, and in the final paragraph above, the third-person narrator takes over as completely as the protagonist in the first paragraph. (In the three pages that follow the excerpt, the narration shifts to the protagonist's first-person again, then back to the impersonal narrator, then to first-person narration by the protagonist's friend and host, Liam Stubbs.)

Something similar but more radical happens in the paragraphs before the Epilogue. Readers come to the end of a discussion between the protagonist and his narratee that moves from unattributed dialogue (the first sentence) to narration by the protagonist (the second sentence) to impersonal third-person narration (the rest of the quotation):

I'm sta-sta-starting to sta-sta-sta-sta-stutter.

The language coming apart in my hands. The way the blue gown shredded when you knelt in the sand beside the lake and pulled the tired cloth over the child's golden crown of curls.

She studies him. She's not sure whether he's playing a game or words are truly sticking in his throat. A silly make-believe to turn back disaster or some awful malady affecting him.

> Either way, something is terribly wrong and he can't do a thing, she can't do a thing to change it, so she says, No matter, no matter, it's fine, baby. You're fine. Letting him know she understands and it's all right. Either way. Everything. Any way. As long as you tried your best, baby. Fine. Fine. Fine. (205–206)

Then three diamond shapes signal a narrative break. Afterwards a sort of narrative conclusion draws many of the main points together, the need to tell and hear stories the most important among them. The narrative shifts somehow between the first and second paragraphs of this conclusion (cited below) from a continuation of the protagonist's narration before the typographic symbols to what seems a return to the writer-narrator's explicit narration from the beginning of the novel's first part.

> One day when it's time to tell the last story and I stutter because it sits like a stone in my throat and carries the weight of all the stories told and untold I wanted to bring you as gifts, stories of my dead to keep you alive, to keep love alive, to keep me coming here each evening to be with you in spite of my dead, in spite of what was missing, lost, unaccounted for....
>
> One day I will tell you about Ramona Africa in her cell and Mandela in his cell and the names we lit candles for in Philadelphia, in Capetown, in Pittsburgh. Here. Take my blind hand. Teach it your features. Forgive me my dead. Loosen their grip on my heart. I breathe through their stories. If I ever kiss you, it will be with lips that form them. My dead in the kiss. (206)

Suddenly the levels of narrative, confusing on the first reading but actually fairly carefully drawn, collapse and with them collapse levels of time as well. However, the collapse of narrative levels does not indicate a pooling of the levels or narrators into one homogenous mess; rather the collapse serves to further stress the importance the novel places on the variety of speakers and levels that reside in the text. Though one character, the protagonist, leads readers through the novel, other voices play roles of equal importance. Ultimately, the multiple and shifting levels operate together in an impossible realm one is tempted to call ghostly.[4]

One of the main reasons for the very confusing nature of the novel's narrative structure is that it collapses onto one plane. This attempt, which allows many voices to speak their experience and draws connections between multiple strands of culture that most people would not ordinarily make, has an important analog, or even an enabling factor: a non-Western treatment of time. This philosophy of time is one Wideman has come to call "Great Time," following John S. Mbiti's *African Religions and Philosophy* ("Storytelling" 267). Wideman explains this theory in an interview about *The Cattle Killing*.

---

[4]   The novel's many voices represent a variety of perspectives on the level of gender, temporality, geography, religion, etc. At the same time, they seem channeled through one dominant voice that makes all of them sound more or less the same.

My notion of history is not linear, but much more like traditional, indigenous versions of history—African, American Indian, Asian—that sees [sic] time as a great sea. Everything that has ever happened, all the people who have ever existed, simultaneously occupy this great sea. It fluctuates, and there are waves, and ripples, so, on a given day, you are as liable to bump into your great-great-great-great-grandmother, as you are to bump into your spouse. That idea appeals to me because it makes problematic concepts like living and dead, concepts like progress. (Interview with Laura Miller, screen 2)

The section near the novel's end is one example of this sort of time. There are more examples, but the theory behind them is more important. This notion of time helps to explain why the African spirit can play such an important role, as it is a figure, a metaphor of time. To wit, there are elements of strong coincidence in the novel involving the spirit. Kate (who disappears while pregnant) and the African woman the protagonist loses track of at the lake (who carries with her a light-skinned infant) could be easily connected, though the encounter with the African woman occurs before the protagonist's meeting with Kate in the novel's chronology. The former occurs during the yellow fever epidemic, the latter after it. Seemingly obvious connections only work if one ignores traditional western teleological models of temporality.

In the novel the collapse of time may be a goal of the text or a uniting idea, but it is also one greatly feared by the two most important male figures in the text, Liam and the protagonist. The protagonist expresses his fear by imagining himself as an infant, shot and thrown in a ditch (199). Even more interestingly, while speaking of his time as a slave in York, England, Liam tells the protagonist about a time he was taken with his student master to view a pregnant African woman's corpse available for sale to the highest bidder.

My legs trembled. I pressed my hands into the wall. I needed the stones for support. Needed their roughness cutting into my skin. The African woman on the table was my sister, mother, daughter. I slept inside her dark stomach. I was gripping her heart with both my hands and it was the world's heart, hard and cold as ice. She'd been stolen from me and now I was about to lose her again. Knives would slice her open, hack her to bits. They'd find me cowering in the black cave of her womb again, dead and alive, alive and dead. (137)

Liam connects all moments of historical time into one bundle in this experience. Through his words he unites himself with all Africans, past, present, and future, denying the imposition of Western modes of time. His discourse throws logic to the wind, insisting on an impossible presence as an adult outside the body of the woman, as a child inside it, and as her relative from the previous, same, and next generations all at once. Here Liam even seems to suggest that this relationship forces him into the predicament seen all over the novel. Both dead and alive, he is somehow neither—he is undead, another of the book's many spirits. Thus the novel puts forward a model of history that forces a sort of ghostliness on its subjects, a ghostliness that carries beyond historical events to personal reminiscences, suggesting that storytelling is complicit in this framework as well.

The text tries not just to collapse levels of narrative and novelistic time, but also works to connect the historical events of the novel with the present day. In this image, with which the novel nearly concludes, past and present come into direct contact. "Ramona lights her candle—passes it to Mandela—passes it to Mumia—passes it to Huey—passes it to Goodman and Chaney—passes it to Gabriel—passes it to the ghost of a woman finding herself, naming herself at one of the rallies in one of the cities where I search for you, to join you, save you, save myself...." (207). The novel does not continue the story of the protagonist any further than an indefinite point in time after the fire at the orphanage for African children, but the search for the spirit and all that her presence allowed the protagonist goes on. In the end, this historical narrative has resonance beyond its pages for many reasons, including that its relevance has been connected to the present and its political struggles.

Another element of the connections drawn by the novel is the variety of texts "sampled" in *The Cattle Killing*. Elements of historical texts are borrowed, twisted, "signified" upon. Wideman uses the term "sampled" on the copyright page of the novel to mention some of his sources, especially the ones he quotes within its pages. He also uses this technique for the story "Fever," one of the texts that led to the writing of *The Cattle Killing*. The verb "to sample" is used frequently in hip hop music to refer to parts of one song—from a refrain to a bass line to a single word—used directly in another. Transposed to literature and reformulated by Wideman, sampling invites expansion to include not just actual historical documents but imagined figures and fictional texts. As such, it resembles the techniques Gates describes under the rubric of "signifyin(g)."

From the early slave narrative of Rev. Richard Allen, Wideman derives many elements of his protagonist's life. In addition, Allen appears briefly in the novel as himself. Using the published texts of the Philadelphia physician and American Declaration of Independence signatory Dr. Benjamin Rush (1745–1813), Wideman introduces events of the Philadelphia yellow fever epidemic of 1793, which also figure in Allen's narrative. From Rush's published letters to his wife, Wideman invents a life for this woman and introduces her servant, Kate. From the historical circumstances of the British anatomist and painter George Stubbs (1724–1806), Wideman develops the characters of Stubbs's inherited slave and companion Liam and Liam's common-law wife. Out of the true story of the cattle killing and subsequent mass starvation of the Xhosa people of South Africa in 1856–57 (especially as told in Noël Mostert's *Frontiers*), Wideman draws the legendary tale of the prophecy that started the killing.

Wideman frequently draws upon historical relationships between his characters to elevate the verisimilitude of his sampling. Both Allen and Rush describe the yellow fever, for instance, and worked together to combat it. For details outside their descriptions, Wideman turns to the standard work on the epidemic,

J. H. Powell's *Bring Out Your Dead* (1949). In other instances the connection is less clear. Rush attended lectures in London by the anatomist and obstetrician Dr. William Hunter (Rush, *Autobiography* 52–53), who later worked with the painter George Stubbs (Doherty 16). Richard Allen's brother, who signed on with a ship bound for the Cape of Good Hope after manumission, is tied in the novel to the events of the cattle killing, which take place not far from the Cape over a half a century later (Wideman, Interview with Derek McGinty 186, 211–12).

Wideman's manipulation of multiple narrators and narrative levels is inseparable from this sampling, as a number of the characters of the novel are drawn directly from historical texts or are postulated or imagined from gaps in the texts. These phantom characters, all but one of African descent, are: the protagonist, Mrs. Thrush's maid Kate, Liam Stubbs, Mrs. Stubbs, and the narrator's sailor brother. They add to the sampling aspect of the novel by suggesting that historical narratives tell part of history, but rarely are all the materials of historical truth available in existing documents. The text suggests that the stories of Wideman's postulated characters fill a need in the historical record; they are raised to the level of the "real" texts in order to complete it. As Wideman manipulates the details of the historical texts he uses—for example, renaming the historical figure Dr. Benjamin Rush "Dr. Thrush," manipulating the details of Rush's biography to make his wife blind and her servant girl black—he raises the postulated characters to the same level as those characters drawn from life. As another element in his effort to allow as many participants as possible to tell their story, Wideman includes some fictional texts in his collage of the ghostly traces of the past.[5]

There are too many possible narratives sampled in the novel to discuss them all here. Beyond those used directly for characters or events, works alluded to in the book, such as Samuel Richardson's *Pamela* and the novel's epigraphs from the biblical book of Ezekiel, could lead to interesting insights, especially due to their ironic use. One main sampling, however, has direct bearing on the ghostliness of the novel, its themes, and its narrative strategies: the story of Nongqawuse of the Xhosa people and the cattle killing.

Wideman's interest in the notion of "Great Time" and his interest in ghostliness connect the story of Nongqawuse to the general narrative line. This central event

---

[5]   As Gates develops in *The Signifying Monkey*, the slave narrative continues the traditions of Africa in its drawing upon, citing and reformulating previous texts. According to Gates (153), the narrative of Olaudah Equiano (1789) exercised tremendous influence on later narratives of American slaves, including that of Frederick Douglass (1845). The neo-slave narratives that began to appear in the 1960s continue many of these tendencies but merge them with contemporary concerns. Bernard Bell describes the neo-slave narrative as a late modernist or postmodernist attempt to "combine elements of fable, legend, and slave narrative to protest racism and justify the deeds, struggles, migrations and spirit of back people" (285). An episodic structure, a fundamentally oral basis for the narrative, and an urge to tell previously untold or unrecorded stories typify the neo-slave narrative (Bell 289–90). See Rushdy for a more extensive discussion of specific works.

emphasizes a key motivation for the novel's historical nature: a new vision of the future. The disaster results from a false prophecy delivered by Nongqawuse, the niece of a Xhosa priest. The survivors of the disaster are ghosts, dead like the ones who failed to survive. Tragedy, in other words, affects both those who perish and those who live to speak of it. The writer-narrator character wants the image of the Xhosa to guide his book, for every word "to be a warning, to be saturated with the image of a devastated landscape," for his book to begin and end with this image (7).

The story of the cattle killing returns within the main narrative, and forces another collapse of temporal levels. The protagonist encounters Nongqawuse in a dream (148) after his last day in Radnor with Liam and Mrs. Stubbs, a day that ends with the whites of Radnor burning down the houses of all the local blacks. After the dream the protagonist awakens as if in a field in Africa, sees the real destruction around him, and leaves Radnor for Philadelphia. Along the road he encounters the African spirit for the first time in the guise of a human form—the woman who disappears in the lake. The dream, too, seems a visitation by the African spirit, but Nongqawuse's words resemble those of a mother speaking to her child. Strangely, the protagonist dreams of the cattle killing before assisting in the care of the ill during the 1793 yellow fever outbreak in Philadelphia, despite the fact that it takes place over sixty years later. Time collapses and narrative levels are crossed through the sampling of and imaginative "signifyin(g)" on a faraway historical event. The dream also suggests a notion of time similar to Wideman's explicit commentary in the interview quoted earlier: time is seen as a sea of events, and it is irrelevant whether the event occurs in the past, present, or future of any one individual. In fact, the sea of time also implies the possibility of individuals stretching beyond single lifetimes, like the spirit dipping in and out of the protagonist's life and later emerging in Southern Africa. Additionally, the spirit's intimation that she will return in a future dream, in which the prophecy has been realized, points to history as a potentially redemptive moment and gives the narrator something to move forward toward, despite the general pessimism of the text as a whole.

Behind the layering of narrative levels, the collapse of time, and the sampling of texts, the crucially important narrative strategy of the novel is the meditation on the nature of narrative itself, or more precisely, on storytelling. An emphasis on oral storytelling over the academic sounding word "narrative" is appropriate to Wideman's techniques: many of his sources originate in the oral tradition, his narration sounds best read aloud, interruptions and hesitations fill his paragraphs, and much of the novel must be understood as spoken. A written document is a step removed from the physical contact so desired within the story between the protagonist-narrator and the spirit he searches for throughout the novel. Though a hierarchy presents itself in the text, with physical contact at one end and the written word at the other, the text places serious doubt on the possibility of real physical contact. In lieu of that contact, then, storytelling takes its place.

Again, the novel's main narrative conceit is that the protagonist's storytelling is chopped into hour-long segments with the convalescing woman. The storytelling thus tends toward a sort of amorphous body similar to the sea of history that resembles less a story line than a story pool. Despite his narrative's disconnectedness, however, the protagonist hopes it holds his listener's attention. He says, "When I omit parts of the story, do I relinquish my hold on you. When the tale jumps to another place, where do you go. Promise you will tell me someday. I pray you are not disappointed when I leave things out. Promise we can return together and sort out what's missing. I can't bear to think this single telling is my last chance, my only chance to be here with you" (39). Narrative becomes a symbol for the serial inhabitation of bodies mentioned above: like those ghosts who move from one body to another, someone chasing behind and losing, then catching the trail, the protagonist's story at times leaves its hearer, or the hearer leaves it. Though they join up again, the protagonist continues to voice his fear throughout the novel. Storytelling becomes a way to reach out to his narratee, to connect with her, and make present his ghostly past through words.

This ghostly element of the protagonist's storytelling emerges explicitly in the text as well. At one point he tells the woman, "Bear with me. Let me relate to you our first meeting, itself also, strangely, a return. To memory, possibility, life. As all stories are" (55). These sentences might be taken as a motto for the text as a whole. They suggest not only that stories allow access to memories, but also that telling stories opens up new possibilities, that new life can be formed out of them. In ways almost literal for this novel, stories can bring the dead back to life and lead to the sort of life suggested by the spirit in the protagonist's dream of Nongqawuse. This fact becomes extremely important when the text suggests that the woman to whom the protagonist has been telling his story has already died. He says, "This enterprise, this speaking into the dark as if it would raise you from the dead. Why am I driven to it. Why don't I lie down beside you. Sleep your sleep. Why the whispering in your cold ear—words, words, words, as if silence isn't enough" (78).

Still the novel offers a glimpse of hope in its epilogue. There the writer-narrator character's son Dan writes a letter to his father after having read the book. He writes:

> sometimes I wish you could hear my thoughts as I read along. Interpolations, interpretations, digressions, footnotes. Factual queries, off-the-wall signifying and rewriting the text. I wish you could eavesdrop on some of that mess.
>
> Sometimes your books seem to anticipate my wisecracks, misgivings, my groans and amens. We're rapping and capping tit for tat. (210)

Someone listens after all, and provides not just an audience but also a theory of the text's composition and how to read it. Reading such a text is an active, uncontrollable process. The text guides the reader to a degree but also allows for digression, commentary, and changes. Reacting to the text equals listening to it. Reacting to the text means signifying on it, building upon it, savoring it, letting it dwell within the reader's mind. Thus the dance of the spirit's trail continues.

Conclusion

Wideman's *The Cattle Killing* presents fundamental challenges to its readers. As a work of fiction, it includes substantial elements of historical accuracy. As a ghost story it departs from Western notions of the ghost and plunges the reader into the spirituality of the African continent. As a narrative it frustrates its readers into playing such an active role that many reject the novel. Wideman calls the novel "a parable about texts. It's a parable about actual life, the fictional life, invented lives... generations who invent lives for their ancestors.... It's also a kind of carnival of texts—of letters, novels, reminiscences, research, historical documents—and how these interact and click together at certain times for readers, writers" ("Benefit" 208). *The Cattle Killing* requires engagement and work, but it also invites a degree of playfulness. It invites its readers to participate in its creation, to answer the call of desire that starts the engine of narrative, to face their ghosts in acceptance, not fear. For, without the ghost, the novel resembles many other fractured, open-ended and collage-style narratives. With the ghost the text acquires justification for its techniques, a motivating spirit, and a guiding metaphor.

Works Cited

Allen, Richard. "The Life, Experience, and Gospel Labours of the Rt. Rev. Richard Allen." Wideman, *My Soul Has Grown Deep* 6–53.

Bell, Bernard W. *The Afro-American Novel and Its Tradition*. Amherst: University of Massachusetts Press, 1987.

Doherty, Terence. *The Anatomical Works of George Stubbs*. London: Sacker & Warburg, 1974.

Douglass, Frederick. *Narrative of the Life of Frederick Douglass, an American Slave*. 1845. Gates, Classic 243–331.

Equiano, Olaudah. *The Interesting Narrative of the Life of Olaudah Equiano, or Gustavus Vassa the African*. 1789. Gates, Classic 1–182.

Gates, Henry Louis, Jr. *The Classic Slave Narratives*. New York: Mentor-Penguin, 1987.

——. *The Signifying Monkey: A Theory of African-American Literary Criticism*. 1988. New York: Oxford UP, 1989.

Genovese, Eugene D. *Roll, Jordan, Roll: The World the Slaves Made*. New York: Pantheon, 1974.

Gomez, Michael A. *Exchanging Our Country Marks: The Transformation of African Identities in the Colonial and Antebellum South*. Chapel Hill: University of North Carolina Press, 1998.

Herskovits, Melville J. *The Myth of the Negro Past*. Boston: Beacon, 1941.

Mbiti, John S. *African Religions and Philosophy*. 1969. London: Heinemann, 1988.

Morrison, Toni. *Beloved*. 1987. Plume-Penguin, 1988.

Mostert, Noël. *Frontiers: The Epic of South Africa's Creation and the Tragedy of the Xhosa People*. New York: Knopf, 1992.

Pitts, Walter F. *Old Ship of Zion: The Afro-Baptist Ritual in the African Diaspora*. New York: Oxford University Press, 1993.

Powell, J. H. *Bring Out Your Dead: The Great Plague of Yellow Fever in Philadelphia in 1793*. Philadelphia: University of Pennsylvania Press, 1993.

Raboteau, Albert J. *Slave Religion: The "Invisible Institution" in the Antebellum South*. New York: Oxford University Press, 1978.

Rush, Benjamin. *The Autobiography of Benjamin Rush: His "Travels through Life" Together with his Commonplace Book for 1789–1813*. Ed. George W. Corner. Princeton: Princeton University Press, 1948.

Rushdy, Ashraf H. A. *Neo-Slave Narratives: Studies in the Social Logic of a Literary Form*. New York: Oxford University Press, 1999.

Stuckey, Sterling. *Slave Culture: Nationalist Theory and the Foundations of Black America*. New York: Oxford University Press, 1987.

TuSmith, Bonnie, ed. *Conversations with John Edgar Wideman*. Jackson: University of Mississippi Press, 1998.

Wideman, John Edgar. "Benefit of the Doubt: A Conversation with John Edgar Wideman." Interview with Bonnie TuSmith. TuSmith 195–219.

——. "Fever" in *The Stories of John Edgar Wideman*. New York: Pantheon, 1992. 239–65.

——. Interview with Derek McGinty. *The Derek McGinty Show*. National Public Radio. WAMU, Washington, DC. 9 October 1996. TuSmith 180–94.

——. Interview with Laura Miller. *Salon*. 24 April 2003 Available at http://archive.salon.com/nov96/interview961111.html (accessed 10 October 2009).

——. "Introduction" in Wideman, *My Soul Has Grown Deep* ix–xvii.

——, ed. My *Soul Has Grown Deep: Classics of Early African-American Literature*. New York: One World-Ballantine, 2002.

——. "Richard Allen" in Wideman, My *Soul Has Grown Deep* 1–5.

——. "Storytelling and Democracy (in the Radical Sense): A Conversation with John Edgar Wideman." Interview with Lisa Baker. *African American Review* 34 (2000): 263–72.

Chapter 8

Ghosts of *Proof* in the Mind's Eye

Mark Pizzato

Hamlet: ... methinks I see my father.
Horatio: Where, my lord?
Hamlet: In my mind's eye, Horatio.

Shakespeare, Hamlet 1.2.184-85

Characters onstage and onscreen are, in a sense, always ghosts. They have a "presence" created by the actors, by other artists involved, and by their audience—transcending the mortal body in theatre or with immortal illusions projected in the cinema and on TV. Yet, such spectral figures also reflect the fictions of self and other in another theatre, that within our brains. These theatrical aspects of our cranial apparatus, staging various selves and others, in dreams and fantasies, but also in representations of reality, reveal the animal energies of our primal ancestors haunting us as well. Long before the emergence of theatre as an art form in ancient Greece and India, our ancestors developed an "inner selective environment" of performance, through the brain's representation of potential actions in the outer world (Dennett 374–76). How did animals' inner environments evolve, through mammalian play and dreaming, through human language and culture, into numerous transformations of the external environment, including the current technologies of theatre and cinema, which reflect the performance spaces of memory and possibility in the mind's eye?

This chapter begins by considering the theatrical and cinematic aspects of the mind, regarding the brain's evolved anatomy and its "extelligence" of culture (Stewart and Cohen), thus summarizing parts of my recent book, *Ghosts of Theatre and Cinema in the Brain*. I will then perform a close reading of *Proof*, a play and film about mental illness, mathematical genius, and patriarchal ghosts, to discern how stage and screen media continue the evolution of human higher-order consciousness, through spectral illusions that also have effects in the Real. How do *Proof*'s ghosts affect the theatre and film viewer differently—given the changes made from stage to screen and the positioning of the spectator, as a phantom also, through such choices? As in my recent book, I will use both cognitive neuroscience and Lacanian psychoanalysis.[1] I hope this will suggest a bridge across the current divide between modernist essentialism and postmodern relativism in theories of

---

[1] Many neurologists, including Mark Solms and Oliver Turnbull, have connected their work with Freudian psychoanalysis. There is even a society for "neuro-psychoanalysis," based in London and New York, with its own journal. Freudian therapists, such as Louis

performative subjectivity.[2] For the current, neomodernist concern with essential structures in cognitive theories of theatre and film—often set against Lacanian influenced poststructuralism—might benefit from a broader view combining both approaches, especially regarding the ghostly expressions of the mind's theatre.

Inner Performance Spaces

The anatomy of the human brain reflects its ancestry: the primal brainstem and basal ganglia as reptilian (or ichthian) core, the emotional limbic system as a later developing paleo-mammalian layer, and the neocortex as outermost mammalian layer, with the further evolution of distinctive right and left hemispheres.[3] The human limbic system reveals the development of an inner performance space of emotions, beyond the homeostatic functions of the brainstem, in our mammalian ancestors and current mammal relatives. Specific circuits of panic, fear, rage, and seeking systems (including lust and nurturing subsystems) are discernible within the human limbic brain, through the corresponding areas of rat and monkey brains (Panksepp). Human dreaming and play function as inner and outer theatres—as threat simulation and rehearsal spaces, for behavioral and emotional exercise.[4] Play involves mock aggression, as when a mammal's snarl turns into a grin or children imitate their elders and experiment with potential adventures, in the competitive aspiration for superior identity. This externalizes the body's inner theatre of fears and desires, from personal dreams to collective play and working "reality." Each human body, while dreaming or awake, bears its own theatre of emotions, interpreted through the higher awareness of feelings in the brain's limbic system and neocortex, plus the self-reflective "feeling of feelings" (Damasio, *Feeling* 231–32). Thus, the brain may also use the body as its playground, projecting bodily emotions or "as if" body states.[5] "Emotions play out in the theater of the body. Feelings play out in the theater of the mind" (Damasio, *Looking* 28).

Cozolino, Daniel Siegel, and Arnold Modell, have also related their work to neurology. But there has not been much consideration of Lacanian theory with regard to neuroscience.

[2]   For other bridges between modernism and postmodernism, see Pizzato, *Edges of Loss*.

[3]   This tripartite model, devised by Paul McLean in the 1950s, is now in common usage. Yet, as my UNC-Charlotte colleague, biologist David Bashor, explained to me, our lower brain areas are actually inherited from fish, via a proto-reptilian or proto-mammalian ancestor. Cf. Shubin.

[4]   Dreaming is "a mechanism for simulating threat-perception and rehearsing threat-avoidance responses and behaviors" (Revonsuo 90). Play serves "to exercise and extend the range of behavioral options under the executive control of inborn emotional systems. In fact, play may be the waking functional counterpart of dreaming" (Panksepp 295).

[5]   Cf. Damasio, *Looking* 117–18: "the body-sensing areas constitute a sort of theatre where not only the 'actual' body states can be 'performed,' but varied assortments of 'false'

The human neocortex has evolved distinct areas to process limbic emotions and bodily perceptions. The right hemisphere is a visuo-spatial, holistic, intuitive, anxiety-biased association area, and thus an anomaly detector or Devil's Advocate scout (Solms and Turnbull; Cozolino; Ramachandran and Blakeslee). The later maturing, left hemisphere is an audio-verbal, sequentially rational, causality-based, executive routine and prosocial controller or war-room general. The right neocortex has stronger ties to the emotions of the limbic system. Hence, the body's theatre of emotions percolates from the brainstem and limbic system through theatrical, mimetic feelings of the right brain and narrative, mythic rationalizations of the left: correlating to the three Lacanian orders of Real, Imaginary, and Symbolic. These areas within and between brains also correspond to the gradual evolution of performance levels in our species: from the episodic awareness of primate ancestors to the mimetic culture of *Homo erectus* two million years ago, to the development of language and mythic culture in *Homo sapiens* a half million years ago to human theoretic culture, starting forty thousand years ago, which eventually produced theatre and cinema as ritual art forms externalizing the brain's inner performance spaces (Donald 260–66, 319–26).

Over 90 per cent of brain activity is unconscious (Gazzaniga 21; Ramachandran and Blakeslee 152). Concepts and percepts are staged, according to cognitive scientist Bernard Baars, in the limited "spotlight" of consciousness by conceptual contexts, deep goals, and interpretive memory traces (plus automatic routines)—like offstage technicians, directors, and audience members in the brain's unconscious (46–47, 144–46).[6] Such theatricality also relates to how we experience ideas, images, and emotions within our heads: both the fictional performances of dreams or imagined events and the representations of external reality through our senses and expectations. Most of what we dream or perceive is absorbed unconsciously and only partially remembered—as imaginative reconstructions—later on. What we consciously perceive as present reality is also staged and screened as representations within the brain. For example, there are thirty visual projection areas, each interpreting distinctive neuronal signals from the eyes, through the conceptual templates of prior experiences and present expectations (Carter 39, 43). There are also cross-modal areas connecting the various perceptual stagings and projective screenings[7] of the five senses—through augmentation, if senses and

---

body states can be enacted as well, for example as-if-body states, filtered body states, and so on."

6   See also Pizzato, *Ghosts* 99–100, 107–108.

7   Of course, the "projection areas" within the brain are not the same as the mechanism of a cinematic projector or the "projection" of one's negative aspects onto others according to psychoanalysis. Yet, the interpretation of visual (and other sensory) signals within the brain also involves projecting personal expectations when viewing theatre, cinema, or other performances of fiction/reality—and this may involve a defensive projection of negative assumptions as well. For a connection between evolutionary psychology and psychoanalytic "projection," plus other defense mechanisms, see Nesse and Lloyd.

expectations agree, or interference, if they do not. Rather than a single stage or screen in the brain, there are many that combine theatrically, using the same circuitry to represent outer reality as they do in presenting imagined scenes and dreams, while filling in gaps and repressing inconsistencies.[8]

Likewise, there is no central playwright, director, or spectator in one area of the brain, as a "little man" or homunculus scripting and watching the show inside. There are many unconscious areas with distinctive functions, converging to form the representation of reality and the inner environment of imagination and dreams—in the stage space of consciousness. Yet, the human brain presents the illusion of a single self perceiving the world around it or imagining and dreaming a world within. Like a director creating a unified mise-en-scene, with the help of actors, designers, technicians, and playwright, the brain fashions an ideal self and seamless reality—through a conscious and unconscious, conceptual and perceptual "filling in" of the gaps in vision (and other senses), including the blind spots where each eye connects to the optic nerve (Ramachandran and Blakeslee 103–104). The brain "interpolates" what might be in the blind spot, using the statistical regularity of its experience of the world, thus economizing on visual processing. And yet, our brains also project fantasies onto the gaps in perception—as exemplified by the hallucinations of James Thurber, which he turned into stories and cartoons. Such fantasy spaces and images are usually masked by "baseline" sensory signals, except when our imagination is given free-play with damage to the brain or eyes, or in the fictional spaces of theatre and cinema.

According to neurologist V. S. Ramachandran, "vivid visual hallucinations," like those of Thurber and others who have Charles Bonnet syndrome, are "fairly common in elderly people with visual handicaps like macular degeneration, diabetic retinopathy, corneal damage and cataracts" (Ramachandran and Blakeslee 105). Perceptions of reality involve both bottom-up sensory signals and the top-down expectations of concepts, memories, and fantasies—between the higher brain regions and primary cortex (110–11). If there is a blind spot due to neural or ocular damage, it may be filled with vivid hallucinations, because the top-down projections receive no countermanding sensory signals. This may also involve the body's other senses, as with phantom limb pain in amputees. The unconscious part of the brain sends a muscle-clenching message but there is no action signal from the missing limb, so the brain commands more clenching, which triggers a stored pain memory: the feeling of a phantom limb (53–54). As Ramachandran puts it,

---

[8]   See Baars 74–75; Solms and Turnbull 209–13; and Ramachandran and Blakeslee 109–12. Cf. Kosslyn, "Einstein's" 263, on the creation of mental imagery as a slower and more "constructive process" than perceptual representation in the brain, because "the backward connections [from frontal lobes to posterior brain areas] are not as precise as the forward." Also, during dreams the frontal-lobe action and inhibition areas are dormant, unlike waking imagination and perception (Solms and Turnbull, 212). "In the absence of the frontal lobes to program, regulate, and verify our cognition, affect, and perception, subjective experience [in dreams] becomes bizarre, delusional, and hallucinated."

"we are hallucinating all the time and what we call perception is arrived at by simply determining which hallucination best conforms to the current sensory input" (112). In Lacanian terms, we construct the theatre of reality through Symbolic and Imaginary orders that we project upon the external materiality (and loss) of the Real, individually and collectively, while also reconstructing and experimenting with such realities in the theatres of dreams, memories, imagination, and art.[9]

The construction of a present, "hallucinated" reality in the brain—through memories, dreams, desires, imagined scenes, and a sense of self—bears aspects of cinema as well as theatre. According to neurologist Antonio Damasio, humans generate not only a "movie-in-the-brain," but also the *"appearance* of an owner and observer for the movie *within the movie"* (*Feeling* 11, 160). Thus, the mind's eye may zoom in and out when viewing an imaginary object (Baars 73). As in the virtual worlds of puppetry and computer graphics, as well as movies and TV, the mind pans, scans, and rotates internal images (Kosslyn, *Ghosts* 128–29). Like conventional cinema, but with a differently shaped screen, the human imagination tends to create a limited visual field, a "flat oval" of about 45 degrees in height and 120 degrees wide, similar to external viewing through the eyes (Baars 73–74).[10] But the brain may also produce a virtual reality theatre, inside and around the self (as reality or fantasy), beyond the limited stage space of consciousness and the screen of vision—as with the imaginative collaboration of theatre spectators filling in the scene onstage and connecting it to offstage events, or of movie viewers suturing a larger diegetic world at the screen's edges and editing cuts.

There are distinctive ways that the technologies of theatre and cinema extend the inner performance environment of the brain. The spectator of a play onstage may zoom the vision in or pull back, while shifting the focus of attention and making connections. However, a movie frames and edits much more of the scene for the viewer (and often shows a greater variety of scenes to make up for the two-dimensional screen and recorded performance). But both media evoke a further theatre within the spectator's brain. Unlike cinema, theatre spectators share space and time with the actors onstage. They breathe the same air across the stage edge. They influence each other's performance and perception, through the internal theatres created simultaneously within each of their brains during the external show. Thus, theatre extends the human construction of reality, involving past, present, and future, from episodic animal experience to mimetic social mirroring to mythic memory ordering to the collective dream/reality space of live performance. It plays upon loss and desire through a shared, womb-like, co-creative space, whereas cinema involves this communal element in the separate

---

[9]   Cf. Solms and Turnbull 23–31, on the projection and association areas of the neocortex, in relation to executive controls, imagined actions, limbic emotions, and Freudian drives.

[10]   The rectangular instead of oval screen in cinema probably developed from the prior proscenium tradition of theatre (and the Cartesian-perspective picture frame in Euro-American art). See Brewster and Jacobs 147, 168.

spheres of production and audience spaces. Yet, both theatre and cinema express the brain's higher-order awareness of change and mortality, of nurture and danger in human culture, as well as the primal emotions of panic, fear, rage, and seeking in the limbic system.

Western theatre evolved a specific lineage of architectural expression for mammalian emotion and higher-order neocortical awareness, from natural being to human lack of being, through certain stages of spatial presence. The flawed Thespian hero, communal chorus, and troublesome gods of ancient theatre's stage, orchestra, and outdoor setting feature the struggle of an individual brain against collective and natural forces, personified by various masks and the open-air scene of the cosmos. The biblical and everyman characters of medieval theatre, with church mansions as well as outdoor platea and processional staging, show a different cosmic extension of the brain's desires and fears, ordering human mortality in relation to paradise and hell-mouth, with a divine king ruling over all and yet with devils and death as persistent threats. The human-measured world of Renaissance theatre, with the poetic effects of spoken décor or the visual magic of proscenium perspectives and vanishing points, reveals an early modern way of playing with prior ideals of gods and spirits, yet also a progression toward acquiring divine power through human technology. This builds—through Enlightenment manners and moral sentiments, through Romantic sublimation, social outcast heroes, and authorial genius, through melodramatic spectacles and good-versus-evil stereotypes, through modern, objective, realist, fourth-wall intimacy and various, subjective, anti-realist experiments, through postmodern fragmentation and self-reflexivity—to the recent technologies of cinema, television, and cyberspace, which include all of the preceding developments onstage. However, these screen media do not "stink of mortality" in the same way that live theatre does (Blau 132).[11]

Cinema moves its spectators through space and time, with mobile cameras and editing cuts—as if the movie viewer were a ghost or god, watching through a divine window. The characters onscreen also appear as ghostly projections, but in a different way from those onstage. Both performance media create presence, aligning past and future, memories and dreams. Yet characters onstage appear this way while tied to the actor's body, in direct communication with the spectator's, creating rare moments that will never be repeated even in the same production on other nights. This also involves the territoriality (a primal animal drive) of shared and yet opposed, actor and audience spaces in theatre. But film characters are displayed transcendently, beyond the mortal actor and material scenery that the camera captured (or computer graphics added), through the reconstructive illusion of a full reality onscreen. Even live television and interactive videogames are not

---

[11]   Cf. Auslander 10–23, 158–62. He deconstructs the notion of "live" theatre and argues that television is today's "dominant" performance medium, having "usurped" theatre's position even more than cinema. I would add that the Internet and videogames are also usurping television, especially in their mixture of live, recorded, and interactive performance. See Zizek 54–55.

embedded in actors' bodies, scenic materiality, and shared spaces as directly as theatre—though they are vulnerable to technological problems and play also in the virtual-reality theatres within spectators' brains, like performances onstage. Thus, theatre and cinema (as well as related screen media) extend specific aspects in the play of emotions within the body, through the evolving theatre of the brain, from animal fear and desire, vulnerability and power, to human cultural spaces. But these technologies also derive from biological risks taken by our ancestors' bodies, under the pressures of survival and reproduction, which created the extreme plasticity of our brains, culture, and artworks, for good or ill.

Big Brains and Hollow Egos

With the decline of the dinosaurs, mammals started to dominate the earth, demonstrating greater risk-taking flexibility in a changing environment. Predatory mammals developed a particularly dangerous but successful strategy. They not only gave birth to exposed offspring, unlike egg-laying dinosaurs and birds, but also to relatively helpless young. The offspring of migrating herbivores were born ready to run from predators and follow the herd for safety. Yet the babies of territorial predators had to be nursed in a safe den or carried by their mothers—until they gradually learned to hunt in the pack or venture out on their own.

The expanding brain-power required for predatory mammals to survive, through the risky strategy of live birth and vulnerable babies, took a quantum leap when four-legged primates evolved into our two-legged hominid ancestors. Mammalian play and dreaming became crucial techniques, not just for expressing joy or fantasy, but for learning and reinventing survival. Two-legged hominids had their hands free for developing tools and sign-language, leading eventually to the verbal language areas of the brain's left hemisphere (perhaps because it operates the right side of the body, with the right hand as dominant for gestures and tool use in most humans).[12] But the birth canal of two-legged females could not evolve past a certain point to bear bigger brained babies—due to gravity's pull on internal organs through a larger pelvic hole (Shlain 4). Hominids then evolved an even riskier strategy: premature birth to a totally helpless infant, so that the enlarged brain could fit through the birth canal. This also allowed for greater flexibility in the hominid infant, as it developed with more parental and cultural, rather than intrauterine nurturing.

In a psychoanalytic view, the "specific prematurity" of human birth (Lacan 6), with half the proportional gestation time of our primate relatives (Shlain 8), produces a lack of being—as the Imaginary and Symbolic orders of nurturing outside the womb vastly transform the Real of nature. The human child develops in an external womb of family and culture, beyond the stable environment of the mother's body, learning social behaviors that reprogram the primal drives and

---

[12]   See Banyas 97.

emotions of its reptilian and mammalian brain. The child acquires its identity and behavior patterns through social mirroring and language orders that train its remnant animal instincts—in a human-made world that has greatly changed the natural environment. Play and dreaming thus become even more crucial in humans for imitation and experimentation, while exercising emotions and rehearsing fears or desires. Humans must struggle not only with basic survival needs and threats, but also with a growing awareness of their mortal, lacking being.

During the "mirror stage," in the first 6–18 months of life, the human child becomes aware of its emerging self in the mirror and in the desires of the Other (Lacan 3–9). But the desires and demands of the Other that form an illusory self—and transform the child's unconscious drives into a discourse of the Other—are also self-alienating. The sense of self in the mirror, in others' eyes, and in the mind's eye involves a misrecognition of the true subject in the unconscious. Thus, an idealized ego (or mask of character) forms around lack. Fantasies develop in the desire for certain lost objects as traces of the Real, which can never be recovered, yet trigger the illusion of bliss and completion. Hence, the limbic brain focuses its panic, fear, rage, and seeking systems on a fragile, illusory ego[13] and on the competition for particular objects of the Imaginary and Symbolic worlds. This occurs through dreams, which organize daily memories while rehearsing threats and desires, through play, which models behavior and exercises emotion, and through other theatrical mirrors inside and between minds.

Parents, siblings, other relatives, friends, and teachers in the child's life, as well as characters in the mass media, become ideal egos mirroring various possibilities of the self. But they may also come to represent the Other as ego ideal, a transcendent spectator for whom the child—and the later adolescent or adult—performs (Leader and Groves 48). The child tries to be the "phallus" for the (m)Other, to fill the Other's lack, as object of desire (94). But eventually, through mirror-stage alienation and Oedipal separation (involving the Name/No of the Father), the child will move from its Imaginary relation with the (m)Other to the Symbolic dimension of social demands and ego ideals, with the phallus as signifier of lack, yet promise of potential power.

Each person does this in a particular way. Neurotics fail to go beyond Oedipal castration, to fully traverse the fundamental fantasy of being the phallus for the (m)Other (Fink, *Lacanian* 72). Perverts transgress and thus reinvoke the law (the Father's No) in a repeated attempt to separate (Fink, *Clinical* 179–81). Psychotics are caught in an earlier structure, prior to mirror-stage alienation, through a failure of the Father's Name. Thus, we have evolved a tremendous burden with our bigger brains and lack of being. Rather than being focused by natural instincts toward survival needs in a fixed environment, we radically transform our environment and develop outside the womb through the higher-order variability of culture. Both the individual and society are re-created again and again—through play,

---

[13]   Cf. Varela 60–66, on the cognitive self as "virtual," in relation to neuroscience, Lacan, Buddhism, and ethics.

dreams, and various forms of theatre—as primal survival and reproduction needs become altered into Symbolic demands, Imaginary desires, and Real drives, with particular lost objects that form symptomatic repetition compulsions.

We humans have been extremely successful on this planet, spreading our immortal aspirations across the globe and altering the environment to suit our needs—like the ghosts and gods that various cultures project as extensions of the hollow yet powerful human ego and its ego ideals. Through its lack of natural being, but its want to be technologically and metaphysically transcendent, the human brain has evolved a volatile mixture of passionate drives, a fragile (or paranoid) ego, and the higher-order consciousness of death, while aspiring toward immortality in competition with other egos and cultures. How is this double-edged sword of power and vulnerability, of creativity and destructiveness in big-brained humans still evolving today through theatre and cinema—as exemplified by *Proof*, which explores ghostly identities, inherited genius, and the terror of madness, in different media?

Genius Haunting the Stage and Screen

Ramachandran speculates that mathematical and artistic genius may have evolved in some individuals when certain brain areas (such as the left or right angular gyrus) became enlarged as part of the general growth of the overall brain for adaptive reasons. "Maybe when the brain reaches a critical mass, new and unforeseen traits, properties that were not specifically chosen by natural selection, emerge" (Ramachandran and Blakeslee 196).[14] David Auburn's *Proof* (2001) focuses on the amazing emergence of mathematical genius in two characters, a father and daughter, Robert and Catherine, who also suffer from traits of mental illness. Onstage together in the first scene, Catherine drinks "champagne" (after discovering it is just wine), which Robert has apparently provided for her twenty-fifth birthday (6). Then he demands that she not "waste" her talent anymore, as with the days, the work, and the discoveries she has already "lost" through laziness and depression (8). They discuss her desire, through his demand, to produce a proof of her mathematical genius—before going crazy as he did at her age, just after producing his "best work" (9). Robert describes his slip from genius into madness as a "sharper... clarity.... No doubts." His ability to work all day on a mathematical problem became an all-encompassing paranoia: "secrets, complex and tantalizing messages.... The whole world was talking to me" (10). This is what Catherine fears will happen to her, at the same age as her father, especially when he reminds her that he is dead now. She is talking to a ghost. Robert tries to reassure her that she is not crazy if she asks herself whether she is. But then he must admit that her talking to him, as a ghost, is a "bad sign" (12).

---

[14]   See Miller on the role of sexual, as well as environmental, selection in evolving the bigger human brain and its extraordinary talents.

Robert may be right, on both accounts. Catherine's wondering about her sanity is different from his former clarity, when Robert had no doubt that the whole world was talking to him. According to Lacanian analyst Bruce Fink, certainty about hallucinations being real (as with Robert's former clarity) is characteristic of psychosis, whereas doubt is the "*hallmark*" of neurosis (*Clinical* 84). Catherine may be just a normal neurotic, doubting her sanity and the influence of her father's spirit or "genius." She projects his ghost from memories in her brain onto the empty spaces around her after his death—like an amputee experiencing phantom limb pain or those who fill in the blind spots of vision with vivid hallucinations, or to a lesser degree like the rest of us who interpolate an ordinary reality. Yet, Robert's appearance to Catherine is a bad sign that his demands upon her in the past have turned into her own desires for and against him in the present, as she extends the mirror stages and projection screens within her brain into the empty home around her—and her future with others.

Through Lacanian psychoanalysis and current neuroscience, we can see that the human evolution of a bigger brain created an internal theatre of familial and cultural demands in the specialized left hemisphere (as executive control area), with alternative ego desires and intuitive anxieties in the right (as devil's advocate), building upon the transformed drives of the mammalian limbic system and the basic bodily needs still signaled by the reptilian brain stem. Auburn's play shows this with Robert's continued *demand*, even after his death, that Catherine develop and express her mathematical genius—as he appears on the porch to celebrate her birthday with champagne. He is a ghost, born from the internal theatre of her brain and projected onto the external screen of reality, through the sutured gaps of perception. The ghost of Robert, offering champagne and companionship, emerges from the basic *need* of thirst in Catherine's brain stem, the primal *drive* to restore his presence as lost object via feelings of mourning and merriment in her limbic system (as his funeral coincides with her birthday), and the various conflicting *desires and fears* of her right hemisphere, while memories of his *demands* mix with others in her left. Of course, desires are not strictly located in the brain's right hemisphere, nor demands just in the left. But these Lacanian terms, like the Imaginary and Symbolic orders, correspond to many of the distinctive functions of the right and left hemispheres, according to current neurology.

Auburn's play engages theatre spectators, and their internal theatres, with the reality of Robert's character—through the device of not letting the audience know he is a ghost until midway through the scene (unlike Shakespeare's strategy in *Hamlet*). He is thus a projection of the Symbolic demands, Imaginary desires, and Real drives within Catherine's brain and theirs. After Robert reminds Catherine that he is already dead, Hal, a former graduate student of Robert's, appears also through the porch door. Spectators might think, at first, that he is a ghost, too. But he then asks the startled Catherine if she was "asleep" and about her drinking "alone" (12). Spectators realize he is a character in the ordinary external reality rather than another hallucination they share with Catherine's brain. Auburn's stage directions indicate that "Robert is gone" by then. Yet this play's quick shift (like a cinematic cut) between subjective and objective realities exposes the neuro-psychoanalytic mixture of perception, fantasy, and memory—of Real, Imaginary, and Symbolic—in any brain's construction of reality. Is Robert gone when the actor playing him leaves the stage? Or is he still present, not only in the theatres within Catherine and Hal, but also between them, through the traces left in memory and projections from the audience?

The film version of *Proof*, directed by John Madden (2005), begins differently. Rain falls on plants outside an enclosed porch, as the camera tracks across the water running down its windows. A TV set is visible inside, through the blurred glass. Images change with channel switching, but certain voices are briefly heard: a commercial for a stain-remover with "power," another for a product that the consumer can "twist," "turn," "fix," and "improve," and further commercials for home weight-lifting equipment and for a realtor. The latter commercials are seen more clearly as the camera moves inside. An enlarged male head appears over the house on the TV screen, as a voice says: "When you're looking for a home, your real estate agent is a big part of your life. You need someone you can count on." Also, in a different TV clip, a commentator (Jimmy Kimmel) appears briefly, saying: "they painted some people up like animals and now it's over."

Unlike the opening of the stage drama, Catherine (Gwyneth Paltrow)[15] is shown alone, sitting in the enclosed porch room, with rain streaking the windows like tears, while she stares at the TV and changes its channels by remote control. Yet, each of the TV images and voices foreshadows specific aspects of her drama. She is stained by grief and guilt, while desiring the power to move beyond her father's genius and madness. She must twist and reshape his ghost inside her, in order to improve her identity and her future relations with others. She has born the weight of caring for her father at home in Boston for five years, after her mother died, while her older sister Claire (Hope Davis) developed her own career as a currency analyst in New York. Catherine will soon learn that her sister is returning home not only for their father's funeral, but also to sell the house where Catherine still lives and then take her to New York, possibly to a mental asylum. Thus, the large male head over the house in the commercial relates not just to Robert's ghostly presence, but to Claire's role as Symbolic agent of the Other outside the home. Claire made a greater separation from her father than Catherine—and from their dead mother, who is only mentioned once in the play and film, yet might be imagined by the audience as haunting the home throughout. We learn that Catherine took on a more maternal role in caring for her mentally ill father, while also bearing more of his potential for genius, and delayed her own schooling for his sake. These sisters were thus "painted" as different social animals while they grew into their twenties. But the film will show, like the play, how Catherine evolves at a crucial point in her life—through mammalian panic, fear, lust, and rage—toward a distinctive human sharing of her genius with others.

---

[15]   Paltrow starred in the same role in a London stage production of *Proof*, also directed by John Madden, prior to making the film with him.

The film's opening montage also shows Catherine riding a bicycle toward and onto the University of Chicago campus (including an overhead "god shot" of her with cars in street traffic), her walking across the quad and inside a hallway, and then her bumping into a young man wearing glasses, who turns out later to be Hal (Jake Gyllenhaal). Thus, the movie viewer sees what Catherine is remembering as she sits alone in the porch room—when Robert (Anthony Hopkins) appears there, startling her, as in the play. Indeed, Robert speaks ("Can't sleep?") before we see him, just at the moment when Catherine bumps into Hal in her memory/fantasy. Initially, this makes us think that Robert is real, snapping Catherine back to reality. But when we learn that he is a phantom, this moment, in retrospect, ties together Catherine's desires for and memories of both men. Robert then gestures with his head toward the kitchen, after telling her it is "after midnight." The movie cuts to a shot from the back of the fridge, while Catherine opens it (with Robert's voice-over of "Happy Birthday") and finds his present of "champagne," instead of seeing it already present on a porch table as in the play's stage directions (5).

These are just a few examples of the many ways the film moves the viewer to various places in Catherine's memory and throughout the house. The movie gives the spectator a ghostly role of observing the theatre within her brain and floating at the edges of reality (even inside the fridge), though not interacting with Catherine as Robert's ghost does. During the "live" version of the drama onstage, spectators also watch as ghostly, fourth-wall voyeurs. Yet they choose how they join the characters vicariously in the stage space, with its three-dimensional actors and props, during this scene and others, all of which take place on the porch, while merely suggesting the activities inside the house and elsewhere. Spectatorship through both media involves "mirror neurons" in the brain, which fire along the same pathways in seeing an action performed as when doing it oneself.[16] But the distinct experience of a shared stage space (involving a single location with this play), or of a moving and cutting dream screen, changes how the viewers re-create the drama within their own internal theatres. Their different experiences and collaborations are also shaped by numerous choices in how Auburn's script, a particular staging of it, or Madden's movie presents this drama about the mixing of subjective and objective realities, evoking spectators' personal identifications with or observations of the characters' genius, sanity, and madness.

---

[16] Various types of mirror neurons have been discovered by Giacomo Rizzolatti and his colleagues in their experiments with monkeys. The same brain cell fires when the monkey makes a particular movement or watches another monkey or the human researcher perform that movement: grasping with the hand (selective for certain grips), grasping with the mouth, holding, and tearing (Churchland 108). In humans, too, unconscious motor commands are made, in the cells of spectators' brains, to mime such movements when seen. Such mimetic actions may be inhibited, yet are "used to interpret what is seen," especially by mirror-stage infants rehearsing self- and other movements (110). See also Ramachandran, *Brief* and "Mirror."

The film cuts Robert's lines demanding that Catherine not waste her talent (moving them to a later, added scene as her memory of him), his wistfulness about the prior "clarity" of madness, and his final line about the "bad sign" of Catherine seeing him as a ghost. Instead, it uses a few lines from a scene later in the script (46) to show her further memory of meeting Hal several years before, after bumping into him, with her father also there during the time when his madness was in remission and he could teach again. This provides a transition to Hal's appearance in the present (without glasses), after he has been looking at Robert's notebooks upstairs. The movie viewer is thus positioned between Catherine's fantasy of a phantom father, which may signify her madness, her memory of Hal when her father was not mad, and the current reality with Hal present but her father absent. By removing most of Robert's lines, the film presents a less demanding paternal ghost, who does not insist that Catherine develop her talent. He just appears as a loving, bumbling father, who offers her a bottle of wine as "champagne" and encourages her to go out with friends on her birthday, asking about a girlfriend whom Catherine has not seen since the third grade. His patriarchal flaws of going "bughouse" before and being dead now are only revealed at the end of the scene, just before Hal interrupts in the present reality. Yet, the father's desire that Catherine move beyond him to be with others on her birthday and the conflict that creates (as he also demands she do math with him) builds from this scene toward the drama's climax, along with the twisted burdens of genius/madness and resentment/guilt that she bears.

The movie viewer experiences Catherine's inner conflict through cinematic cuts between reality and memory, like intrusions of the past (and present phantom) in the theatre of her brain. The theatre spectator, on the other hand, witnesses more complete scenes of dialogue in just one location, framed as present or past, and is thus invited to refocus, edit, and project personal associations between the lines, bodies, and objects palpably present onstage or absent there. After the initial gift of a wine bottle as champagne, the key object, both onstage and onscreen, becomes a notebook. For the drama revolves around the mystery of whether Robert regained enough sanity to use his genius again before he died and created another sublime truth in one of his notebooks, as he did in his twenties, or whether Catherine has done that. When Hal interrupts Catherine's hallucinatory meeting with her father, she accuses him of stealing such a notebook, after he expresses his envy of Robert's genius. She demands to inspect his backpack; he calls her "paranoid" (16). The audience is challenged to judge, at that moment and at later points, whether she is crazy or he is villainous.

Onstage, Catherine's sense of territoriality is more immanent than in the film, even though the movie shows the audience much more of the house. Catherine has allowed Hal into her home (like the audience at the fourth wall). She has given him access to her father's personal remains, in a private area that theatre spectators do not see, but can imagine near them. There, Robert left 103 notebooks with his "graphomaniac" writings and yet possibly a nugget of genius (13). Hal's demand for permission from Catherine to return again and again, to mine those remains, reveals his drive for the sublime that was once in Robert's mortal brain and may have been left on paper as "proof" of his continued genius beyond madness. "I don't believe a mind like his can just shut down" (14). But Catherine loves Robert in a different way. Fueled by limbic panic, fear, and rage at the loss of her father and the threat of Hal as her father's student (who might publish Robert's proof under his own name), Catherine demands an inspection of the backpack, revealing her mammalian drive to protect the family territory and its ghostly possessions.

The film cuts Catherine's explanation to Hal of her different experience of Robert as his daughter and caretaker, and of her more complete knowledge of his genius and madness. It moves some of those lines to an added scene of Catherine, later in the movie, shocking the mourners at Robert's funeral with her resentment that they cared only for his greatness. She took care of him at home, she says, during his mind's decay, and now she is "glad he's dead" (17). In the stageplay, she just tells this to Hal and insists she does not want "any protégés around." But he warns: "There will be others." With these lines cut in the film, there is more emphasis on how the notebooks trigger Catherine's memories of her father, rather than the potential invasion of her home (and the stage space) by other math geeks hungry for her father's work. There is also more focus on Hal's attempt to ask Catherine out: to listen to his band that night or go jogging later to help with her mental stress. In the stage version, Hal mentions that his own mother died "a couple years ago" (18), but that line is cut, too, from the film, giving the audience a simpler judgment of whether Hal just wants the prize notebook or a date, not a deeper commiseration.

Once again, the movie draws the audience directly into Catherine's internal theatre of memory. In both versions, she calls the police, after she finds a notebook Hal has stolen, under his jacket, not in his backpack. But Hal tries to explain to her that he was just taking it in order to wrap it for her birthday. He shows Catherine what her father wrote several years ago in the notebook about her drive to take care of him at home, rather than letting him be institutionalized, as having "saved" his life (20). In the film, this triggers Catherine's memory (and guilt) of telling her father that she was going to school at Northwestern, separating from him to live there, because he had been well "for almost seven months" (44). The film moves up some dialogue from Act 2 to create this brief flashback at the end of the first scene, showing shock and woundedness on Robert's face, instead of the longer argument and various emotions, between him and Catherine, with the full scene of 2.1 later in the play.

Thus, the film audience receives fragments of memory from within Catherine to solve the mystery of her guilty attachment to the paternal ghost, her inheritance of his genius or madness, and her personal evolution of limbic drives, through neocortical desires and demands, concerning an object (another notebook) that she has hidden offscreen. Theatre spectators dwell more fully in the memory scenes and present conflicts on the porch—while working on the problem (or proof) of something sublime, lost and re-created, in the shared stage space with their mortal bodies and other material objects.

Audience Ghosts

In both versions, Catherine falls in love with Hal, opening her heart, body, and father's desk drawer to him. She gives him a key to the drawer the morning after they have sex, so that he can find the notebook of his dreams. In the stage version of the initial seduction, he kisses her and apologizes. Then she flirts with him and kisses him more passionately, showing her drive of limbic lust beyond the fears of territorial invasion and the demands of the father's ghost (31–33). In the film, however, Catherine is more hesitant, with additional lines expressing her inner conflict, perhaps due to the co-writing of the screenplay by David Auburn and Rebecca Miller, daughter of Arthur Miller.[17] The film shows Hal playing the drums with his band in Catherine's home after the funeral (at the party arranged by Claire), whereas the play only refers to this, with the music heard offstage. The film also shows the band performing a John Cage-like number called "i" (several minutes of silence since "i" means "imaginary number") in honor of Robert, although the play only refers to that in dialogue (14, 29). The film uses visuals and music much more to involve the audience in Catherine's attraction to Hal, in relation to her father's absence. The movie even goes upstairs to Catherine's bedroom, where Hal uses the excuse of being "drunk" to give her the first kiss (31). But the film shows Catherine as painfully reticent about becoming intimate with Hal, giving her further lines for this. She moves away when he kisses her the first time, saying she is "a little out of practice." She covers her face after he kisses her again, saying that she feels like an egg ready "to crack open." He makes love to her on her bed, though not much of their bodies are shown. The focus instead is on Catherine's face, experiencing pleasure yet also torment, as she covers it with her hand after the brief orgasm.

When Claire tells Catherine, the morning after the party, that she has already sold the house, Catherine indeed cracks—as in an earlier scene of rage against Claire for trying to control her life. In that earlier scene, Claire had encouraged Catherine to visit her in New York, questioning her rage at the police the previous night, and doubted that Hal really existed, until she met him. Now, Claire not only doubts her sister's sanity, but also takes her home away. Catherine's fragile identity explodes with rage against Claire's demanding use of the Symbolic order against her. (Claire paid off the mortgage for the house while working in New York, so she has the right to sell it now.) Catherine blames Claire for abandoning her and her father. But Claire claims that both of them might have saved their sanity if Robert had been institutionalized. When Hal returns with the precious notebook that Catherine gave him the key to find, with its "historic" proof, he

---

[17] In the DVD commentary, director John Madden gives Rebecca Miller credit for an additional scene, later in the drama, when Catherine meets with a professor at Northwestern about her failure to complete a math assignment.

does not believe she wrote it and neither does Claire (41).[18] This misrecognition sends Catherine even further into limbic panic and animal rage against her sister and lover. Both her domestic territory and her remnant object of connection to her father's genius have been negated.

The stage play shows this cracking of Catherine's ego in two scenes: at the end of Act 1, with her rage at Claire and revelation that she wrote the proof, and in the second scene of Act 2, after a memory scene with Robert, about Catherine's choice to move away and study at Northwestern. The film also shows Catherine's rage at Claire and her claim that she wrote the proof. But it then adds a god shot of her walking across the Northwestern campus in winter several years ago. Scenes are also added of Catherine meeting with her math professor, trying to work on a problem set, and driving home with great concern for her father who has not answered her calls for days.

This extended flashback culminates in another scene, partly moved up from 2.4, the penultimate scene of the play. Catherine finds her father working outside in freezing weather (at night in the film). Robert claims to be "in touch with the source" again, on a "geyser" of inspiration, like thirty years ago when he was in his twenties. He admits that he thought he was finished, "terrified" that he would never work again. But now he wants Catherine to work with him. He shows her the "general outline for a proof" in one of his notebooks. "It's very rough," he says after handing it to her.

Next, the film shows Catherine's argument to Claire and Hal that she wrote the notebook's proof. It thus brings together the climactic scenes of Acts 1 and 2 in the play. But the movie suggests more ambiguity about which notebook holds the proof of genius: Catherine's or Robert's. It gives an extended sequence of added scenes (plus the demand of Robert from the play's first scene that Catherine not waste time), mixing past and present to show her working with her father on her notebook, while he writes in his. In the flashbacks, Robert also helps Catherine with a mathematical idea while staring at a horror movie on TV. (The TV movie shows a woman fleeing from a male zombie.) However, the film saves the grand finale of the play's climax, when Robert demands in the past that Catherine read aloud the nonsense in his notebook, until after she breaks down in Claire's arms, crying that she "killed him."

In this added scene, Catherine denies that she wrote the proof, interpreting her success in that genius-work as an Oedipal murder of her father. Her guilt for that, along with the rejection of her work by Claire and Hal, triggers her ego collapse. She stays in bed and does not speak (as Claire reports to Hal), so Claire arranges to fly her to New York to care for her there. But Hal brings back the notebook before they leave. Having checked with several "geeks," young and old, he decides that Catherine did write it after all. She tells him he is too late, but he gives it back to her by throwing the notebook through the open window of the limousine as

---

[18]   The historic proof is never explained in detail, which some critics see as a flaw in the play. See Hornby 112 and Klaver 6.

it drives away to the airport. The film then shows Catherine in the past reading Robert's mad proof and Catherine in the present deciding not to submit to her sister's control (by refusing to get on the plane with her). The concluding scene has Catherine sitting with Hal to check the proof of her genius and sanity, as she enables herself to move beyond her father's ghost.

The movie thus weaves together a different climax from the play, adding images and lines that suggest Catherine worked with her father to write her proof, yet could not help him with his delusion of doing his own great work once again. After her nervous breakdown, Catherine is willing to let the world think that Robert wrote her proof—until Hal's drive to make her know the truth (by throwing the notebook through the car window) helps her fight once again, against Claire, for her own sanity and genius. Catherine crosses the fundamental fantasy of having her father return through the notebook as a lost object of *jouissance* and thus accepts her own split subjectivity with its potential for greater truth. In Lacanian terms, this sacrifice of a prior castrative sacrifice[19] enables Catherine to move beyond the loss of Robert, reconfiguring the fundamental fantasy of a ghostly father and his immortal proof, toward her own possibilities of genius.

However, the original stage play gives a different sequence as the climax and resolution. In a scene cut from the film, Hal visits the day after denying Catherine's genius, but Claire will not let him see her and blames him for her collapse. Claire gives Hal the notebook, suggesting that he cares more for it than for Catherine (58). This positions the audience on the outside of Catherine's genius/insanity split, judging it with Claire and Hal, and judging them as concerned caretakers or opportunistic villains. The play then shows a full scene of Catherine in the wintry past with Robert, as she encounters his renewed, yet delusory enthusiasm and the gibberish of his notebook. But it shows this without the film's montage of her developing genius in the past and breakdown in the present. The audience is left with the task of imagining such connections through their own internal theatres.

The final scene of the play shows Hal visiting a week later, with his confirmation that the proof is genuine and his new belief in Catherine's genius. But first, Claire argues with Catherine about having missed a week of work to stay with her and care for her, because Catherine would not get out of bed. Claire even tells her to stay in Chicago if she hates her help. This allows the audience to see more of Claire's inner conflict than in the film: how she struggles to combine maternal responsibility for her sister's well-being and her business world ambitions (especially after being away for years instead of helping to care for their father). The audience can also judge more about Hal's love for Catherine or his sublime self-interest, in his longer dialogue with her about accepting the notebook, with its proof of both her identity and a new mathematical truth. She says, too, that she

---

[19]   According to psychoanalytic theory, we each sacrifice infantile jouissance (erotic, ecstatic joy) to enter the social order of language and culture. But this produces symptomatic problems, which may then be "cured" by a further, therapeutic sacrifice. See Fink, *Clinical* 69–71. See also Pizzato, *Theatres*.

could not work with her father on the proof because of his madness—unlike what is shown in the film.

The movie of *Proof* may not involve the audience as much in the protagonist's subjective reality, of genius and madness, as *A Beautiful Mind*, Ron Howard's 2001 film about John Nash (a mathematical genius who suffered from schizophrenia like the fictional Robert). And yet, a comparison of *Proof*, the film, with the original play demonstrates how cinema's ghosts, like and unlike theatre's, extend certain aspects of the brain's internal, Imaginary and Symbolic environments. By cutting lines, adding montage and music, and restructuring scenes to quickly interweave subjective and objective viewpoints, *Proof* shows the cinema's extension of our brain's inner theatre, where memories and fantasies merge, through emotional, intuitive, and rational circuits, to fill in the fragmentary modes of reality perception and ego identity.

Both versions of *Proof* demonstrate how dreams inside the brain, rehearsing scenes of (im)mortal desire and fear, may combine with the physical and emotional exercise of mammalian play—to become the artful experiment of a shared, stage or screen performance. *Proof* shows the lack of being in prematurely born humans opening a painful void and yet creative space in the ego, especially with the loss of a father who then becomes a ghostly influence. Catherine's memories of Robert turn into a tragically flawed fantasy, involving the notebook's proof—through a desire to resurrect the ideal ego of his genius and thus deal with his demands on her as ego ideal. But the audience also plays a role as ego ideal, as ghostly Other to the stage or screen, although each spectator may identify in different ways with the drama's flawed characters. The theatre or movie audience thus becomes an external version of the audience inside the brain: a ghostly form of the unconscious Other, mirroring the characters' deep goals, conceptual contexts, and interpretive memory traces. Yet, spectators may also continue a personal and collective evolution of the ghost theatres within the brain—through a greater awareness (or catharsis) of the characters' tragic flaws.

With its realistic style and postmodern issues, *Proof* posits no divine spectator, as in earlier stages of theatre's history. But the spectators watching it evolve our human culture by striving for a divine viewpoint—a higher order of awareness, or perhaps genius, to deal with and reintegrate the animal passions that may otherwise twist into madness and destructiveness, given our lack of natural being and egos competing for power. The mind's eye of the audience aspires to a spectral teleology, involving godlike, inner and outer theatres, through the material spaces and live bodies of the stage or the subjective suturing of time onscreen.[20] This expresses

---

[20]   Cf. Blau 133–34, on "the versatile negotiability of cinematic time: arrest, reversal, speedup, and various kinds of optical exchange, the synthetic time-warp of montage, splicing, segmenting,... a virtual suspension of time, in the intoxicating control of succession, the feeling that time, after all, is possessed by the cinematic machine...." Theatre, however, involves a "much more conscious... overlay of playing time upon lifetime," which includes "the ghost of a ritual pretense... [and] the actor's mortality... dying in front of your eyes."

the Symbolic and Imaginary, narrative and mimetic orders of the human brain's inner theatre, plus its Real animal heritage, shared in the cultural womb of stage or screen performance. Yet, as *Proof* shows, human genius emerges today not just through bigger brain power or new mathematical and scientific discoveries. It also evolves through the communal sharing of math, science, theatre, and cinema—transforming the ghostly influences within us in nurturing, creative, and sublime ways, despite the dangers in our selective drives of competition and control.

Works Cited

Auburn, David. *Proof.* New York: Dramatists Play Service, 2001.

Auslander, Philip. *Liveness: Performance in a Mediatized Culture.* London: Routledge, 1999.

Baars, Bernard J. *In the Theater of Consciousness: The Workspace of the Mind.* Oxford: Oxford University Press, 1997.

Banyas, Carol A. "Evolution and Phylogenetic History of the Frontal Lobes." *The Human Frontal Lobes.* Ed. Bruce L. Miller and Jeffrey L. Cummings. New York: Guilford, 1999.

Blau, Herbert. *Blooded Thought: Occasions of Theatre.* New York: PAJ Publications, 1982.

Brewster, Ben, and Lea Jacobs. *Theatre to Cinema.* Oxford: Oxford University Press, 1997.

Carter, Rita. *Exploring Consciousness.* Berkeley: University of California Press, 2002.

Churchland, Patricia Smith. *Brain-Wise: Studies in Neurophilosophy.* Cambridge: MIT Press, 2002.

Cozolino, Louis J. *The Neuroscience of Psychotherapy.* New York: Norton, 2002.

Damasio, Antonio. *The Feeling of What Happens: Body and Emotion in the Making of Consciousness.* New York: Harcourt, 1999.

——. *Looking for Spinoza: Joy, Sorrow, and the Feeling Brain.* Orlando: Harcourt, 2003.

Dennett, Daniel. *Darwin's Dangerous Idea.* New York: Simon, 1995.

Donald, Merlin. *A Mind So Rare: The Evolution of Human Consciousness.* New York: Norton, 2001.

Fink, Bruce. *A Clinical Introduction to Lacanian Psychoanalysis.* Cambridge: Harvard University Press, 1997.

——. *The Lacanian Subject.* Princeton: Princeton University Press, 1995.

Gazzaniga, Michael S. *The Mind's Past.* Berkeley: University of California Press, 1998.

Hornby, Richard. "Mathematical Proof." *Hudson Review* 54.1 (Spring 2001).

Klaver, Elizabeth. "*Proof, Pi,* and *Happy Days.*" *Journal of the MMLA* 38.1 (Spring 2005).

Kosslyn, Stephen Michael. "Einstein's Mental Images." *The Languages of the Brain*. Ed. Albert M. Galaburda, Stephen M. Kosslyn, and Yves Christen. Cambridge: Harvard University Press, 2002.

——. *Ghosts in the Mind's Machine: Creating and Using Images in the Brain*. New York: Norton, 1983.

Lacan, Jacques. *Écrits: A Selection*. Trans. Bruce Fink. New York: Norton, 2002.

Leader, Darian, and Judy Groves. *Introducing Lacan*. New York: Totem, 1996.

Madden, John, dir. *Proof*. Miramax, 2005.

Miller, Geoffrey. *The Mating Mind*. New York: Doubleday, 2000.

Modell, Arnold H. *Other Times, Other Realities: Toward a Theory of Psychoanalytic Treatment*. Cambridge: Harvard University Press, 1990.

Nesse, Randolph M., and Alan T. Lloyd. "The Evolution of Psychoanalytic Mechanisms." *The Adapted Mind*. Ed. Jerome H. Barkow, Leda Cosmides, and John Tooby. Oxford, Oxford University Press, 1992. 601–24.

Panksepp, Jaak. *Affective Neuroscience: The Foundations of Human and Animal Emotions*. Oxford: Oxford University Press, 1998.

Pizzato, Mark. *Edges of Loss: From Modern Drama to Postmodern Theory*. Ann Arbor: University of Michigan Press, 1998.

——. *Ghosts of Theatre and Cinema in the Brain*. New York: Palgrave, 2006.

——. *Theatres of Human Sacrifice: From Ancient Ritual to Screen Violence*. Albany: SUNY Press, 2005.

Ramachandran, V. S. *A Brief Tour of Human Consciousness*. New York: Pi Press, 2004.

——. "Mirror Neurons and Imitation Learning as the Driving Force Behind 'the Great Leap Forward' in Human Evolution." *Edge* 69 (June 1, 2000). Internet.

Ramachandran, V. S., and Sandra Blakeslee. *Phantoms in the Brain: Probing the Mysteries of the Human Mind*. New York: William Morrow, 1998.

Revonsuo, Antti. "The Reinterpretation of Dreams: An Evolutionary Hypothesis of the Function of Dreaming." *Sleeping and Dreaming*. Ed. Edward F. Pace-Schott, Mark Solms, Mark Blagrove, and Stevan Harnad. Cambridge: Cambridge University Press, 2003.

Shlain, Leonard. *Sex, Time and Power*. New York: Penguin, 2003.

Shubin, Neil. *Your Inner Fish*. New York: Pantheon, 2008.

Siegel, Daniel J. *The Developing Mind*. New York: Guilford, 1999.

Solms, Mark, and Oliver Turnbull. *The Brain and the Inner World*. New York: Other Press, 2002.

Stewart, Ian, and Jack Cohen. *Figments of Reality: The Evolution of the Curious Mind*. Cambridge: Cambridge University Press, 1997.

Varela, Francisco J. *Ethical Know-How*. Stanford: Stanford University Press, 1999.

Zizek, Slavoj. *On Belief*. London: Routledge, 2001.

PART III
Reanimating the Dead

Chapter 9
"For the Union Dead": Robert Lowell's American Necropolis

William S. Waddell

No reader should be surprised at the ubiquity of memorialization in Robert Lowell's volume *For the Union Dead*. His concern with the people and places of his (and his country's) New England past marks his work from its very start: the Lowells and Winslows of his personal genealogy, the names to conjure with from American history (Salem, Concord), his family graveyard in Dunbarton, and the resting places of representative people from our past ("At the Indian Killer's Grave," for example). Still, the pervasiveness of motives and strategies in the 1964 volume is striking, as is their range. The opening two poems, "Water" and "My Old Flame," offer personal memorials—a particular rock in the former, a house now sold to new owners in the latter—markers that could, in effect, be icons from anyone's experience.[1] These are sites merely of nostalgia. But elsewhere in the book, Lowell includes memorial treatments that address the passing of whole cultures, and do so not only through the rhetoric and materials of the poems themselves, but by invoking as well the public rhetoric of monuments. Both the artifacts (poems and monuments) and their rhetoric raise questions of what, if anything, survives of those cultures—what, in spite of their passing, may be passed on. The title poem is by far the best known, but "Florence" also provides a gloss on Lowell's strategies and attitudes that is provocative in itself and illuminating in comparison with "For the Union Dead," the poem under primary consideration here.

My analysis does not propose an understanding of that poem dramatically different from the prevailing consensus. If, as Guy Rotella observes, there is critical disagreement over the poem's degree of affirmation or despair (53–54), there is little over the principal terms of its drama. That consensus view of the poem has always recognized the figures of Colonel Shaw and the dozen or so members of the regiment represented in Saint-Gaudens's bas relief, dead and long absent themselves, as representing a spirit of American promise now similarly absent, whether irrevocably dead or merely betrayed. The challenge and resonance of that premise doubtless help to explain why readers and critics keep coming back to "For the Union Dead" as one of the touchstones of Lowell's career. The

---

[1]   If Paul Mariani is right about the genesis of "Water"—a poem based on a scant few hours alone one day with Elizabeth Bishop in 1948—the threshold for memorialization is slight indeed (167).

poem's virtually simultaneous affirmation and undercutting of values, motives, and the possibility of fidelity to ideals (and perhaps even to any continuous self) sustain the kind of postmodernist reading so effectively executed by Rotella. They also mirror, in this overtly political poem, the ambivalence toward tradition and authority that Alan Williamson and Robert von Hallberg, among others, have located at the center of Lowell's political attitudes. This tension between affirming and undercutting ideals precisely parallels that between the heroic and the democratic that Michael North locates running through virtually all American monuments and attitudes toward them, both public and individual.

Placing Lowell's poem in the context of representations of death, however, creates a different opportunity, one that connects with these other readings without choosing between or merely repeating them. Descriptively, I will go further, observing the ways Lowell tries to produce Shaw and his soldiers as, to use Judith Butler's phrase, bodies that matter. Lowell works from the substitute materiality of the bronze bas-relief, which is itself a discursive monument. He does so in the service of other bodies that matter, including Lowell's own body and those of the black schoolchildren, and thus the symbolic body politic of mid-twentieth century America. We arrive at a view of the poem as an instructive instance of Ronald Schleifer's analysis, in *Rhetoric and Death*, of death as an ineluctable, embedded part of the language and vision of modernism.

Butler's and Schleifer's provocative arguments share a marked similarity in describing the psychological and psychosocial mechanisms that shape the anxieties they explore. Schleifer sees the recognition of death in opposition to life as Butler sees the recognition of an opposite sex within the realm of the body: in fundamentally psychoanalytic terms, with glosses from Foucault and Baudrillard, as a problematic "other" that is a difference within the same. As Schleifer observes, "'death' both is and is not a 'part' of life; it is a 'stage' of life (a part) and the negation of life altogether (its 'other')" (5–6). As Butler describes the dynamics of such a relation, "the question is whether the forms which... produce bodily life operate through the production of an excluded domain that comes to bound and to haunt the field of intelligible bodily life. The logic of this operation is to a certain extent psychoanalytic inasmuch as the force of prohibition produces the spectre of a terrifying return" (54). If the difference of an opposite sex seems this threatening, the sense of terror and haunting along the boundary between the intelligibility of "our ordinary lives and the nothingness or pure non-sense of death" (Schleifer 228) must be even clearer and more dramatic, wherever it appears.

The concept of intelligibility, of course, connects these issues inextricably to human discourses and the rhetoric thereof. I do not have the space here to rehearse a fair summary of Schleifer's complex analysis of the late nineteenth-century shifts in the conditions of value, physical and metaphysical, that provoke this defining modernist anxiety. But I agree with his argument that "at the heart of modernism lies the felt sense of contradiction between material accident and seeming transcendental ('mythic') truth" (80). Such truth would be immortal, at least in comparison to any individual human life, but through relation to that truth, those brief, individual lives might achieve transcendent meaning. The threatened replacement of enduring, transhistorical values by contingent, merely historical, accidental ones thus invokes the terror of death without meaning, without transcendence. For Schleifer, such a "contradiction cannot be resolved" (80). Given that situation, he examines the ways modernist writers and postmodern theorists have called upon and investigated the resources of rhetoric, in applying and arranging the power of language, to respond to this new circumstance, experienced as both external-historical and internal-psychological.

One such response is founded on the power of language to represent what is not there, especially the dead. Here we see exactly what Sarah Goodwin and Elisabeth Bronfen would have us expect in treatments of death. "That which aligns with death in any given representation is Other, dangerous, enigmatic, magnetic.... To study representations of death is to study how not only individuals but also groups have defined themselves against what they are not but wish to control" (20). Schleifer concludes his study with this "rhetoric of mourning" and describes its reach toward the intelligibility of enduring value in language through reference to Derrida. "In other words, the violence of language for Derrida is the violence of the 'restricted economy' of meaning... that wrests from the play of language and the more terrible play of time a semantic 'reserve' of the 'timeless simplicity of an intelligible object'" (209, interior citations from Derrida's *Writing and Difference*). The "violence" here is an assertion of power, as Schleifer describes a primal urge, in language and representation, toward monumentality and the kind of transhistorical significance always implied by monuments.

In the pair of poems from *For the Union Dead* that I will treat here, Lowell's handling of monuments and other representations of death illustrates the complex *agon* Schleifer describes and shifts this particular crisis of modernism, in the title poem, to American ground. What Lowell perceives and fears in "For the Union Dead" is that the material requirements of machines and commercial activity may have replaced enduring, transhistorical ideals, individual and communal—even that the values of mechanism and material acquisition are emerging as transhistorical.[2] In the poem, Lowell transposes this fear into his own specifically American moment. Saint-Gaudens's sculpture survives, materially and rhetorically, though propped. It communicates a possibility of engagement and vision: the heroism of commitment to transcendent values and the aesthetic construction of that message. But Lowell's foregrounding of the monument contains the acknowledgement of

---

[2]   The ground of Lowell's concern with machines is plain enough in the poem's urban context, but it shows as well a striking similarity to the emphasis of a bleak passage from Benjamin's *Illuminations*, cited by Schleifer (45–46). In it, Benjamin calls attention to the inhuman scale and rapidity of technological change, singling out the lethal horrors of mechanized combat in World War I. Benjamin's emphasis on warfare reminds us how consistently the horrific technological threat of nuclear war was on Lowell's mind during the early 1960s. Recall, for example, the lines from "Fall 1961": "All autumn, the chafe and jar / of nuclear war; / we have talked our extinction to death" (ll. 6–8).

death inevitably within it, since it is a commemorative monument and is further undermined literally and materially by the garage excavation. It is also undermined by the poem's competing rhetorical construction, which represents the bas-relief surrounded by determining representations of racism, capitalism, and mechanism. In the end, the speaker gazes on a brute, spectral city: Boston as necropolis.

The title poem is, however, not the only poem in the volume to explore large-scale cultural expression and transition through important representations of death, especially monumental ones. "Florence," appearing early in the book (the seventh poem of thirty-five), offers a revealing series of comparisons to "For the Union Dead" that extend to matters of content, structure, and strategy. In both poems, Lowell's first-person speaker looks, in memory or in real time, at and through both casual and deliberate representations of a city—that is, some that are individualized and contingent and some at least expected to be in some way transcendent—to a layered past, and situates himself in a problematic relation to that past, and its implications for the present and the future. Juxtaposing these two poems demonstrates the importance to Lowell of the issues involved as well as their more comprehensive and consistent treatment in "For the Union Dead."

"Florence" opens with a first person expression of "long[ing]"for a series of things—incongruous but effectively concrete—representing the city, at least for this speaker. Since one can only long for things that are not present, that single verb represents an absence, though not one of death. Later in the poem's first section, Florence is a "there," compared favorably to an unspecified "here." In this way the opening of the poem memorializes the speaker's experience and, in the sequence of the volume if not of the poem's composition, anticipates Lowell's use of the aquarium at the beginning of "For the Union Dead." The cuttlefish and communists constitute a casual and individualized experiential representation of Florence.

The poem turns in its second half to some of the city's more official representations, those more intentionally proffered as elements of the city's public discourse (and discursive identity), specifically the Old Palace and three pieces of sculpture from its courtyard. The palace itself clearly represents Florence's civic and political history: at the time of its erection in the fourteenth century, it represented the triumph of the Guelph supporters of papal authority over the Ghibelline party of the Holy Roman emperors, and it remained the seat of Florentine government for centuries. Its fortress-like appearance further suggests an authority maintained by vigilance and force, if necessary. The three pieces of sculpture that Lowell mentions depict directly only mythic and legendary figures and events. They express Florentine cultural power and authority indirectly, as the products of Donatello, Michelangelo, and Cellini (none of whom is mentioned by name), with an authority derived from a few hundred years' worth of judgments of artistic merit. Yet, through the sculptors' commissions and the controversies over the placement of the sculptures themselves, they are associated with two different eras of Medici rule in Florence (Donatello and Cellini) and with the brief Republican interval between (Michelangelo). The statues also reflect the palace's aggressive vertical thrust and warlike mien. All three depict scenes of revolutionary violence: Perseus, David, and Judith as heroic killers, types of the "lovely tyrannicides" for whom Lowell sees Florence as the "patroness." These statues commemorate heroes in their moments of triumph—over Medusa, Goliath, and Holofernes, respectively—in victories that meant freedom or safety to the heroes and to the peoples they represented.

In Lowell's description, the heroes' monuments repeat the lean singularity of the Old Palace's tower, which "pierces the sky / like a hypodermic needle." They

> rise sword in hand
> above the unshaven,
> formless decapitation
> of the monsters, tubs of guts,
> mortifying chunks for the pack. (ll. 26–30)

Lowell's rhetoric further recuperates these mythic and legendary figures into the actual history of Florence via a remarkably economical reference to their ability as sculpture, pieces of art, to embody the defining Florentine Renaissance impulse to fuse classic and Christian terms:

> Perseus, David and Judith,
> lords and ladies of the Blood,
> Greek demi-gods of the Cross.... (ll. 23–25)

The language asserts the success of this fusion in the equivalence implied by appositional substitution. By this discursive means, Lowell identifies in this display of materials signifying Florence—the palace, the sculptures—the kind of viable transmission of values that makes them transhistorical. Hence, these monuments accomplish the kind of operation called into question more skeptically in the contemporary American context of "For the Union Dead."

Lowell's description of the statues emphasizes their dramatic and aggressive silhouettes, their distinctness of line and form that seems to express the concentration of their subjects' will, contrasting dramatically with his description of their vanquished enemies. Lowell's representation of death here—"formless decapitation," "tubs of guts"—foregrounds the consequences of butchery, a deliberate violation of bodily form and degradation of flesh to the status of food for the hero's dogs or scavenging wolves.[3] The speaker's reaction to his own brutal

---

[3] It is worth noting here that of the three statues named, only Cellini's Perseus, standing over Medusa's twisted and headless body, fits Lowell's description. That is perhaps why he picks up the reference later in the poem, as he shifts back to the speaker reporting his own experience. Donatello represented Judith at the moment just before she brings the sword down on Holofernes, and though the doomed and drunken king is kneeling and bestridden, his body is still whole. Michelangelo's David, of course, drapes his slingshot over his left

portrait is sympathy for the victims, first expressed almost oratorically—"Pity the monsters! / Pity the monsters!" (ll. 31–32)—and then more quietly and reflectively, as the poem modulates back toward first-person, experiential reference points. The repeated injunction expresses misgivings about the heroes' attitudes at least, if not the event of their enemies' destruction. And the more personal perception identifies allegiance to the heroes—"Ah, to have known, to have loved / too many Davids and Judiths!"—with taking "the wrong side." (ll. 34–35)

For Alan Williamson, who took his title from the climactic cry in this poem, this ambivalence regarding decisive (and often violent) action expresses a central anxiety in Lowell's political attitudes about the tendency of ideology to deny— and, if necessary, to exterminate—the non-rational elements of human nature (97–99 for "Florence"; 107–10 for "For the Union Dead"). This is a Freudian version of an argument at least as old as Burke's critique of the Jacobins and probably older. For our purposes here, however, it is more important to notice two things. First, even when Lowell returns to the personal perspective in "Florence," it remains identified with the heroic realm projected by the sculptures. Second, the poem's conclusion in mere description rather than action suggests a kind of open-eyed paralysis. The speaker casts his own experience in the archetypal terms proposed by the statues: taking the wrong side by loving Davids and Judiths (that is, people like them, heroic but ruthless, arrogant), claiming himself to have "seen the Gorgon." The repeated injunction to "pity the monsters!" has already suggested identification with the defunct vanquished rather than the energetic heroes. The fixed stare that produces the poem's final images—still informed by the figures in the Perseus sculpture but seeming now a more generalized metaphor of domination and threat—suggests an abject stillness. The speaker appears to have learned, or at least to have recognized, something communicated by the Florentine monuments. But in the poem's language, Lowell leaves the speaker stuck, self-projected into that alternate realm.

The speaker is subjected, not a subject—and unable to cross back to effective action in his own world. The message implied by the monuments is the survival of values like righteousness and sureness of purpose across the centuries' ebb and flow of history within a single city, even across the passing of classical and biblical civilizations. This seems to have inspired the speaker primarily with anxiety about what the authors of that survival had to do to accomplish it. As we shall see, when Lowell, repeating the structural movement of "Florence," has his speaker in "For the Union Dead" turn from the heroic realm represented by Colonel Shaw's monument, his perspective moves pointedly back to the quotidian surroundings of Boston. As many readers have seen, that speaker also sits, similarly paralyzed.

For Lowell, Florence was familiar but still foreign. The monument to Colonel Shaw and the Massachusetts 54th on Boston Common, however, was doubly domesticated: it was not only a sculpture commemorating an American theme,

---

shoulder, but the sculpture includes no representation of Goliath's body whatever. Nor are actual packs of dogs or wolves part of any of the legends celebrated by these works of art.

but was a familiar part as well of the poet's life experience. Even going back to his childhood, Saint-Gaudens's bronze bas-relief, not unlike the South Boston Aquarium with which the poem begins, was part of the furniture of Lowell's life. The Civil War, its monuments, and particularly its racial questions were part of the cultural furniture of his nation. Moreover, Lowell's poem responds to a representation of death, of the dead, that had been already designed and produced—that is, aestheticized—by Saint-Gaudens. It already had a rich cultural significance, broadly as a Civil War commemoration and more specifically as Boston icon and event, inscribed by William James and others, during both the genesis and display of the statue.[4]

In fact, Lowell's poem responds to a second precursor as well. The subject and title amount to an exhumation of his first poetic loyalty, as the title parallels and the thematic substance echoes those of mentor Allen Tate's "Ode to the Confederate Dead" (1928).[5] The return to the Civil War context, the transposing of Tate's title (Confederate/Union), the quatrains that persist even in the absence of regular meter, and the general thematic similarity to Tate's ode, all gently register his friend's influence. But a single contrast matters more than all those similarities. Tate's speaker can ask, at the end of the rhetorical run up to his conclusion, "What shall we say who have knowledge / Carried to the heart?" (ll. 82–83). If this speaker is uncertain what language can do, he is *not* uncertain about having the knowledge, and having it as one among at least some small community (something to justify the "we"). There is no suggestion of any analogous confidence in Lowell's speaker. From the mesmerized boy recalled by the abandoned aquarium to the helpless poet-professor watching the news, Lowell surveys a landscape of death and ruin, and does so from a point of view so flat and distant as to seem almost postmortem. The speaker seems a merely accidental attribute of the place, very nearly as much of a statue as the sculpture he observes. In "For the Union Dead," knowledge carried to the heart may be imputed to Colonel Shaw, who "rejoices in man's lovely, / peculiar power to choose life and die," or to Shaw's father, but it is never

---

[4]   Details of that history need not concern us here, but Rotella's discussion of the poem includes an interesting summary (64–66), which is based in turn on Kirk Savage's more extensive treatment (193–207).

[5]   One might quarrel with the drama of the word "exhumation" here: Lowell and Tate, after all, remained friends and correspondents throughout Lowell's life. (The older poet in fact outlived him.) I would argue, however, that the relationship irrevocably changed after Tate's disparaging judgment of the *Life Studies* poems, when he saw them in manuscript. The style and manner of Lowell's work from *Life Studies* on clearly represents a break with the dense, uncompromising formalism that drew him to choose Tate for a mentor in the first place. Tate regarded it, according to Ian Hamilton, as "a personal—even filial—betrayal" (237). Whatever degree of *personal* reconciliation the two men managed, my point here is that one of the deaths represented, mediated, and memorialized in "For the Union Dead" may be the death of Lowell's allegiance to Tate as a *craftsman*.

claimed by the speaker (ll. 37–38). That, apparently, like Shaw himself, "is out of bounds now."

This domestication is the ground of Lowell's own primary aesthetic strategy for controlling the structure of his poem: the metonymic juxtaposition of experiential observations—the "now," "once," and "last March" of the poem's identifiable perspectives in time. Lowell's speaker is more definitely situated in space and time—more "at home," so to speak—in "For the Union Dead" than he had been in "Florence." This familiarity allows as well a much more naturalistic introduction of the monument, which occupies, as do the sculptures in "Florence," the middle of the poem, bracketed by representations of personal experience. (Think, for a moment, how out of place an exclamatory apostrophe "Oh Boston, Boston"— echoing the one in "Florence"—would sound in this poem.) The familiarity of the scene, however, does not triumph over, but rather underscores the speaker's detachment from all that he sees. Throughout "For the Union Dead," Lowell's speaker seems confounded, suspended in a state like the one that Schleifer calls, for his more general context, "a chilling 'sense,' never fully articulated, of anesthesia" (8). To the extent that that striking paradox might ever be "fully articulated," the voice of "For the Union Dead" surely comes very close. The similarity among the speaker's memories—the very foundation of their metonymic link—lies in the speaker's recognition of a barrier between himself and what he observes, between himself and what he wants to understand. The glass wall of the aquarium, the "barbed and galvanized / fence on the Boston Common," and the television screen function as discrete material emblems of a psychological detachment (ll. 5, 12–13, 59).

The speaker's desultory gaze drifts in the opening stanzas through space and time in Boston, noting the ruin of the boarded up aquarium and the steam shovels' siege of the Common. The longing from the beginning of "Florence" is replaced by the less energetic, more resigned "sigh[ing]... / for the dark downward and vegetating kingdom / of the fish and reptile" (ll. 9–11). The imagination, it seems, can reach no further than the (seemingly) playful transformation of those steam shovels into dinosaurs. But then Shaw's monument "sticks like a fishbone / in the city's throat" (ll. 29–30), as it sticks in the middle of the poem, arresting the speaker's attention for a full five stanzas, eight if we count the extension to the old churches, to "frayed flags" (l. 43), and to Shaw's father's ruthlessly physical preference for the bare ditch (ll. 49–52).[6] The monument has power, but how much? Is it serving its purpose? Lowell's image—the fishbone, choking—simultaneously diminishes the monument in size but insists that it remains a threat, aptly invoking consumption as a metaphor for the process going on around it. The monument, or something about it, remains, at least potentially, a skeletal but intractable "reserve" of intelligibility,

---

6   One way to gauge the dramatic value of Shaw's monument to the poem is to compare it with "The Mouth of the Hudson," also focusing on the decline and decay of a Heraclitan flux, but lacking the tension produced by the counterweight Lowell has made of Saint-Gaudens's sculpture.

in the Derridean sense already alluded to for mourning. It represents the enduring rhetoric of monuments generally, the motivating desire for transhistorical values. Shaw's monument, like others, including those from "Florence," acknowledges death—the absence of the person or persons represented. But it also challenges death by presenting in its material substance a simulacrum of their bodies and by asserting, even in a detail like a Latin motto in an English speaking country, authority and cultural identifications that endure in spirit even across centuries.[7]

In this context, the statue performs the traditional monumental version of resurrection, restoring bodies that matter to (and through) substitute matter. In Saint-Gaudens's design, the dead convey the impression of solidity and mass: not that of mere "tubs of guts... mortifying chunks," but images retaining the clear lines of human form. The sculpted bodies of Shaw, his horse, and about a dozen of his African American infantry represent their living presence. Saint-Gaudens cast them marching, and the fact that the black foot-soldiers are so close-packed behind Shaw and his horse in the foreground emphasizes their massed and militant physicality. Their faces and postures are, moreover, individualized—the feature that has traditionally been said to have inspired William James's remark, cited in Lowell's poem as evidence of the success of the sculptor's restoration, that he "could almost hear the bronze Negroes breathe" (l. 28).

Shaw's body is presumably the only one sculpted, as we say, "from life." But all the figures in Saint-Gaudens's monument are at least a little less generic, less "abstract," than the typical statues that Lowell alludes to later, possibly mass-produced for hundreds if not thousands of local cemeteries. The singular figure of Colonel Shaw still rises above this mass. Lowell's language recalls the sharp verticality of tower and statue in "Florence." Shaw appears "lean / as a compass needle," his posture rigidly erect ("he cannot bend his back"). But there are two reasons why this image does not challenge the sky the way the Florentine monuments do. The first inheres in bas-relief as a form. Rather than free-standing figures set against the surrounding landscape and horizon, it produces a panel in which figures are set apart from a background of the same monumental bronze. The entire representation lies within a frame, in this particular case a rectangle with a gently rounded top. But even within the memorial's design, Saint-Gaudens both ratified (ideologically) and limited (physically) his hero's implied ascending ambition. Above and slightly behind the figures of Shaw and his men extends the bronze mass of an angel, representing the goodness and justice of their cause yet simultaneously confining any heavenward aspiration. Interestingly, however, Lowell's description of the statue in his poem ignores the angel in the sculptor's design. In the terms of his poem, Colonel Shaw and his men earn their heroic status not because their mission is ordained of heaven, but by the contrast between

---

[7]   Lowell's revision of the monument's motto for the epigraph to his poem—changing the subject from singular to plural—actually makes it match more accurately the number of bodies represented. As Rotella points out, this change has important political implications as an assertion about which bodies matter (56).

their human moral commitment and the cheapened values of the speaker's mid-twentieth-century present.

The observer's sympathy for and admiration of Shaw and his regiment—attitudes implicit in representing them, even in death, as retaining their bodily as well as moral integrity (distinct and lively images, not tubs of guts)—can be unambiguous and unironic because they are not triumphant conquerors in the way of Perseus, David, or Judith. Saint-Gaudens's monument to Shaw and his regiment represents recent history's actual dead, not distant and legendary killers or victims, heroic sacrifice rather than the triumph of revolutionaries or the forcible overthrow of tyrants. In this way the ideological leanings of "For the Union Dead" illustrate Robert von Hallberg's contention that, in the difficult calculus of Lowell's fascination with politics and power, "the most noble, intelligent accomplishment is renunciation, not conquest" (154). Shifting to the terms of Michael North's analysis, I would add that whatever there is of the heroic sublime in Saint-Gaudens's monument, it is not inherently undemocratic. The sculptor has reanimated Shaw and his men in *preparation* for their crucial act rather than representing them in its execution. Thus, for Lowell or any observer, the knowledge of their eventual fate is also experienced in looking at the monument. Their deaths become a parallel phantom image alongside the mass of the bronze, a phantom image that Lowell gives a more concrete form in the poem by recalling Shaw's father's bitter consecration of the ditch. That the bronze effigies of Shaw and his men perpetually march toward their fate emphasizes both the choice and determination in their sacrifice. In spite of being formed of inanimate material, they seem, famously, the most vital element in the scene. As Lowell's speaker surveys the landscape, every other human presence has been erased, or perhaps more accurately, absorbed into our machines. Voluntary movement belongs only to "giant finned cars" (l. 66) and "dinosaur steamshovels" (l. 14).

But to say that the speaker's sympathy and admiration may be unambiguous is not to say that the transhistorical gesture in the statue's rhetoric is successful and effective. What, in this poem or in this world, can sympathy and admiration accomplish? In the poem, we judge the monument's power by its effects on the speaker, by its motive force of inspiration, by its place in the aesthetic balance of the poem. The speaker looks closely, singling out Colonel Shaw himself, the figure on horseback raised above his men. The speaker responds to the strength projected by the combination of the statue itself and the accumulated knowledge of how one is supposed to respond, and he gives as much motion and energy as possible to what remains, in fact, stillness: "an angry wren-like vigilance, / a greyhound's gentle tautness" (ll. 33–34). Yet the motion inheres solely in the downward comparisons to birds and dogs. Lowell saves his speaker's greatest tribute for the specifically human act of judgment, in this case the choice of sacrifice. But Shaw's "rejoic[ing]" in that power—inferred or projected by the speaker—is what puts him "out of bounds now." When Shaw leads his soldiers to death, "he cannot bend his back" (l. 40). The speaker himself, alas, is unable to follow the direction of Shaw's "compass-needle." As he confronts America's racial division a century later, he "crouch[es]" to his television set. For the last image of the speaker's body that we see in the poem, Lowell has chosen to emphasize his bent back.

Before that visual contrast, Lowell allowed his speaker's impression of Shaw's monument to dwindle into nostalgia, with revolutionary-era churches and the cemeteries where the Union dead are buried, described in ways that emphasize age and frailty. The "old white churches hold [only] their air" of principled rebellion; the flags at the graveyards are "frayed" (ll. 42–43). Even the stone statues, intended to carry the memory and ideals of the dead forward, turn out to be mortal, growing slimmer each year, literally ground down, if slowly, by time and the elements. This nostalgia drifts into the poem's lone ellipsis, and then is halted by a new association. The speaker remembers the attitude of Shaw's father to the very idea of a monument, a challenge also, perhaps, to the ideologies such a monument represents. This grieving man's insistence on the brute corporeality of the facts of death shatters the speaker's reverie and undermines reverence.

> Shaw's father wanted no monument
> except the ditch,
> where his son's body was thrown
> and lost with his "niggers." (ll. 49–52)

This, too, is knowledge carried to the heart. The bitter rejection of the civic-minded displacement inherent in heroic commemoration propels Lowell's speaker back, in the most thrilling leap in the poem, to his own time, and a despairing recognition (ll. 53ff). The ditch, indeed, is nearer. It is simultaneously the common grave of Shaw's regiment, the garage excavation in downtown Boston, and, via the poem's immediate reference to World War II, the cemeteries at Normandy and the ash-heaps of Auschwitz. Ultimately, it represents the vast ditch under the shadow, in 1960, of nuclear annihilation. Lowell's ditch is a representation of death that is inclusive and metaphorical, yet vividly and grimly physical.

But it is not merely physical. This cold scar in the ground, this place dedicated only to rot, is a moral space as well. The speaker's assertion has come before the evidence. The ditch is nearer, but the reason he knows that is revealed in the next observation: "There are no statues for the last war here," he says (l. 54). Such heroic representations of death and commemorations of noble sacrifice have been replaced by the "commercial photograph... [of] Hiroshima boiling / over a Mosler Safe, the 'Rock of Ages'/ that survived the blast" (ll. 55–58). The equivalence of photograph and statue is asserted simply by Lowell's semi-colon, and the matter-of-factness of his tone first delays, then intensifies the horror of the image. "Festering within the pride that led to this commercial use of mass death," as William Logan has said, "lies an accusation deeper than anything by Marx" (125). This commercial photograph has emptied the representation of death of all its human physicality, all its historicity, and posited a "Rock of Ages" that is a monument only to capitalist accumulation. It is a sealed emptiness, simultaneously a mocking tomb and the perverse ark of a new covenant. Here, bodies do not matter. Here is the contemporary emblem of monumental ideologies of authority, instruction, cultural identification, and inspiration. Here is the moral ditch.

The metonymic leaps from bas-relief to ditch to commercial photograph bring the poem back to Lowell's contemporary American moment. When he makes the connection between racial issues involved a century earlier in the Civil War and the civil rights movement in 1960, we see a pointed contrast in the images as well. His television screen does not give us images of leaders or mass demonstrations actively opposing injustice. Instead, he represents the vulnerable pawns in the game: black school-children filmed, presumably, trying to integrate a school. However ironic the "bell-cheeked" vitality of Saint-Gaudens's black infantry may be, given their fate, their image contrasts markedly with the deathly images of "drained faces" on those living children, fragile as "balloons," rising on the wind only (l. 60). Are they drained of blood, of energy, of hope? The contemporary medium of television, commemorating events as they unfold and theoretically so much more lively and life-like, has not preserved any sense of agency for these children or for the speaker who sees them. They are distanced and abstracted by the television set, removed not in time, but by another glass barrier, absorbed by a different kind of machine.

With this substitution of one representation of death for another, Lowell navigates his poem, as he did in "Florence," away from the contemplation of monuments of the past and back toward the speaker's experience. Yet, we're still reading the power of Saint-Gaudens's sculpture through its effects on the poem's speaker. A particular sight of that sculpture has been an occasion of the dependably, if intermittently, startling recognition of the heroic standing within the ordinary, even within the banal. Set against material transformations of the Boston landscape and calling forth memories from the speaker's past experience—Shaw's father's words, the many statues and cemeteries, the experience of the aquarium—the monument has the power to lead the speaker to a moral realization. But it does not have the power to inspire him toward a remedy, or indeed toward any action. The failure of Shaw's heroic sacrifice in the Civil War—construed in the monument and in the poem as his willing and wholly human act of renunciation—is a failure to reconstitute American race relations on the basis of mutual respect and justice. This failure is signified by the violent struggles for integration and civil rights in the poem's contemporary frame, calling into question the possibility of any future characterized by progress and instructed by the past.

In Schleifer's terms, Saint-Gaudens materially and rhetorically posits Shaw as a pre-modernist, synecdochic emblem—a celebrated part, adequately representing a viable whole—of democratic vision and commitment to ideals. But this cannot overcome Lowell's metonymic links to a ruined aquarium, a threatened statehouse, and a devolving world. What the poet and speaker offer as an answer for this deep challenge to transcendent value, this sense of personal and cultural loss, is only rhetorical performance, i.e., new representations. In mourning, according to Schleifer, this circumstance is inevitable: "For mourning is the scene of rhetoric, the place where the 'rhetoricity' of rhetoric cannot be erased, where there is nothing else between our ordinary lives and the nothingness or pure non-sense of death than the gestures of rhetoric" (228). In "For the Union Dead," Lowell's performance is bitterly brilliant, as it illustrates and articulates despair. Lowell already figures a futurelessness in his transformation of contemporary Boston into that "dark downward and vegetating kingdom / of the fish and reptile," and ultimately includes himself in the "savage servility" that triumphs "everywhere" at the end (ll. 65–68). This "servility" also implies that we have lost the "lovely, / peculiar power to choose life" and so must live in a city of the dead.

The perspective that I have been describing in "For the Union Dead" parallels Lowell's own perspective on his art, at least when he is in a doubting mood. It lies behind the tone and the epistemology of *Life Studies* and extends all the way to "Epilogue," that eerily titled poem that closes *Day by Day*. Even when he observes and represents life, the result seems static, monumental, and finally memorial.

> But sometimes everything I write
> with the threadbare art of my eye
> seems a snapshot,
> lurid, rapid, garish, grouped,
> heightened from life,
> yet paralyzed by fact. (ll. 8–13)

By Saint-Gaudens's hands and by Lowell's words, materials may be "heightened from life," may reach toward some transcendence. But in "For the Union Dead," transcendence fails, paralyzed by the facts of Shaw's father's iconoclastic bitterness and by the processes and new icons of contemporary Boston. In the stillness of the artistic frame, it is *life* that eludes representation. The poem's synchronic projection of its speaker's own life allows our awareness of another, more noble, and existentially committed past. What the moments in time share is the condition of observing from behind a barrier. That projection also evokes our recognition of a separation that literally denies contact and participation, and figuratively undermines meaningful, purposeful action. From the Ozymandian snowfields at the beginning to the "savage servility" suggested by the cars at the end, Lowell's speaker finds hollow lassitude everywhere, including within himself. He presents Boston as a necropolis, a city shadowed by the failure of human ideals. The numb suspension of his detachment connotes a death in life, a condition bounded and haunted (to return to Butler's words) by the lost prospect of meaningful death.

Works Cited

Butler, Judith. *Bodies That Matter: On the Discursive Limits of "Sex."* New York: Routledge, 1993.

Goodwin, Sarah Webster and Elisabeth Bronfen, eds. *Death and Representation.* Baltimore: Johns Hopkins University Press, 1993.

Hamilton, Ian. *Robert Lowell: A Biography*. New York: Random, 1982.

Logan, William. "Lowell's Bubble." *Salmagundi* 141/142 (2004): 125–28.

Lowell, Robert. "Epilogue." *Day by Day*. New York: Farrar, 1977.

——. "Florence." *Selected Poems*. New York: Farrar, 1976.

——. "For the Union Dead" *Selected Poems*. New York: Farrar, 1976.

Mariani, Paul. *The Last Puritan: A Life of Robert Lowell*. New York: Norton, 1994.

North, Michael. *The Final Sculpture: Public Monuments and Modern Poets*. Ithaca: Cornell University Press, 1985.

Rotella, Guy. *Castings: Monuments and Monumentality in Poems by Elizabeth Bishop, Robert Lowell, James Merrill, Derek Walcott, and Seamus Heaney*. Nashville: Vanderbilt University Press, 2004.

Savage, Kirk. *Standing Soldiers, Kneeling Slaves: Race, War, and Monuments in Nineteenth-Century America*. Princeton: Princeton University Press, 1997.

Schleifer, Ronald. *Rhetoric and Death: The Language of Modernism and Postmodern Discourse Theory*. Urbana: University of Illinois Press, 1990.

Tate, Allen. "Ode to the Confederate Dead" (1928). *Norton Anthology of Modern Poetry*, 2nd edition. Eds: Richard Ellmann and Robert O'Clair. New York: Norton, 1988.

Von Hallberg, Robert. *American Poetry and Culture 1945–1980*. Cambridge: Harvard University Press, 1985.

Williamson, Alan. *Pity the Monsters: The Political Vision of Robert Lowell*. New Haven: Yale University Press, 1974.

Chapter 10

Locating the Front Line: War, Democracy, and the Nation in Toni Morrison's *Sula* and *Song of Solomon*

Kathryn Nicol

In *On Violence*, Hannah Arendt contrasts the lonely, isolating and "antipolitical experience" of the individual death with the "vitality" of death "faced collectively and in action," where the loss of individual life is compensated by the continued survival of the group, a survival that transforms death in action into an experience of "life itself" (67). Death in Arendt's account appears Janus-faced, presenting itself as at once an experience that marks a falling out of the political realm, into absolute privacy, and an experience that marks an energetic appearance within and intrusion upon the political, through participation in violent action carried out in the name of "the species" (68). Such a distinction suggests that to be understood politically, the death of an individual takes on meaning according to the circumstances in which it occurs, and in particular in relation to conflict, and to the group, as "death in action." This essay argues however, that the boundaries constructed around an understanding of context (the limits placed upon the contextual circumstances that legitimately contribute to our understanding of events as political) have themselves been subject to political and historical forces that render the possibility of reading death as a political event ambiguous at best. Through her fictional representations of death, and in particular violent death, Toni Morrison's work seeks to analyze this ambiguity and, in the process, to redefine the contours of the political and its relationship to violence as experienced by black Americans in the twentieth century.

Arendt's political theory is examined here as an example of the ideological relocation of death to the borderlands of the political, a relocation that occurs as a consequence of her conception of public space and critique of violence as a political tool. My motive in focusing on Arendt's work is not primarily to provide a critique of her political theory, but to suggest that her conception of political (non-violent) public space coheres with a dominant national narrative of the United States as democratic, peace-loving, and life-giving. Such a narrative depends crucially upon the geographical and ideological relegation of death and violent conflict to the borders of the nation. This is achieved not by denying that death and violence occur, but rather through the identification of violent death as personal and individual rather than political, as the concern of a minority, rather than the nation as such, or through the location of violent events within political and historical narratives that subsume the potential oppositional force of such violence beneath the narrative of the nation. In contrast to such accounts of violent death I offer a reading of Toni Morrison's fiction as a complex attempt to re-present violence and through this re-presentation to bring to light the ambiguities and contradictions that lurk within national narratives of conflict and peace, civility and incivility.[1] In particular, I believe that Morrison's work challenges us to contest the boundary suggested above between the private death of the individual and the collective nature of "death in action" in the experience of black Americans in the twentieth century.

In Arendt's political theory, primacy is given to the search for a public life and common world that can provide a basis for commonality among disparate individuals. This shared common world does not require that all members of this world be similar in nature, but that they are capable of "sameness in utter diversity" through a shared world view and orientation towards "the same object" (*Human* 57–8). One example of this category of shared objects is the democratic nation, which creates the conditions for democratic pluralism, unlike the conditions of totalitarianism or mass consumerism that, Arendt argues, render individuals "entirely private" (58). It should be noted that the American Republic holds a particular place in Arendt's account of democracy. The American Republic forms the prime example of the democratic state in Arendt's work. In the Declaration of Independence and the Constitution, she finds evidence of "an entirely new concept of power and authority, an entirely novel idea of what was of prime importance in the political realm" (*Revolution* 166). This "new concept of power and authority" rests upon the role that "we the people" have in the Declaration of Independence, a declaration that Arendt identifies with the discovery of a new constitutional entity, the modern republican citizenry.[2] The force through which the American Republic was founded therefore was not armed force, but the will of the collective.

---

[1]   As John Keane notes in his study of war and nation building in the twentieth century: "Uncivility was the ghost that permanently haunted civil society. In this respect, civilization was normally understood as a project charged with resolving the permanent problem of discharging, defusing and sublimating violence; uncivility was the permanent enemy of civil society. Civilization therefore denoted an ongoing historical process in which civility, a static term, was both the aim and the outcome of the transformation of uncivil into civil behaviour" (19).

[2]   Bonnie Honig's analysis of Arendt's account of the founding of the American Republic informs my argument throughout. As Honig argues: "For Arendt then, the problem of politics in modernity is, how do we establish lasting foundations without appealing to gods, a foundationalist ground, or an absolute? Can we conceive of institutions possessed of authority without deriving that authority from some law of laws, from some extrapolitical source? In short, is it possible to have a politics of foundation in a world devoid of traditional (foundational) guarantees of stability, legitimacy, and authority? Arendt answers *yes*, and she turns to the American revolution and founding as a model of this possibility" ("Declarations" 98).

The desire to find, or found, a public space and public body out of which a democratic polity could emerge is clearly related to the traumas of twentieth-century European history. Such a conception of the United States as foundationally democratic, however, has consequences for Arendt's understanding of the history of race in America. An instructive example of this can be found in her identification of black rights protesters in the 1960s as a special interest group (*Violence* 18–19) in contrast to the "global phenomenon" of student rebellion (15). While student "rebels" (19n32) seek to develop the available forms of democracy and justice for all, interest groups seek only to increase their access to privilege within the present system. While the complexity of Arendt's argument and the validity of some of her comments should not be underestimated, what is important to my argument is the continual privileging of the American democratic system as the means by which all political development must take place and the apparent impossibility of a "white special interest group" at work within the nation. Her comments in an essay on conflicts over school desegregation are instructive here. "The color question was created by the one great crime in America's history and is soluble only within the political and historical framework of the Republic" ("Reflections" 233). Segregation is an issue in which "the law of the land and the principle of the Republic are at stake" (235). Yet what is presumed within this argument is that "the law of the land and the principle of the Republic" are in fact at variance with slavery and racial injustice, rather than historically implicated in these systems of power. Hence, Arendt's work forms part of a tradition of American political commentary that identifies race and racial difference as secondary to and divisible from the origins and nature of American politics (Mills; Smith "Liberalism").[3]

By suggesting that we can only understand the history of segregation and racial conflict as being at variance with the narrative of the democratic nation, the violent struggles of the Civil Rights Movement appear in this account to be in ideological conflict with, rather than an attempt to address the faults in, national democracy. Therefore, the belief that the United States is already, indeed from its foundation, home to a collective "public," in whose name correctly political rather than personal action can be carried out, renders any political protest against the state suspect and any violent protest against the status quo illegitimate. It is in the gaps and fault-lines between the narrative of the nation as democratic or pluralistic and the historical reality of segregation and oppression that Morrison's characters struggle to survive.

The relationship between the democratic nation and the use of armed force opens an *aporia* between the "peaceful" nature of the democratic nation and the forces that guarantee this peace. This *aporia* is a structural feature of Arendt's account of the democratic nation. As she suggests, "A theory of war or a theory of revolution... can only deal with the justification of violence because this justification constitutes its

---

[3]   Evidence of a similar displacement or subsumption of race within United States politics can be found the representation of the Civil Rights Movements in narratives of the Cold War. See Dudziak 13.

political limitations; if, instead, it arrives at a glorification or justification of violence as such, it is no longer political but antipolitical" (*Revolution* 10). Therefore, while a theory of war may justify localized instances of violent conflict, war itself cannot be a political act in the sense Arendt suggests is appropriate to a democratic nation such as the United States. Crucially, Arendt suggests that it is only "as though" life is nourished through death in action (*Violence* 68). While the experience of death in action may *appear* to be life-affirming, this experience in Arendt's account is transitory, not transformational, and achieves only a metaphorical rather than political significance (69). Against Marxist-influenced accounts of revolutionary violence in the work of Georges Sorel, Jean Paul Sartre and Frantz Fanon, Arendt argues in *On Violence* and *On Revolution* that violence cannot play a long-term role in the transformation of politics. The ends of violence, the effects which violent action will have, cannot be predicted or controlled by the political actors who aim to use violence as a means (*Violence* 4). Arendt certainly does not argue that political action can exclude violence (*Revolution* 10) or that violence must always be expelled to the realm of the irrational (*Violence* 65–66). But her work counters organic metaphors of "natural" violence and argues that violence must be theorized in opposition to the political, rather than as a continuation of the political (49). Political violence is not only unstable but in fact undemocratic. This identification of violence as the opposite of democracy is a key feature of modern International Relations theory.[4]

In part, Arendt's critique of violence as a political tool results from her identification of violence as a silencing force, in contrast to the dependence of politics on the possibility of free speech.

Where violence rules absolutely, as for instance in the concentration camps of totalitarian regimes, not only the laws—*les lois se taisent*, as the French Revolution phrased it—but everything and everyone must fall silent. It is because of this silence that violence is a marginal phenomenon in the political realm; for man, to the extent that he is a political being, is endowed with the power of speech (*Revolution* 9).

Not only does violence render speech impossible, but attempts to articulate the meaning and experience of violence will always fall short of the experience itself. As Bat-Ami Bar-On suggests, for Arendt:

> At close distance, violence, due to its vigorously coercive character, stills and hushes since it cannot be contested with public speech. Moreover, the closer one is to the lived experience of violence, thus to destruction and pain, the less one

---

[4]   See, for example, Russett. As Kenneth Waltz suggests, the belief within International Relations theory that democracies "are the one peaceful form of the state" has played a significant role in the justification of force used by democratic powers in "exporting" democracy to other territories, where violent intervention is justified in the name of furthering peace (x).

can communicate to others about it through speech, and, therefore, the less one can make public. (12)

However, while violence certainly problematizes articulation, this division between violence as silence and the political as speech risks a failure to acknowledge the silences created by a concept of the political based on a collective public to which many lack rights of access.

Arendt's political theory therefore suggests a way of thinking about the democratic nation as pluralistic, as "sameness in utter diversity." This depends upon the collective will of the people expressed in the founding moment of the nation and relegates to history the armed conflict from which that foundation emerged. While Arendt's critique of violence as a political tool remains persuasive in many respects, this account of the democratic nation, applied to the history of the United States, begs the question of the extent to which the democratic nation extended its rights to *all* citizens. The historical and legal inequality of black Americans throughout much of the twentieth century not only puts the democratic nature of the nation into question, but also raises questions about the displacement of violent conflict to the borders of the nation—and about the negation of the ideological and political meaningfulness of "deaths in action." It is at this point that I wish to turn to the work of Toni Morrison.

Morrison's work also theorizes the American nation and American democracy. It consistently problematizes the collective nature of this body of citizens by highlighting the question of racial identity and racial difference within the nation. An essential aspect of this project can be found in Morrison's fictional accounts of death, in particular violent deaths. She raises profound questions about the representation of death as a private and individual experience, the inscription and location of violence within and outside the borders of the nation, and the democratic nature of the American Republic. While Arendt's account of the democratic nation pushes the case of violent death to the borders of the nation, in conflict with the democratic experience and suspect within the collective life of the nation, Morrison's work repeatedly and insistently explores case histories of violent death through the lives of her black American characters. Furthermore, Morrison's work strives to *articulate* moments of violent conflict (both physical and ideological), bringing these moments of conflict into proximity with the reader rather than allowing them to remain at a safe distance.

Morrison's work is grounded in a historical reading of national and racial experience, which emphasizes the possibilities of writing the nation "otherwise," counter to the authoritative narratives of nation, democracy and peace. As Robert Vitalis notes in his study of US international relations, Morrison's work contests the "norm against noticing" racial issues in American political and cultural life (333). In addition, Morrison's non-fiction challenges and rereads both canonical American literature and authoritative national narratives (Morrison, *Playing*; Morrison and Lacour, *Birth*). Many critics take this deconstructive turn as a point from which to initiate a critical reading of Morrison's work.[5] I want to emphasize, however, that despite the deconstruction of authoritative narratives of national identity in her work, Morrison's fiction must also be read as a commentary on the durability of such authoritative narratives. She demonstrates how the modern nation returns to and remains invested in normative narratives of its own identity. In the case of the United States, this involves an identity that makes iconic use of the concept of democracy. Therefore, I would argue that Morrison's work, though committed to the deconstruction of authoritative narratives of the nation, remains skeptical of the effectiveness of these deconstructive literary strategies. Her novels engage in postcolonial and postmodern dislocations of the status of the nation and of individual subject as primary. Yet, they repeatedly emphasize the extent to which power adheres to concepts of national identity—and the persistently racial, but undisclosed, contours of "individual" identity.

This essay will focus upon the ideologies of death, war and national identity in two early novels, *Sula* and *Song of Solomon*, and particularly on the role of black war veterans as pivotal characters in these novels. In these novels we find the experiences of black American men as soldiers, involved in conflicts abroad and at home. By bringing war veterans into her fiction, Morrison telescopes the distance between conflict on the borders of the nation and conflict within national boundaries, and draws our attention to other lines of conflict in the boundaries of segregation. By creating equivalences between international warfare and racial conflict within the nation, Morrison's novels do not merely challenge the identification of the nation as a place of life and peace rather than death and violence. She also destabilizes distinctions between the legitimate, political nature of national conflicts and the illegitimate, personal nature often ascribed to conflicts over racial differences within the nation.

At the beginning of the twentieth century, the armed forces of the United States were strictly segregated, with black servicemen restricted to a limited number of black battalions and to the least skilled occupations (Berry 313). Not only did black servicemen face segregation and discrimination within the armed forces, but they were also denied the right to participate in victory parades. Particularly in the South, they faced violence from white populations on their return to the United States (Berry 315–18). While the armed forces organized their its troops according to racial differences, the social function of war in the United States also brought to the surface racial tensions. As Gary Gerstle comments in *The Racial Crucible*, a social study of race and American identity in the twentieth century, war provided an opportunity to delineate and affirm national identity, through the exposition of "cherished ideals" and the intensification of efforts to consolidate the identity of national "insiders" and expel "outsiders" (311–12). The "cherished ideals" around which the nation organized itself in the wars of the twentieth century were those of freedom and democracy, projected as the character of the American nation through

---

[5]   The critical consensus on this aspect of Morrison's work is extremely strong. Some notable examples of this approach are Harding and Martin; Duvall; and Page.

its resistance to the aggressive and imperialist campaigns of European powers, and later Communism.

While the nation identified itself through war with democracy and freedom, the debate over entry into the armed forces on the basis of race highlighted the paradox of democracy in a segregated and racialized society. In the early twentieth century, the ideology of democratic participation continued to be based on ideas of capability, as developed within a liberal democratic tradition in which access to democratic rights was defined by ability. In the context of American society, such rights of access were inevitability racialized, and debates over the participation of immigrant Americans in the armed forces often centered upon their fitness for citizenship as much as their fitness for military service. Within these debates, black Americans functioned as an "invisible racial other" (Gerstle 121). Definitions of their difference structured the terms in which other "white" immigrants could be assimilated into the American nation. One result of the segregation of the armed forces therefore was the partial expulsion of black Americans from the identity of US citizenship—and the reinforcement of American identity as "white" (Gerstle 189). Compounding the work of segregation laws on the one hand, and Garveyite separatism on the other, the experience of war in the early twentieth century demonstrated what Berry and Blassingame call the "paradox of loyalty" for black veterans (295), whose participation in national defense involved a social pact of national identity, allegiance and death that the state failed to fulfill. Therefore, if in twentieth-century America, what Bonnie Honig calls the "dream of a place called home" ("Difference" 258) gained institutional power through the production of narratives of the nation at war, for black servicemen war in the name of the US was a potentially destabilizing experience, emphasizing the unhomely nature of the homeland they were defending. Crucially, the violence of war for black veterans in this period does not stop at the boundaries of the nation, and in part this is because the civic (civilized, therefore peaceful) nation continued to exclude black Americans from full citizenship and full access to public life.

War enters *Sula* directly through the presence of Shadrack, a traumatized veteran whose experiences of battle in Europe continue to haunt him on his return to the US and his home town. He is unable to locate the town in his own memories and is remembered imaginatively rather than intimately by others: "even the most fastidious people in the town sometimes caught themselves dreaming of what he *must have been like*" (7, emphasis added). Shadrack remains apart from the community after his return from war, distanced spatially and socially, as an "uncivil" man in society (116). As a veteran, Shadrack has become, as Patricia Hunt suggests, "stateless" (451), and his experience of international conflict and the trauma of war renders him separate from the nation and community for which he fought.

Shadrack's experience of battle is an experience of spatial and epistemological dislocation, in which orientation is impossible and reference points take on arbitrary meanings:

For several days they had been marching, keeping close to a stream that was frozen at the edges. At one point they crossed it, and no sooner had he stepped foot on the other side than the day was adangle with shouts and explosions. Shellfire was all around him, and though he knew this was something called *it*, he could not muster up the proper feeling—the feeling that would accommodate *it*. He expected to be terrified or exhilarated—to feel *something* very strong. (7)

This experience of the battlefield signals both a crisis of form and a crisis of language from which Shadrack must recuperate meaning. The trauma of separation from his own materiality; from the material existence of his body as spatially fixed, experienced in the loss of control of his "monstrous" hands (9, 12), is later stabilized by the sight of his reflection. "There in the toilet water he saw a grave black face. A black so definite, so unequivocal, it astonished him. He had been harboring a skittish apprehension that he was not real—that he didn't exist at all. But when the blackness greeted him with its indisputable presence, he wanted nothing more" (13). Shadowed against the sun, reflected in water, Shadrack's appearance takes on an existential blackness through which his presence is secured. Yet this victory is not complete. Upon his return to the community, no social substitute for his own reflection appears. Another solution must be sought.

The solution is National Suicide Day, a celebration of death whereby Shadrack seeks to control and contain his fear, which is not of death but of its unexpectedness (14). This annual event sets Shadrack, the outsider, at the heart of the community and also brings the presence of war into the civic text. Shadrack's introduction of death (and not just suicide but also murder) into the community reproduces in ritualized fashion the violence of war. Therefore, through his "National" celebration, Shadrack brings the potential violence of war within the borders of the community, an act that inverts the civilizing process of the civic state, which seeks to expel violence to its border zones. By attempting to make static the threat or promise of violence, Shadrack allows the violence of war—now linked to and in some ways indistinguishable from the violence of everyday life—to become present within the civil community by his destabilization of national boundaries. In his stateless location, Shadrack no longer respects the official boundaries of the nation state. In his attempt to stabilize violence temporally rather than spatially, through its location in one day rather than on the borders of the nation, Shadrack brings his community into intimate proximity with the threat of death normally associated with war rather than peace.[6] National Suicide Day therefore challenges national narratives of peace and civilization (as the overcoming of violence and death) in the same way that Morrison's veterans haunt the civic narrative of US history cleansed of racial violence through the location of violence elsewhere,

---

[6]   An excellent analysis of the use of the categories of "war" and "peace" in the novel can be found in Hunt.

in the fields of international war.[7] Shadrack's "National" holiday disrupts the boundaries of the nation as these boundaries relate to him as a black veteran and to the community of the Bottom as a segregated community.

Shadrack's festival of the containment of violence is not only marked as national, but also as "Suicide Day." Suicide here acts as a problematic sign, in that it indicates something that is gestured to but not performed (at least by Shadrack). The call to suicide that Shadrack performs, instead of the act itself, implies a number of different registers of interpretation. The literalization of the meaning of Suicide Day at the end of the novel, when the march leads the community to death rather than triumph over death further challenges the epistemological status of Shadrack's celebration.

Suicide is often read in terms of both self-harm and individual psychopathology, but sociological readings have challenged this relegation of suicide to the status of an individual and apolitical act. Émile Durkheim suggests that war, through the act of military service, exists as an anomaly in the modern sociology of the individual. The self-actualization of the individual—necessary for the conception of the individual as a modern, democratic, political actor—is compromised by identification with the group (197). Suicide is a term that has been relegated to dishonourable deaths in modern society, yet, as Durkheim asks, "When does a motive cease to be sufficiently praiseworthy for the act it determines to be called suicide?" (199). Implicit within Durkheim's argument is the suggestion that war forms a limit case in the modern distinction between suicide and the "praiseworthy act." War implies the conscious choice of the possibility of death. But this cannot be called suicide in a society that pathologizes suicide and yet requires its citizens to fight. For the black veteran whose risk of death for the sake of the nation is not rewarded by full citizenship, the distinction between suicide and heroic death becomes all the more problematic.

In her analysis of Black women's writing and the Civil Rights Movement, Melissa Walker reads National Suicide Day as relating directly to the protests of the Civil Rights Movement. Reading the violence in the tunnel at the end of the novel as "a delayed consequence of official policies that denied the African American World War I veterans and defense workers the full participation in American society they expected" (121), Walker argues that any interpretation of the fate of the townspeople as protest or suicide must remain undecidable. This ambivalence destabilizes the boundaries drawn around suicide as a specific,

---

[7] David Marriott notes that one of the cinematic responses to World War II was an attempt to introduce images of black soldiers into war films of the period, in an effort to represent "the race problem" through the theme of the trauma of war. Critics of these films argued that the representation of the effects of racism in relation to a universalized idea of trauma founded in war decentered the specificity of experiences of racism from black characters (75). I would argue that Morrison inverts this movement from the particular to the general by positioning the national within the local, and the experience of war within the experience of race.

personal and apolitical form of self-harm. It extends not only to the rewriting of suicide as "revolutionary"[8] in later twentieth-century black political struggles, but also to the non-violent protests that played such a crucial part in the earlier years of the Civil Rights Movement. These protests were not themselves characterized by the avoidance, or the absence, of violence, but rather by a "planned sacrifice of the flesh" (Haag 27). While civil rights protesters practiced non-violence, they were frequently the victims of violence perpetrated by others. By publicly displaying the violence suffered, rather than practiced, by protesters, civil rights marches and demonstrations exposed the racial, anti-democratic motivation behind such acts of violence. As a result, the non-violent nature of the Civil Rights Movement could be understood as an attempt to identify these protests as political, in the sense Arendt argues for, despite a continuous struggle necessary to maintain this non-violent identity.

The violent impulses and desires of the townspeople in *Sula*, however, disconnect their actions from such a conception of political protest. The spirit of the town is repeatedly characterized as a murderous rage (118, 122). The desire of the town, when confronted with the tunnel that represents their exclusion, is to "kill it all, all of it" (161). Unlike the "planned sacrifice of the flesh" exhibited in civil rights marches, this march is not witnessed by anyone outside the community and is self-destructive rather than sacrificial. As a result, this violent anger destabilizes both the identity of their actions as political and the boundaries between suicide and protest. Likewise, Shadrack's introduction of violence into the civil community raises questions about the status of the violence he experienced during warfare and the extent to which it is distinct from the violence suffered by black Americans "at home."

As a result of this disruption of national narratives of life and death, Shadrack's National Suicide Day emerges as multiple and irrational to the extent that it conforms neither to the boundaries of the nation state nor to the forms of political protest sanctioned by it. As a result, the death of the townspeople in the tunnel signifies the disconnection of the town from black politics and the Civil Rights Movement, as Walker suggests (110–11). Yet it also shows that the relationship to violence experienced by the townspeople, like Shadrack's unspeakable experience of the moment of war (*Sula* 7), cannot be expressed in terms of the rationality of protest politics. The novel suggests that when conflict is described through a distinction between peace and war, where peace is associated with the democratic nation, there is no available language that does justice to conflict within the nation. This is particularly so outside the bounds of legitimate protests made in the name of the state—the model of the Civil Rights Movement. By transforming Shadrack's experience of war into the rhetoric of suicide, the novel creates a linguistic bridge. Shadrack's marginal, irrational and apparently illegitimate discourse gains the potential to be a structuring ideology in the novel. In this rhetoric, suicide is no

---

[8]   For a discussion of the relationship between images of suicide in Morrison's fiction and black power ideology, see Ryan.

longer individual, politically passive and pathological. It may in fact be a response to the paradoxical position of black Americans within the nation in this period. This rhetoric of suicide describes the action of the townspeople as both self-destruction and protest. In their local loss and destruction, the nation and national democracy are also implicated.

Song of Solomon foregrounds the experiences of black veterans in the United States through references to the historical violence (82, 155) and exclusion (233) suffered by black veterans returning from World War I. As in *Sula*, the reaction of the veterans to these experiences questions and destabilizes national narratives of belonging and exclusion, life and death. Whereas *Sula* foregrounds an alternative, "carnivalesque" narrative of the nation in National Suicide Day (Grant 94), *Song of Solomon* represents historic episodes of white violence and imagines the possibilities of black political reaction to these life-threatening forces.

The inclusion within the text of historical episodes of white racial violence, such as the lynching of Emmett Till in 1955 and the bombing of the 16th Street Baptist Church in Birmingham in 1963, allows Morrison the opportunity to reflect on the competing narratives through which these violent events may be understood. While Morrison's texts forcefully highlight the presence of black life in the American scene, through the representation of self-identified black communities, this concentration on black presence never leads to a straightforward and unambiguous understanding of the events in question. The cultural matrix of black American life cannot resolve these conflicts, if only for the simple reason that they are not created by nor contingent upon the presence of black Americans as such. While Morrison clearly insists upon the pluralistic nature of American life, her work also problematizes pluralistic readings of the nation that imagine agonistic political relations as a potential solution, however limited, to national conflict.[9]

As discussed above, the commonality of Arendt's "public" is based not on natural affinity but on affinity across difference. Yet, this affinity across difference depends upon a participation in the political life of the nation that was not guaranteed for black Americans for much of the twentieth century. Political models that seek to create ideological space for conflict and difference within the democratic polity struggle to identify national and political boundaries that do not impose problematic limits on difference within the nation. Chantal Mouffe's work on agonistic politics stands as one of the most serious and complex engagements with this question in contemporary political theory. Yet even here I would suggest that the necessary distinction drawn between "insiders" and "outsiders" raises questions about the status of black Americans in the nation as Morrison depicts them. While theories of democratic pluralism attempt to negotiate conflict *within* the nation, war once again remains a limit case—and a metaphorical substitute for the conflict of the polity.

---

[9]   For a succinct description of agonistic politics, see Mouffe, "Democracy."

Throughout her work, Mouffe identifies a distinction between the "enemy" and the "adversary" as crucial to an understanding of agonistic politics. She suggests that the enemy is one with whom we share "no common symbolic space" (*Paradox* 13). But adversaries can be defined "in a paradoxical way as 'friendly enemies,' that is, persons who are friends because they share a common symbolic space but are also enemies because they want to organize this common symbolic space in a different way." While Morrison's black American characters certainly share the geographic space of the nation with others, the extent to which they share, or are allowed to share, a "common symbolic space" remains seriously in question. This "common symbolic space" is crucially shaped by the nature of the democratic nation itself. "An adversary is an enemy, but a legitimate enemy, one with whom we have some common ground because we have a shared adhesion to the ethico-political principles of liberal democracy: liberty and equality" (Mouffe, *Paradox* 102). To share this symbolic common ground, black Americans would require access to the full implications of a shared commitment to "liberty and equality," access which was historically denied for much of the twentieth century. As a result, for black Americans in this period, the democratic nation did not possess the characteristics necessary to ground a pluralistic politics. Any claims to this by the white mainstream were of necessity based on a refusal to take seriously the exclusion of black Americans and other ethnic minorities.

As a result of this exclusion, American democracy could not perform the function of defusing violence that Mouffe, and to some extent Arendt, assign to it. As Mouffe suggests:

> the parliamentary system exploits the psychological structure of struggling armies and should be conceived as a struggle in which the contending parties renounce killing each other and accept the verdict of the majority on who has won. (*Return* 5)

Before, and even to some extent after, the Voting Rights Act of 1965, the power of the "actual vote" was not a weapon available to black Americans in this metaphorical battle. As Morrison's fiction, set in this period, persistently reminds us, the conflict faced by black Americans was as likely to be physical as to be symbolic. It often resembled "killing each other" rather than a metaphorical replacement.

Morrison's novels represent an irredeemably pluralistic society and show that the moral connotations of this term are significant. Yet they pay equal attention to the racial contours of this pluralism, demonstrating the energy and force associated with attempts to submerge, negate and destroy the radically other within the plural.[10] As living representatives of the willful falsehood of a common

---

[10]   I think it is important to note here that Morrison's work pays as much, if not more attention to intraracial conflicts. While this reading focuses upon violent confrontations between black characters and a "white" mainstream, this is not to suggest that it is the only, or even the most significant, site of conflict in Morrison's work.

(white) American national identity, the deaths of Morrison's black characters take on ideological significance.

The lynching of Emmett Till in 1955, an event also memorialized in Morrison's unpublished play, *Dreaming Emmett*, takes on an iconic status in *Song of Solomon*. This event is first announced on a radio news show and the delayed revelation that the death is Till's creates an uncanny moment of the intrusion of the real into the novel. The report of Till's death leads to the eruption of arguments among the listening men over the rational or irrational nature of his violent murder and the likely response to it by the white authorities and population. Once again, international conflict provides a frame of reference for Till's death, at least in the eyes of the men who "witness" this announcement. The imagined commemoration of Till's murderers by the white community echoes the victory parades denied to black veterans. The listeners also speculate that Till's father was probably a war veteran, whose death by lynching on his return to the US seems as likely as death in service in the South Pacific (82).

Milkman, the novel's central character, initially lacks both racial and political consciousness. It is perhaps significant that, as a result of his class privilege, he is able to avoid military service (69). Hearing of Till's death, he is unable to comprehend either the event or the discussion that follows it, dismissing both Till and his killers as "crazy" (88). He later repeats this accusation: "'But people who lynch and slice off people's balls—they're crazy, Guitar, crazy'" (155). By locating these acts of violence in personal pathology, as irrational acts which can neither be explained nor understood, Milkman shows his ignorance of the extent to which lynching, among other forms of white violence, represents a political response to black emancipation and later movements for citizenship and civil rights—a response Angela Davis describes as "undisguised counter insurgency" (185). Understood as collective, lynching can be seen in the context of the political structure of the nation rather than an impulsive act of an individual or localized group. This reduction of white racist violence to the response of the pathological individual is echoed in Milkman's inability to comprehend the absurdity of seeking legal justice for his grandfather's death (*Song* 232)—and in the debate over the possibility that Till's killers will be prosecuted. One of the barbershop men asserts that this will happen: "'The law is the law'" (82). This depersonalization of the law, in contrast to Guitar's insistence that the law is always the white law (82, 160), is the structural correlative of the association of white racist violence with the pathologized, but deracialized, individual. The rational (and by implication colorblind) law opposes the irrationality of individual violence and so secures the stability of the state. The intrusion of racial difference and racial politics destabilizes this opposition by questioning the rational ability of the law to function in a colorblind way and the location of violence in the deracialized individual. Yet it also brings into question the role of the state as mediator between the law and the individual—and potentially exposes the historical complicity of the state in anti-black violence (James 104).

While Milkman understands Till's death only through the idea(l) of the individual, Freddie's response is characterized by a racially-informed knowledge of violence. But this is a knowledge that does not oppose the racial basis of violence, which he locates in the South. Freddie, a "born flunky," (24) blames Till for his "northern" inability to obey the racial rules of the South. "'What'd he do it for?' asked Freddie. 'He knew he was in Mississippi.... Who the hell he think he is?'" (81). Freddie echoes accounts of lynching that have located the instigation of violence in the conduct of the black victim, as Till's historical murder was "instigated" by a whistle received and repeatedly constructed as an act of violence.[11] Freddie's response implicitly legitimates the violence of lynching as a "natural" feature of a region that is notably American, but elsewhere, in "Bilbo country" (81), named after the Governor, Senator, and committed segregationist, Theodore G. Bilbo. Here, Freddie provides a defense for Till's attackers as being provoked, a defense which continues to operate in contemporary public explanations of "white riot" in response to black actions (Williams 141–42). Freddie's response to the lynching implies that a "common understanding" of the geography of the United States would have saved Till's life. Through this understanding he indicates a symbolic reading of the nation that may be shared, but depends upon a shared belief in a "natural" racial violence, and thus saves the nation from its violent hinterlands. By dividing the North from the South, Freddie divides the nation and locates violence elsewhere, outside the nation as such, a distinction later challenged by Guitar's refusal to recognize a distinction between North and South (*Song* 114).

The oppositional representations of violence examined here are centered on distinctions between violence as rational and structured by racial identity versus violence as irrational and the possession of an individual whose identity is subsumed beneath it. A passage in Morrison's novel meditates on the black Southside community's beliefs about black and white rationality and violence— after news of the murder of a white boy and the invocation of "Winnie Ruth," a murderous and criminally insane woman held to be responsible for this crime.

> Such murders could only be committed by a fellow lunatic of the race, and Winnie Ruth Judd fit the description. They believed firmly that members of their own race killed one another for good reasons: violations of another's turf (a man is found with someone else's wife); refusal to observe the laws of hospitality (a man reaches into his friend's pot of mustards and snatches out the meat); or verbal insults impugning their virility, honesty, humanity and mental health (100).

The ironic tone of the distinctions made within this ideology of rational and irrational violence is deepened by the gradual revelation of the existence of the Seven Days and their part in the acts of violence attributed to Winnie Ruth. The Seven Days are a group of black men, almost all war veterans, who are committed

---

[11]   Susan Brownmiller's second-wave feminist account of the event continues this tradition by describing Till's whistle as "just short of physical assault" (247). For a detailed response to Brownmiller, see Davis.

to retaliating to white violence through reciprocal acts of murder. Their alternate narrative retrospectively alters a number of significant and ambiguous events of the novel, among them the suicide that opens the novel, Porter's drunken suicide attempt and Empire State's reaction to the news of Emmett Till's lynching on his "Day." This provides an apparently rational account of such acts through a thesis of white violence and black resistance. However, the alternate narrative of the Seven Days is not in itself enough to account for the presence or nature of violence, or the deaths which result from it. The novel does not rest on, but complicates and contests the political thesis the Seven Days present. Here, Morrison's work problematizes both the democratic politics of the nation *and* the revolutionary politics of violence.

The ideology of the Seven Days presents a Manichean world of black/white racial difference in which black violence is a necessary and legitimate response to white violence (155–60). As suggested in relation to Shadrack's march, the possibility of "legitimate" violence within the boundaries of the nation state destabilizes the distribution of violence at its boundaries and questions the authorizing identity of the state. Echoing the ideology of black nationalist and black power movements of the later twentieth century which related the struggle against racism in the United States to anti-colonial struggles elsewhere (Carmichael 5), Guitar's suggestion that his "whole life is geography" (114) is a challenge to the authority of the state to judge his actions.[12] Ralph Story suggests that, through their opposition to the state, the Seven Days are engaged in a "revolutionary praxis" (156) whose violence is the only logical response to the extremes of white racism. Story focuses on the ideology of love expressed by Guitar (159) and Porter (26) as the revolutionary connection between the community and the secret society of the Days. Yet I would argue that this ideology of love is compromised, throughout the novel, in the divisions between the Days, in their "community" and in Guitar's final acts of violence against Pilate and Milkman.

Initially, the ideology of the Seven Days appears to bear a resemblance to the strategies and effects of revolutionary violence described by Frantz Fanon in *The Wretched of the Earth*. Fanon locates the violence of anti-colonial struggles primarily in colonial regimes themselves, which structure the relationships between colonizer and colonized as violent (29). Fanon's suggestion that the violence the colonized subject takes up is initially the same as that practiced by the colonizer (31) seems to reflect the Seven Days' attempt to perform a reciprocal rather than oppositional violence, through their "mathematical formula" of matching black

---

[12]   This association between Guitar/the Seven Days and black nationalist ideology has led to readings of the text that compare Guitar's position with Malcolm X and Milkman's with Martin Luther King. See for example Walker and Story. Though the divisions between the politics of Malcolm X and Martin Luther King are certainly relevant to the novel, I would argue that such readings are overly schematic and imply an endorsement of one or other of these political stances, which the novel does not appear to support, even to the extent of Walker's suggestion that Guitar and Milkman are "unfulfilled" versions of these political figures (142–44).

and white deaths in an attempt to construct a racial parity of violence. However, Fanon's more radical suggestion is that revolutionary violence is necessary to transform the colonial subject into an individual existing outside the economy of desire of colonial power structures (48). The Seven Days' ideology of violence contains no such transformational effect. Restricted in numbers and by secrecy, the Seven Days' longevity is achieved through repetition rather than progress (*Song* 155). When Milkman challenges Guitar on the possibility of his own victimization, Guitar turns to this tradition of repetition as a means of evasion (161). The development that this evasion conceals is Guitar's turn to violence against other black Americans.

Lacking the transformational power that Fanon associates with revolutionary violence, the program of the Seven Days conforms more closely to the abyssal structure of vengeance. Each act of violence provokes another act indefinitely, in the absence of a system of public justice that replaces private vengeance (Girard 15–7). The final "Dead end" of the cycle of violence of the Seven Days occurs in Guitar's assaults on Pilate and Milkman. In attacking Milkman, Guitar negates his own ideology of impersonal and abstract violence directed against an undifferentiated white world (*Song* 155–57). He attacks Milkman in anger and apparently out of vengeance (295). Motivated by the desire for wealth, even in the name of the group, Guitar extends his violence beyond the practices of the group. He embodies the unpredictability of violence as a means extending beyond its ends.

Adrift between international conflicts on the borders of the nation state and the possibilities of a political collective that historically has excluded them, Morrison's black veterans are neither "enemy" nor "adversary." As a result their identity becomes politically unspeakable and doubly ambivalent. Denied full rights within the military and refused recognition on their return home, their conduct as soldiers on the front line of racial violence lacks any context within which it can be understood as political. These novels give voice to the unlivable position the black veterans inhabit within the democratic nation. By representing their lives and deaths, Morrison does not simply reject the politics of the democratic nation, or attempt to found a new, revolutionary politics. She engages in what might be called a politics of pessimism. As Sheldon Wolin suggests in his essay, "What Revolutionary Action Means Today":

> In a land where optimism is virtually a patriotic duty, pessimism is still taken as a symptom of resignation and despair. But pessimism is, I think, something else: a sign of suppressed revolutionary impulses. Pessimism is the mood inspired by a reasoned conviction that only revolutionary change can ward off the consequences that are implicit in the tendencies of contemporary American society, but that such a revolution, while politically and morally justifiable by democratic standards for legitimate authority, is neither possible nor prudent— if by revolution we mean launching a campaign of insurrection or civil war.

Revolutions of that nature are plainly pathological under contemporary conditions of interdependency. (249)

Optimism, encoded in national narratives of democracy and peace, is not available to Morrison's war veterans, or many of those who follow them. Such a patriotic optimism would require that they ignore the evidence of the extent to which they are excluded from the civil rights and public realm of the nation. Optimism, as a belief in the democratic and peaceful nature of the nation, is itself a component of the "shared symbolic space" of the United States. Yet, the wartime and peacetime experiences of these veterans provide evidence for their ideological as well as legal exclusion from full citizenship and from the right to a public voice. By setting theories of democratic pluralism in the context of the history of segregation and the role of racial difference in representations of the nation at war, I argue that Morrison crucially expands the contexts in which the deaths represented in her novels can be understood as personal or political events. Through this strategy, Morrison's work contests the privileging of an ideological identification of the nation as essentially democratic over a historical understanding of the struggles for citizenship experienced by black Americans in the twentieth century.

Works Cited

Arendt, Hannah. *The Human Condition.* Chicago: University of Chicago Press, 1998.

——. *On Violence.* London: Penguin, 1970.

——. *On Revolution.* London: Faber, 1963.

——. "Reflections on Little Rock" in *The Portable Hannah Arendt.* Ed. Peter Baehr. London: New York, 2000. 231–246.

Bar On, Bat-Ami. *The Subject of Violence: Arendtean Exercises in Understanding.* Oxford: Rowman and Littlefield, 2002.

Berry, Mary, and John W. Blassingame. *Long Memory: The Black Experience of America.* New York: Oxford University Press, 1982.

Brownmiller, Susan. *Against Our Will: Men, Women and Rape.* London: Secker and Warburg, 1975.

Carmichael, Stokely, and Charles V. Hamilton. *Black Power: The Politics of Liberation in America.* London: Jonathan Cape, 1968.

Davis, Angela Y. *Women, Race and Class.* London: Women's Press, 1981.

Dudziak, Mary L. *Cold War Civil Rights: Race and the Image of American Democracy.* Princeton: Princeton University Press, 2000.

Durkheim, Émile. *Suicide: A Study in Sociology.* Trans. John A. Spalding and George Simpson. Ed. George Simpson. New York: Routledge, 2002.

Duvall, John N. *The Identifying Fictions of Toni Morrison: Modernist Authenticity and Postmodern Blackness.* New York: Palgrave, 2000.

Fanon, Frantz. *The Wretched of the Earth.* Trans. Constance Farrington. Harmondsworth: Penguin, 1967.

Gerstle, Gary. *American Crucible: Race and Nation in the Twentieth Century.* Princeton: Princeton University Press, 2001.

Girard, René. *Violence and the Sacred.* 1972. Trans. Patrick Gregory. Baltimore: Johns Hopkins University Press, 1977.

Haag, Pamela. "'Putting Your Body on the Line': The Question of Violence, Victims, and the Legacies of Second-Wave Feminism." *Differences: A Journal of Feminist Cultural Studies* 8.2 (1996): 23–67.

Harding, Wendy, and Jacky Martin. *A World of Difference: An Inter-Cultural Study of Toni Morrison's Novels.* Westport: Greenwood Press, 1994.

Honig, Bonnie. "Declarations of Independence: Arendt and Derrida on the Problem of Founding a Republic." *American Political Science Review* 85.1 (1991): 97–113.

——. "Difference, Dilemmas, and the Politics of Home." *Democracy and Difference: Contesting the Boundaries of the Political.* Ed. Seyla Benhabib. Princeton: Princeton University Press, 1996. 257–77.

Hunt, Patricia. "War and Peace: Transfigured Categories and the Politics of *Sula.*" *African American Review* 27.3 (1993): 443–59.

James, Joy. *Transcending the Talented Tenth: Black Leaders and American Intellectuals.* New York: Routledge, 1997.

Keane, John. *Reflections on Violence.* London: Verso, 1996.

Marriot, David. *On Black Men.* Edinburgh: Edinburgh University Press, 2000.

Mills, Charles W. *The Racial Contract.* Ithaca: Cornell University Press, 1997.

Morrison, Toni. *Conversations with Toni Morrison.* Ed. Danille Taylor-Guthrie. Jackson: University Press of Mississippi, 1994.

——. *Playing in the Dark: Whiteness and the Literary Imagination.* Cambridge: Harvard University Press, 1992.

——. *Song of Solomon.* 1977. London: Vintage, 1998.

——. *Sula.* 1973. London: Vintage, 1998.

Morrison, Toni, and Claudia Brodsky Lacour, Eds. *Birth of a Nation'hood: Gaze, Script and Spectacle in the O.J. Simpson Case.* London: Vintage, 1997.

Mouffe, Chantal. "Democracy, Power and 'The Political'" in *Democracy and Difference: Contesting the Boundaries of the Political.* Ed. Seyla Benhabib. Princeton: Princeton University Press, 1996. 245–56.

——. *The Democratic Paradox.* London: Verso, 2000.

——. *The Return of the Political.* London: Verso, 1993.

Page, Philip. *Dangerous Freedom: Fusion and Fragmentation in Toni Morrison's Novels.* Jackson: University Press of Mississippi, 1995.

Russett, Bruce M. *Grasping the Democratic Peace.* Princeton: Princeton University Press, 1993.

Ryan, Katy. "Revolutionary Suicide in Toni Morrison's Fiction." *African American Review* 34 (2000): 389–412.

Smith, Rogers M. *Civic Ideals: Conflicting Visions of Citizenship in U.S. History.* New Haven: Yale University Press, 1997.

———. "Liberalism and Racism: The Problem of Analyzing Traditions" in *The Liberal Tradition in American Politics: Reassessing the Legacy of American Liberalism.* Ed. David F. Ericson and Lousia Bertch Green. New York: Routledge, 1999. 9–27.

Story, Ralph. "An Excursion into the Black World: The 'Seven Days' in Toni Morrison's *Song of Solomon.*" *Black American Literature Forum* 23.1 (1989): 149–58.

Vitalis, Robert. "The Graceful and Generous Liberal Gesture: Making Racism Invisible in American International Relations." *Millennium* 29.2 (2000): 331–56.

Walker, Melissa. *Down from the Mountaintop: Black Women's Novels in the Wake of the Civil Rights Movement, 1966–1989.* New Haven: Yale University Press, 1991.

Waltz, Kenneth N. *Man, the State and War: A Theoretical Analysis.* New York: Columbia University Press, 2001.

Williams, Kimberlé Crenshaw. "Color-blind Dreams and Racial Nightmares: Reconfiguring Racism in the Post-Civil Rights Era" in *Birth of a Nation'hood: Gaze, Script and Spectacle in the O.J. Simpson Case.* Eds. Toni Morrison and Claudia Brodsky Lacour. London: Vintage, 1997. 97–168.

Wolin, Sheldon. "What Revolutionary Action Means Today" in *Dimensions of Radical Democracy: Pluralism, Citizenship, Community.* Ed. Chantal Mouffe. London: Verso, 1992. 240–53.

Chapter 11
Televised Death in Don DeLillo's America

Andrew J. Price

It is a common assumption of our contemporary culture that the body is an inescapable feature of our humanity, the most enduring reminder of our locatedness in time and place, the locus of life's greatest joys and sorrows. Advertising urges us to rejoice in our embodiment and adopt the attitude that the body is the source of our ultimate pleasures. And while pain, disease, and death can make it seem that embodiment is a weight that drags us down, it is hard to imagine what human life would be like without a body. Simultaneously, though, technological advances are making it increasingly possible to regard embodiment as superfluous. In the 1990s, an ad for MCI Internet service invited consumers onto the Web with the assurance that on the Internet there are no bodies (or even genders or infirmities, for that matter), "only minds." Scientific work in the area of the human genome and DNA has encouraged the tendency to see human life not in terms of materiality but information, in terms of the "code" of our DNA, with significant consequences for the ways in which crime scenes are examined and surrogacy cases are decided in the courts.[1] N. Katherine Hayles addresses this tension of postmodern life:

> On the one hand we all experience ourselves as embodied creatures, living in specific times and places and limited by the biological, cultural, and historical inheritances that define us. On the other, contemporary technology... has given us the sense that we can transcend these limitations and live a disembodied, free-floating existence made possible in part by the near-instantaneous transfer of information from one part of the globe to any other. ("Postmodern" 394)

For Hayles, the challenge awaiting the contemporary author is to interrogate this "parataxic juxtaposition" and to exploit its instabilities in order to "intervene constructively in postmodern culture, exposing the play of power and suggesting opportunities for change" (419).

Following Hayles, I wish to look at the ways in which Don DeLillo's *White Noise* speaks to this "postmodern parataxis." I, too, see DeLillo as a writer whose body of work presents readers with constructive "opportunities for change." In particular, I want to examine more closely how the strain between embodiment and weightlessness informs Jack Gladney's narrative of his impending death. Midway through the novel, Gladney is exposed to a toxic cloud, the result of

---

[1]   For insightful readings of these issues, see Hayles, "Virtual," and Rose.

an accident in a train yard outside his hometown of Blacksmith, which will possibly result in his premature death. "It won't happen today or tomorrow," he tells his wife Babette, "But it is in the works" (202). In his post-exposure life, Gladney struggles with how to relate to medical authority and technology, which complicate his efforts to see the ending of life as natural, meaningful, and possibly the occasion for what Ivan Illich might call "virtuous performance."[2] Gladney discovers that in postmodern times the materiality of the body has been thoroughly effaced, relations between clinicians and patients have been redefined, and death has been rendered meaningless. The priorities of postmodern culture collide with Gladney's own modernist assumptions about embodiment, identity and death. Sensing that something important is being lost, Gladney laments to his colleague Murray Siskind, "They ought to carve an aerosol can on my tombstone" (283). By the end of the novel, Gladney rejects what might be called "postmodern dying," arguing that there can be no humanity without embodiment, no human life worth caring about without the awareness of death.

Such humanistic affirmations, however, will be a long time in coming for Jack (in fact, he'll have to be pushed to the very brink in order to offer them) because he and Babette both have a difficult time contemplating death in any manner. As the opening chapters of *White Noise* illustrate, death is an ever-present concern for the Gladneys, which, in true American fashion, they have spent considerable energy trying to evade. Thus, the Gladneys choose to reside in the quaint small town of Blacksmith because it is far removed from the decay of city life and the "path of history" (85). Jack seems to believe that if he and Babette choose a suitable place to live, they can somehow avoid the "deft acceleration" of time that would bring them closer to death (18). For his part, Jack's professional life at the College-on-the-Hill is an accomplished work of evasion. The field of Hitler Studies, which he invented, allows him to submerge the fear of his own inevitable death in the unspeakable horrors of the Holocaust. As Siskind explains, "helpless and fearful people are drawn to magical figures, mythic figures, epic men who intimidate and darkly loom.... Some people are larger than life. Hitler is larger than death" (287). In short, Siskind tells Jack, the stark reality of six million deaths "would leave no room for your own death" (287). In the classroom, Gladney takes the everyday practice of evasion and invests it with theoretical respectability. While guest-lecturing in Siskind's class on Elvis Presley, he tells the students that the crowds that once assembled to see Hitler "came to form a shield against their own dying. To become a crowd is to keep out death.... Crowds came for this reason above all others" (73). In Jack's analysis, the death-evading behavior of the Nazi crowds is part of the "continuing mass appeal of fascist tyranny," making Nazi parades

---

²   Illich contrasts traditional cultures that empower individuals to face death "virtuously" (through a combination of language, ritual, myth and drugs) with cosmopolitan cultures that rely on a "system of techniques" in which all aspects of the human experience are medicalized. Agency is key in Illich's analysis: traditional cultures promote individual agency in the face of death; cosmopolitan cultures disable it.

and rallies something at once remote and "close to ordinary" to the postmodern American (25, 73). "We *know* all this," he concludes (73).

The Gladneys both turn to avid consumerism as a way of furthering their evasions. Jack and Babette practice shopping as if it were a religious ritual—as if it were, in fact, an alternative to death. Siskind makes the connection between shopping and evasion hilariously explicit: "Here we don't die, we shop" (38). Siskind's wry comment echoes DeLillo's own description of our consumerist ethos: "If you could write slogans for nations similar to those invented by advertisers for their products, the slogan for the U.S. would be 'Consume or Die'" (Nadotti 93). Significantly, then, *White Noise* opens with the yearly return of the students to the College-on-the-Hill, the so-called "day of the station wagons" (5). Perched atop a nearby hill, Jack watches as the students and parents unload their wagons, each vehicle a testament to consumer excess: "students sprang out and raced to the rear doors to begin removing the objects inside; the stereo sets, radios, personal computers; small refrigerators and table ranges; the cartons of phonograph records and cassettes" (3). Surrounded by the sheer plentitude, the parents exude the youth and death-defying good health befitting members of their social class. The women stand "crisp and alert" in their "diet trim," and "conscientious suntans" abound (3). Gladney will later report to Babette that they "glow a little" (6). Picking up on the distinctly American connection between conspicuous consumption and eternal youth that Jack observes, Babette remarks to Jack that she has "trouble imagining death at that income level" (6). Responding with a one-liner of his own, Jack argues that the eventual death of the parents would not be accompanied by any deterioration of the physical body (surely their immense purchasing power will spare them *that*), but would simply be a matter of "documents changing hands" (6). While Jack obviously finds humor in his exchange with Babette—seeing their conversation as a satirical sort of affair—it is not beside the point that, as Babette reminds her husband, they, too, drive a station wagon. Jack's own narrative will belie how deeply implicated he is in the values he satirizes.

The depth of the Gladneys' investments in American consumerism is made plain by their attachment to the supermarket. If shopping is religious ritual, the supermarket stands as Blacksmith's cathedral. (Though Jack is quick to point out the many churches located in Blacksmith, he never enters one of them.) So central is the supermarket to the Gladneys' efforts to evade death that at one point Jack is moved to confess his belief that "Everything was fine, would continue to be fine, would eventually get even better as long as the supermarket did not slip" (170). His narrative will repeatedly connect the supermarket with a life-affirming brightness. "Look how bright" (37), Siskind exclaims to Gladney, referring to the shelves of colorful consumer products. The supermarket, Gladney exclaims later, is "well-stocked, musical and bright" (170). The effect of such brightness seems to be to make shoppers feel comfortably "sealed off" from the world of time outside (38). Emerging from the supermarket one day, Gladney will give credence to Siskind's theory that the supermarket "recharges us spiritually" (37).

> It seemed to me that Babette and I, in the mass and variety of our purchases, in the sheer plenitude those crowded bags suggested, the weight and size and number, the family bargain packs with Day-Glo sale stickers, in the sense of replenishment we felt, the sense of well-being, the security and contentment these products brought to some snug home in our souls—it seemed we had achieved a fullness of being that is not known to people who need less, expect less, who plan their lives around lonely walks in the evening. (20)

Without a trace of satire, Gladney implies that contemporary supermarket shoppers, much like their German counterparts in the 1930s, assemble to "form a shield against their own dying" (73).

Roaming the aisles with the Gladneys, Siskind lectures to them about the contrast he sees between Tibetan culture, where "Dying is an art" to be perfected, and the American denial of death. For Tibetans, death simply signals "the end of attachment to things" (38). Guided by *The Tibetan Book of the Dead*, they learn to see this simple truth "for what it is," thereby reaching a level of awareness and acceptance of death that most Americans would "find hard to fathom" (38). If American shoppers cannot come to see death as Tibetans do, it is largely because for them commodities are not *things*: they are imbued through and through with life. So thoroughly are consumer products fetishized that even the fruit arranged in bins have a "self-conscious quality" to them (170). For the American shopper, consumer products do more than satisfy material needs: they promise longevity. And whereas Tibetans are instructed in the art of dying by sacred texts, American consumers are instructed in evasion by the supermarket tabloids where, fearful of the end, readers can always look forward to "life after death, everlasting life... and personalized resurrection through stream-of-consciousness computer techniques" (144).

It is important to point out that the Gladneys' evasions do not lead them to disregard the body, to reject it as a fearful reminder of mortality. For they are deeply invested in received notions of embodiment. (The many references to food and eating in *White Noise* underscore the importance Jack places on the body and its unceasing needs.) The Gladneys' understanding of the body is thoroughly modernist; that is, they see it as a "relatively unambiguous locus of identity, agency, labor and hierarchialized functions" (Haraway, "Biopolitics" 14). Committing to the body becomes another way for them to fortify themselves against the end. Early on, Jack confides to readers that what he adores most about Babette is the "girth and heft" of her body (3), claiming that there "is an honesty inherent in bulkiness" (7). It is Babette's weight that grounds her to the material world of "dense life" (5). Gladney's former wives, as Hayles points out, were all thin and implicated in the informational world of the intelligence community ("Postmodern" 410), a line of work that Gladney feels left them "estranged from the objective world" (6).

Following the cultural imperative that middle-aged women must not "let themselves go," Babette watches her diet by eating yogurt and wheat germ, and works her hips and thighs by running the stadium steps at the local high school.

Gladney frequently parallels his professional career to the ample proportions of his own body. Thus, he describes the field of Hitler Studies as something to "grow into" (17). When he adopts the pretentious academic name of J. A. K. Gladney, he adds "badly needed bulk" to his frame in order to achieve an authoritative "hulking massiveness" (17). Consumerism, too, is tied to embodiment, for the Gladneys see their consumer lifestyle as a way of magnifying their physical presence in the world, a claim Jack substantiates when he goes on a wild spending spree at the Mid-Village Mall. Spending with a gusto that astonishes his family, Gladney feels that he has achieved greater material being in the world: "I kept seeing myself unexpectedly in some reflecting surface.... Brightness settled around me.... I filled myself out" (83–84). As Arthur Saltzman maintains, consumerism becomes the ritualistic practice by which Jack and Babette "defend their sense of presence" in the world and achieve a life-sustaining "personal density" (812).

The function of Murray Jay Siskind is to tutor the Gladneys in the nature of postmodern life and its privileging of information over embodiment. While the Gladneys weigh down their shopping cart with their purchases at the local supermarket, Siskind reads labels and studies consumer packaging, looking for the symbolism concealed "by veils of mystery and layers of cultural material" (37). As Hayles puts it, what counts for Siskind "is not the material reality" of the products themselves, but "the hidden codes embodied within" them ("Postmodern" 409). In contrast to the connections the Gladneys draw between shopping and embodiment, Siskind connects shopping to the invisible realm of "psychic data" (37). "Everything is concealed in symbolism," Siskind exclaims, "Energy waves, incident radiation" (37–38).

The full implications of Siskind's teachings are not immediately clear to Gladney. But later, when he watches Babette on TV teaching one of her classes to the elderly, Jack sees the emphasis Murray puts on "waves and radiation" as both exhilarating and frightening. "Was this her spirit, her secret self, some two-dimensional facsimile released by the power of technology, set free to glide through the wavebands, through energy levels?" (104). Released from the body and its locatedness, Babette appears to Jack as if she is "coming into being, endlessly being formed and reformed as the muscles in her face worked at smiling and speaking" (104).

If the image of his wife suggests the freedom that comes with becoming "disembodied" (104), Gladney is also gripped by "strangeness." "A two-syllable infantile cry *ba-ba* issued from the depth of my soul," suggesting that the image of Babette makes him yearn all the more for the familiar physicality of her body. Paradoxically, the televised image of Babette signifies for Jack both presence and absence, at one and the same time a joyous release from the burdens of embodiment and a kind of death.

Murray's teachings, however, might be said to merely formalize for Jack a troublesome redistributing of priorities that he seems to have been noticing for some time. Early in the novel, for example, Jack watches Babette update the family phone book, noticing the absence of addresses, the sites which would fix their acquaintances in physical space, and, in a revealing sign of the times, their subsequent reinscription as information. "Her friends had phone numbers only, a race of people with seven-bit analog consciousness" (41). Likewise, chapter 10 concludes with Jack's evocative account of his interaction with an ATM machine that succinctly captures the complex issues and discomfort engendered by our "postmodern parataxis." "The system had blessed my life," Jack notes after the ATM confirms his own questionable estimates of his account balance. If the interaction is a "pleasing" one, it is because of the "support" and "approval" he feels from the "system hardware," whose mainframe, Jack knows, is not located in Blacksmith but is "sitting in a locked room in some distant city" (46). Gladney senses that "something of deep personal value, but not money... had been authenticated and confirmed."

That something, Gladney's narrative hints, is identity. The slippage his account reports is between a time-honored notion of identity, one dependent upon an embodied subject located in time and place, and an emerging notion of identity as informational and disembodied, embedded in a technological system that is not centrally located but dispersed. Such a slippage makes interactions with an ATM machine "disquieting" (46). As if to underscore this "disquiet," Jack contrasts his own interactions with the ATM—with the appropriate emphasis on the invisible "networks, the circuits, the streams, the harmonies" that mediate the process—and the "deranged person [who] was escorted from the bank by two armed guards" (46). Perhaps not all citizens are quite so willing to be interpellated as subjects into a dispersed informational system, to have their personal identity and locatedness replaced by a PIN number. Siskind pronounces technology to be our savior. It is, in his words, "what we invented to conceal the terrible secret of our decaying bodies" (285). But Jack already senses that the change of priorities portends something more ominous. After all, it might be a short step from the seemingly innocuous reminder to "Know your code" to a more sinister assertion that we *are* our codes (295).

The informational world celebrated by Murray is here to stay, like it or not. That is made clear after Jack is exposed to Nyodyne Derivative while refueling the family car during the evacuation of Blacksmith. Not sure what his exposure means, Gladney checks in at the SIMUVAC station to report his situation. While he waits passively, an anonymous technician begins entering information about Gladney into a computer, producing "coded responses" (139) and a "massive data-base tally" (141). With access to data pertaining to Gladney's body—his entire medical and psychological history as well as the information stored in his genes—the official begins the process of reinscribing his material body into a coded readout, an informational profile.

The official's power to obtain this information initially heartens Gladney. "I wanted this man on my side. He had access to data" (139). But Jack soon becomes disturbed by the refiguration of his body as information, about the implications of being said to possess an identity and personal history that can be "stored" in a computer network, and about the consequences of defining authority in terms of access to data. Disturbing, too, is the nature of Nyodyne Derivative itself. No everyday chemical, but rather "a whole new generation of toxic waste," Nyodyne D is a "state of the art" toxin (138–9). Gladney's narrative suggests that it might be the chemical counterpart to the informational waste plaguing his life, a connection reinforced when the cloud is referred to as "a high-definition event" (138). Silently, discretely, like the waves and radiation described by Siskind, this postmodern death has "entered" Gladney's bodily system (141).

The issues that emerge during this scene, though, go beyond the problems of identity and authority. For Gladney begins to understand that the switch to an informational paradigm enforces far-reaching notions concerning dying and death as well. That is to say, he comes to put his finger on the "work" that discourses of the body perform. The work they carry out is essential: they tell us not only what it means to be a self, but how that self comes to its end. At the heart of his encounter with the SIMUVAC official is the question of whether death, like the body, is merely a matter of "codes" and "data." If it is, then what is the role of the self in the process of dying? Gladney's exchange with the official fails to enlighten:

"Am I going to die?"
"Not as such," he said.
"What do you mean?"
"Not in so many words."
"How many words does it take?" (140)

Ultimately, Gladney is told only that he possesses a "situation," a linguistic abomination that will later cause him to declare to Murray that he is already "technically dead" (283).

As an inheritor of the language of the humanities, Gladney would like to believe that death in not merely a matter of the body but of spirit as well, a matter that, as such, calls fourth our best efforts. In chapter 5 he asks, "Shouldn't death... be a swan dive, graceful, white-winged and smooth, leaving the surface undisturbed?" (18). Similarly, while he strolls through "THE OLD BURYING GROUND" of Blacksmith Village, much in the manner of a graveyard poet, he awaits "the light that hangs above the fields of the landscapist's lament" (97), some hopeful signal that might be taken as a saving response to the numbing roar of the postmodern highway that sounds in the background. In the SIMUVAC scene, such hope and belief are dismissed as quaint literary devices, throwbacks to the days when Blacksmith was actually a village in which real blacksmiths toiled. Understanding that his own dying promises to be a different affair from what he would have imagined, he begins to sense a "horrible alien logic" at work (142). This logic signals that an entire humanist tradition of death and dying has come to an end and is in the process of being replaced by one in which the ending of life is coldly technological.

As his narrative unfolds, Gladney becomes increasingly alert not only to the break with the past that the switch to an informational understanding of the body enacts and the self-alienation it produces, but also to the ways in which that rupture can be concealed by language. Indeed, new understandings of the body often rely on metaphors that can obscure the full implications of their newness. For instance, as Mark Rose notes, the metaphor of a "genetic imprint" recalls both fingerprints and the familiar technology of printing, misleadingly suggesting that the new discourse of DNA is continuous with the past (232). When Gladney returns home after nine days of evacuation in Iron City, he is sent by his physician for extensive testing at Autumn Harvest Farms. The suggestion that its clinical practices are organically related to those of the past, in true postmodern fashion, obscures the total break from the old.

At Autumn Harvest Farms, Gladney is subjected to an array of dehumanizing tests that effectively turn his body into a text to be managed by experts. His body is inserted into new visualization technologies while computers scan his body, producing reams of coded printouts. Later, the very materiality of the body is overcome: "Someone sat typing at a console, transmitting a message to the machine that would make my body transparent" (276). With new technologies that can "see more deeply," the entire body is available to the visual inspection of the technician (277). Visualization, of course, is often the first step in justifying intervention. But DeLillo suggests that in clinical settings, visualization is often its own justification, constituting the very authority of the clinician. The power of the clinician is the power to visualize, the power to explore the interior spaces of the body and to interpret the information that lies within. Sensing the increasing importance of images and information in the care of his body, Gladney experiences what might best be described as a near-total decoupling of body and subject. His narrative suggests that this might be the very goal of his treatment.

In fact, Gladney is counseled not to show too much interest in his own case, lest his involvement become personal, "almost like a hobby" as one technician puts it (278). The shift to an informational discourse of the body redefines what counts as data in the management of a patient's case: the subjective experience of the embodied patient is negated by data generated by computers and visualizing technologies. Patients and clinicians are now involved in new relations of power. Though Jack's physician, Dr. Chakravarty, tells him that "Together, as doctor and patient, we can do things that neither of us could do separately" (261), his folksy maxim conceals the privileged role that the physician now enjoys in such a partnership. After running routine tests on Gladney, for example, Chakravarty notes his concern over Jack's blood potassium levels and invites him to inspect the computer printout with its "bracketed number[s] with computerized stars" (260). When Jack asks what the symbols mean, he is advised that "There's no point [in] your knowing at this stage," and, later, "The less you know, the better" (261). Chakravarty's authority, like all of the technicians in *White Noise*, resides in his ability to generate images, to access data and to decode information. "Your doctor knows the symbols," Jack is told at Autumn Harvest Farms (281). Yet, if Chakravarty derives his power from the construction of the doctor as a decoder of information, then what of the material bodies that he treats? Are the images of

Jack's body related to all the other TV and media texts that litter the pages of his narrative—mere images, simulacra? Is his body, too, a copy without an original?

The fear that the body is mere information obsesses Jack, eventually leading to his elaborate plan to assassinate Willie Mink, a.k.a. "Mr. Gray," the inventor of Dylar, the psychopharmaceutical that supposedly rids humans of the fear of death.[3] For some time, Mink has been providing Babette with Dylar in exchange for sex at the Roadway Motel. Although Gladney's plan to orchestrate Mink's demise begs to be read as a classic revenge narrative, Jack's evocative imaginings of Mr. Gray suggest that there is more to it. As Leonard Wilcox has argued, Jack associates Mink with "multinational capitalism" and, more significantly, "informational flow" (359), the very things Gladney has come to feel are pushing him closer to the edge.

> I sat up late thinking of Mr. Gray. Gray-bodied, staticky, unfinished. The picture wobbled and rolled, the edges of his body flared with random distortion. Lately, I found myself thinking of him often. Sometimes as Mr. Gray the composite. Four or more grayish figures engaged in pioneering work. Scientists, visionaries. Their wavy bodies passing through each other, mingling, blending, fusing. A little like extraterrestrials. (241)

Jack draws explicit parallels between Mr. Gray and the postmodern construction of the body as information—leading readers, in fact, to thematically connect this "extraterrestrial" to the "alien logic" that he first discovers at the SIMUVAC camp and now associates with his own postmodern dying. Mr. Gray's body is, after all, no body at all, for it is so totally dematerialized that it has become pure information. In fact, its "blending" and "fusing" nature bears considerable resemblance to the futuristic cyborg described in the work of Haraway. "Why should our bodies end at the skin?" Haraway asks playfully, inviting her readers to consider emerging "lived and bodily realities" in which people will not be afraid of their "joint kinship" with machines ("Manifesto" 208). Bodies are no longer imagined to be the bounded objects of modernity, possessing a clearly demarcated "inside" and "outside," for they can be interfaced wherever there is a will to do so. "No objects, spaces, or bodies are sacred in themselves; any component can be interfaced with any other if the proper standard, the proper code, can be constructed for processing signals in a common language" (205). Underwritten by a view of the body as a "biotic

---

[3]   Mink's research into the fear of death entails an understanding of the brain as an informational structure. Explaining to Jack how Dylar works, Winnie Richards puts it this way: "Your brain has a trillion neurons and every neuron has ten thousand little dendrites. The system of intercommunication is awe-inspiring" (189). By intervening in this communication system, Mink can rid his patients of the fear of death, though as Richards puts it, doing so would result in a life distinctly inhuman. "You have to ask yourself," she states, "whether anything you do in this life would have beauty and meaning without the knowledge you carry of a final line, a border or limit" (229).

component or cybernetic communication system" (211), the future promises to be one in which the home, the workplace, and the body can be "dispersed and interfaced in nearly infinite, polymorphous ways" (205). Perhaps Murray has such a future in mind when he proclaims to Jack that technology has the means of investing the body with "Light, energy, dreams"—nothing less than "God's own goodness" (285). Jack simply wishes to be restored to his flesh and blood body, connected once again to "earth [and] sky" (283).

As it turns out, Gladney's plan marks both the depths to which his despair has taken him as well as the beginnings of redemption. Encouraged by Murray's theory that one can immunize oneself from death by taking another's life, Jack proceeds to the Roadway Motel to not only kill Mink but to procure a stash of Dylar. The meaning behind his plan to kill Mink is now startlingly clear: kill Mink, control fear; cancel out your adversary, reclaim your body. Employing the conventions of a B-movie, Gladney's narrative insists on his own irrefutable embodiment and agency, implying that he constructs this narrative in imaginative response to the clinicians who would deny the urgency of the material body. Making his entrance, Jack heavy-handedly notes that he "tried to see [himself] from Mink's viewpoint. Looming, dominant, gaining life-power" (312). On the other hand, his narrative associates Mink with the "free-floating" world of information. Accordingly, Jack makes reference to the noise of the room, "faint, monotonous, white" (306), while he presents Mink as a subject formed entirely from the tidbits of American television, less a person than a collection of informational garbage. When Gladney asks his imagined opponent "Where are you from *originally*?" he receives no answer, for reasons his own clumsy allegory all too readily supplies (307, italics mine).

Mink is the postmodern body, the body as text, as simulacrum. There can be no question of origins. Yet once Jack shoots Mink—and then is subsequently shot in the wrist by him—the allegory, much like the tablets of Dylar both men covet, implodes. Suddenly, Mink appears as he truly is: a victim of many of the same forces as Jack. Perhaps sensing this connection, Jack tentatively rediscovers his humanity, a humanity that manifests itself in his embrace of Mink's body. As he prepares to give mouth-to-mouth to his former foe, Jack stumbles upon the essence of redemption: "Get past disgust. Forgive the foul body. Embrace it whole" (314). What Gladney now sees in Mink, as Tom LeClair suggests, is "a colored double... to recognize and accept," another embodied individual whose fear of death has driven him to desperate measures (222).

Gladney's redemption at the Roadway Motel brings him closer to an acceptance of the mystery of death and of the joys and sorrows that accompany embodiment. Death cannot be informationally represented as mere "bracketed number[s] with computerized stars," just as surely as embodiment need not be reduced to self-aggrandizement and violence. Gladney's embrace of death's mystery—and the key role that he will ascribe to narrative in sustaining it—is subtly foreshadowed earlier in the novel. In chapter 18, Jack arrives at the local airport to pick up a daughter from an earlier marriage. While waiting, he is drawn to a crowd of passengers who have just survived a near disaster when their plane lost power in all three of its engines before safely landing. Soon, Jack joins the crowd, intrigued by the nameless narrator's tale of the harrowing experience. The narrator recalls the words of the pilot:

> "Now we know what it's like. It's worse than we'd ever imagined. They didn't prepare us for this at the death simulator in Denver. Our fear is pure, so totally stripped of distractions and pressures as to be a form of transcendental meditation. In less than three minutes we will touch down, so to speak. They will find our bodies in some smoking field, strewn about in the grisly attitudes of death." (90)

The words of the pilot remind readers that death defies any attempt to simulate it through technological means. Death is human, existential and real. However, it can be approached and rendered understandable through narrative.

Appropriately, DeLillo foregrounds the literary nature of the pilot's narrative. For example, in the pilot's tale, the falling plane becomes "a silver gleaming death machine" (90). As Hardin notes, in order to underscore the compelling nature of narration, Jack observes that many of those listening to the narrator are the passengers who were aboard the plane—those who, because they experienced it firsthand, would have no need for the story (42). Yet, "No one disputed his account or tried to add individual testimony," Jack notes. "They trusted him to tell them what they'd said and felt" (91). The fellow passengers intuitively sense the role that narrative plays in keeping their feelings alive, of capturing their terror and awe before death, and promoting community. The fact that the media is not present to record the event is important as well—not because, as Hardin suggests, it signifies that the experience of the passengers "will fade" (43)—but because it now survives only in Gladney's own evocative narrative. Despite our technological advances, it seems that narrative is best equipped to provide a framework for an understanding of death.

In the last chapter of the novel, the Gladneys gather with the other residents of Blacksmith to watch the spectacular sunsets that have begun occurring each evening, most likely the result of the Nyodyne D spill. No one knows what the sunsets mean, whether they are a passing phenomenon or prefigure the End. "Some people are scared by the sunsets," Jack notes, "some determined to be elated, but most of us don't know how to feel, are ready to go either way" (324). Simply put, they do not know if they "are watching in wonder or dread." Wonder and dread, though, are both appropriate responses to death—an insight that marks the closest Gladney comes to the language of religion. The aura of certitude that accompanies the technological mastery of time, space, and the body conceals the plain fact that our wonder and dread in the face of death is not a condition best addressed through technological intervention.

Sensing this, Gladney resists the entreaties of Dr. Chakravarty to schedule further follow-up appointments. Realizing that he is no more than an "interesting case" to his doctor (325), Gladney dismisses those who would monitor his dying to ensure that it is "progressing" according to a normalizing sequence of stages. What he upholds in the place of the false technological faith held out to him is not only an acceptance of the mystery of death but also an understanding of the connectedness to other humans implicit in embodiment. Looking out at the crowds huddled together at one of the sunsets, Jack notices for the first time those whose embodied experiences differ from his own, those "in wheelchairs," fellow men and women "twisted by disease" (325). Whereas his earlier views of embodiment were associated with self-magnification and, later, ruthlessness, he now moves on to embrace a sense of kinship, an appreciation of the living contexts that link him with those like himself who are trying their best "to work their way through confusion" (326).

Jack's new beliefs about death and the body go on to inform his deliberations about the kind of narrative he would compose. Gladney dismisses the possibility of constructing out of his experience the kind of novel that so preoccupied a former wife—"long serious novels with coded structures" (232), perhaps because they bear too much resemblance to contemporary discourses of the body and the emphasis they place on informational codes. Not surprisingly, such novels left his wife alienated from her body, rendered her "irritable, rarely able to enjoy food, sex or conversation" (213). Such narrative pleasures, it seems, are intended exclusively for a disembodied mind. Simultaneously, though, he avoids the kind of novel that would implicate him in the white noise of his culture. Walking out into the busy streets of Glassboro after his testing, Gladney thinks, "How literary.... Streets thick with the details of impulsive life as the hero ponders the latest phases in his dying" (281). It is better not to write at all than to offer nothing new.

Gladney's solution, LeClair contends, is to construct an accessible but politically subversive narrative out of his dying, one that resists the complex "coded structures" of many works of postmodernism but which seeks to restore wonder and a little bit of dread—that is, newness—to our lives (232–33). To the extent that this remains Gladney's agenda, it is true, as Siskind claims, that "to plot is to live" (291). Yet Siskind's formulation is too simplistic, for Gladney understands the paradoxical nature of narrative. While it is a truism that narrative is a life-affirming endeavor, Gladney knows all too well that "All plots tend to move deathward" (26). What is true of the body turns out to be true of narratives. Just as all bodies must die, so must all narratives cease, give way in time to the blank page.

The last fragment of the novel—"the cults of the famous and the dead" (326)—is fitting for its recognition of the awesome finality of death, the final limit for the body and for narrative. Just as importantly, it marks Gladney's contention that narrative is never an undertaking done alone. Just as he studies the apocalyptic sunsets alongside his fellow citizens, Gladney composes his narrative in the imaginative company of writers who have gone before him. As Laura Barrett notes, *White Noise* contains references to a wide variety of texts—Hitler's *Mein Kampf*, Winthrop's "A Model of Christian Charity," *The Tibetan Book of the Dead* to name a few—as well as to literary genres such as the western, science fiction, and the epic. The novel's last phrase, as Barrett sees it, might also be read as an allusion to Joyce's masterpiece about death, "The Dead," suggesting that Jack seeks out a literary kinship with writers like himself who wish to use their texts to provide a framework "in which death is poetic and biological rather than numerical and technological" (105).

Narrative, Gladney suggests, is the most salient way in which humans can address the mystery of our mortality, "the gravitational leaf-flutter that brings us hourly closer to dying" (303). Of course, serious narrative can no more explain or master death than can technology; but, unlike the drug Dylar (or television and supermarket tabloids, for that matter), it does not offer readers evasion. Rather, fiction is conceived by Jack as a way in which "the dead speak to the living" (326). What the dead seem to speak about most is the awareness of the end. In doing so, these literary voices restore weight to our bodies, situate us back into a world where death has the last word, but where we also have the opportunity to truly live.

Works Cited

Barrett, Laura. "'How the dead speak to the living': Intertextuality and the Postmodern Sublime in *White Noise*." *Journal of Modern Literature* 25.2 (Winter 2001–02): 97–113.

DeLillo, Don. *White Noise*. New York: Penguin, 1984.

Haraway, Donna. "The Biopolitics of Postmodern Bodies: Determinations of Self In Immune System Discourse." *Difference* 1 (Winter 1989): 3–43.

——. "A Manifesto for Cyborgs: Science, Technology and Socialist Feminism in the 1980s." *Simians, Cyborgs, and Women: The Re-invention of Nature*. London: Free Association, 1991.

Hardin, Michael. "Postmodernism's Desire for Simulated Death: Andy Warhol's *Car Crashes*, J. G. Ballard's *Crash*, and Don DeLillo's *White Noise*." *Literature, Interpretation, Theory* 13 (2002): 21–50.

Hayles, N. Katherine. "Postmodern Parataxis: Embodied Texts, Weightless Information." *American Literary History* 2.3 (Fall 1990): 394–421.

——. "Virtual Bodies and Flickering Signifiers." *October* 66 (1993): 69–91.

Illich, Ivan. *Medical Nemesis: The Expropiation of Health*. New York: Pantheon, 1976.

LeClair, Tom. *In the Loop: Don DeLillo and the Systems Novel*. Chicago: University of Illinois Press, 1987.

Nadotti, Maria. "An Interview with Don DeLillo." Trans. Peggy Boyers. *Salmagundi* 100 (1993): 86–97.

Rose, Mark. "Mothers and Authors" in *The Visible Woman: Imaging Technologies, Gender, and Science*. Eds. Paula A. Treichler, Lisa Cartwright and Constance Penley. New York: New York University Press: 217–39.

Saltzman, Arthur. "The Figure in the Static: *White Noise*." *Modern Fiction Studies* 40 (1994): 807–26.

Wilcox, Leonard. "Baudrillard, DeLillo's *White Noise*, and the End of Heroic Narrative." *Contemporary Literature* 32 (1991): 346–65.

Chapter 12

"Everything now is measured by after"[1]: A Postmortem for the Twenty-First Century

Lisa K. Perdigao

As I write the essay that is to conclude the collection, I, like the writers studied throughout this work, find myself struggling with endings. In a sense, this piece performs as a type of postmortem by allowing one last gaze at the textual body of *Death in American Texts and Performances*. Yet it is more than that because, like the collection itself, it works not only at studying the corpse but also at tracing ghosts and reanimating the dead, revisiting sites of loss and exploring what can be recovered. The essays in this collection suggest that conventional representations of death are no longer viable in the twenty-first century. In this final chapter, I will return to some of the sites of loss evoked in the earlier essays to explore how postmodern film and television signify not only the death of traditional narrative (to echo Andrew Price) but also the emergence of performance texts that present death as a point of origination. This point of origination is not the start of an afterlife but the beginning of narrative itself, the story's source, so that the scenes of death become sites for reanimating the dead and recovering meaning.

Sharon Patricia Holland's statement that the "dead truly acknowledge no boundary" illuminates an aspect of this collection's approach to representations of death in texts and performances (171). Within and between the essays, boundaries between genres and categories are crossed, consistent with the ominous idea of death at the center of this project, haunting its pages. As the artists considered in this collection attempt to represent death, they chase at ghosts, deal with corpses, and yet reanimate the dead, the absent presence of once living bodies and meaningful language. Throughout this collection, our writers explore the conventions of fiction, poetry, theatre, film, and television, highlighting the difficulties and possibilities of each medium's ability to represent loss. As the works under analysis here represent death, their experiments in style and form suggest their subject. Boundaries are crossed and conventions are dismantled. Death becomes a trope for cultural change.

In the 1990s and early 2000s, contemporary narratives have demonstrated a focus, even an obsession, with death and dying. While critical works in this field have treated textual representations of death, many have not included studies of theatre, film, and television. Yet, as children of the twentieth century, film and

---

[1]   DeLillo 138.

television offer new means for exploring how death can be represented in the space between word and image. According to Peter Brooks, "If the motor of narrative is desire, totalizing, building ever-larger units of meaning, the ultimate determinants of meaning lie *at the end*, and narrative desire is ultimately, inexorably, desire *for* the end" (52). But in contemporary film, endings do not always yield revelations. Brooks notes the problems with the teleology of narrative in relation to its ending: "We need to think further about the deathlike ending, its relation to origin, and to initiatory desire, and about how the interrelation of the two may determine and shape the middle—the 'dilatory space' of postponement and error—and the kinds of vacillation between illumination and blindness we find there" (96). In television, this "dilatory space" is expansive. It may span from the ending of individual episodes to the ending of a series. Thus, when television turns to the representation of death, it may present new ways for the culture to conceive and appropriate the presence, the inevitability of death.

Despite the need to express responses to the monumental losses felt in the twentieth century, and particularly in response to the more recent events of 9/11, we bear witness today to an uncertainty, an instability about how to represent death. While Jon Rossini's and Andrew Price's chapters discuss other examples of Don DeLillo's work, I turn now to his novel *Falling Man* (2007), a text that represents 9/11 through its central figure. This will illuminate what is at work in a postmodern landscape littered with corpses and haunted by ghosts, yet offering the possibility of recovery, of reanimating its dead.

DeLillo describes the post-9/11 landscape as being inscribed with loss: "The dead were everywhere, in the air, in the rubble, on rooftops nearby, in the breezes that carried from the river. They were settled in ash and drizzled on windows all along the streets, in his hair and on his clothes" (25). DeLillo's setting is like T. S. Eliot's *The Waste Land*; his protagonist Keith who emerges from the falling towers is like one of Eliot's Hollow Men. When he is being treated, Keith is told that survivors of suicide bombings often develop bumps caused by small fragments of the bombers' bodies, "literally bits and pieces," "organic shrapnel" (16). It is America in the twenty-first century and the dead are everywhere, even embedded in the bodies of survivors.

While Keith is an everyman like Philip Roth's title character who contemplates his life's meaning in the face of death, DeLillo's protagonist is also like Falling Man, a performance artist in the novel who appears throughout the city after the tragedy. DeLillo describes Falling Man as being "suspended from one or another structure, always upside down, wearing a suit, a tie and dress shoes" and says that he "brought it back, of course, those stark moments in the burning towers when people fell or were forced to jump" (33). When Lianne, Keith's wife, discovers Falling Man's obituary—"Dead at 39, apparently of natural causes" (220)—she contemplates what his performances, those spectacles, mean:

> There is some dispute over the position he assumed during the fall, the position
> he maintained in his suspended state. Was this position intended to reflect the

body posture of a particular man who was photographed falling from the north
tower of the World Trade Center, headfirst, arms at his sides, one leg bent, a man
set forever in free fall against the looming background of the column panels in
the tower? (221)

Researching other articles on Falling Man, Lianne finds the results of his autopsy
and toxicological report, his "chronic depression due to a spinal condition" (222).
She tries to study his body after death and while he was performing, comparing
the picture of the man falling from the north tower to the pictures taken of Falling
Man.

Other chapters in this collection consider DeLillo's earlier novels and plays. In
Falling Man, his most recent novel, DeLillo struggles to represent the dead body
alongside the performative body, reminding us that representations of death are
always performative. David Janiak's training before becoming known as Falling
Man includes the study of "acting and dramaturgy at the Institute of Advanced
Theatre Training in Cambridge, Massachusetts," and a residency at the Moscow
Art Theatre School (220). This narrative thread connects with Keith's story as
well; Lianne's study of Falling Man allows her some insight into what happened
to Keith as a result of the 9/11 tragedy. Yet, she feels its effects in more subtle
ways. As she leads a group of Alzheimer patients in a writing group, she reveals
her fear of the loss of memory. When Lianne suggests to Dr. Apter that she wants
to increase her group's meetings to twice a week, he tells her, "From this moment
on, you understand, it's all about loss" (60). Here, he ostensibly speaks of the
patients' condition but, more tellingly, he also describes the landscape that they
are both enmeshed in.

Falling Man performs at the center of the novel to remind survivors about their
losses. When Keith remembers trying to save his friend Rumsey from the falling
tower, a memory reserved for the novel's end, he presents a version of Falling
Man, another type of performance in the retelling: "Things began to fall, one thing
and then another, things singly at first, coming down out of the gap of the ceiling....
Then something outside, going past the window.... Debris in clusters came down
now.... Something came down and there was a noise and then the glass shivered and
broke and then the wall gave way behind him" (242). When Keith emerged from
the ruins, he found everything "falling away, street signs, people, things he could
not name" (246). DeLillo's language here reads like Yeats's "Second Coming,"
highlighting how language itself, that center, does not hold. While postmodernist
theory also offers terms for discussing how language fails to signify, DeLillo's
description of 9/11 in *Falling Man* shows the specific failures of language, with its
gaps, to represent such a pervasive loss.

DeLillo's novel can be read as a trope for what the writers in this collection have
identified in different works because it differentiates between the representations
of the corpse as object and the body as performative. Thus, his representation of
death tackles some of the issues that Jorge Huerta's, Mark Pizzato's, Jon Rossini's,
and Anne Fletcher's chapters on theatre raise in relation to the presence of death

onstage. Yet, as Alasdair Spark, Elizabeth Stuart, and Mark Pizzato suggest in their chapters, cinematography—in both television and film—presents other possibilities and limitations for the performance of death. Analyzing narratives in film and television offers a different vantage point for studying the dead body as well as ideas about narrative closure and resolution.

While we grouped the chapters of this book into the categories of corpses, ghosts, and the reanimated dead, these categories are not so easily and readily distinguishable. In his novel *Specimen Days* (2005), which consists of three novellas spanning different periods (Victorian, late twentieth century, future), Michael Cunningham illustrates how, from the vantage point of the twenty-first century, we culturally conceive of death through a blurring of categories. Cunningham weaves together three storylines with different central protagonists (whose roles and identities change), interrelating them with Walt Whitman's poetry, which haunts each section. Thus, Cunningham continually circles around the concept of death. Ghosts haunt characters as Whitman's presence and lines appear throughout their stories, and the dead, while appearing as corpses, are also reanimated from one novella to the next. In the first novella, a Victorian ghost story, Cunningham writes, "The dead might be present and absent like this, in the world but not of the world" (76). I turn to Cunningham here, like with DeLillo earlier, to suggest how novelists in the early twenty-first century are representing a haunted America by mixing traditional categories. As DeLillo experiments in his novel with the idea of performance art to represent loss, Cunningham uses the haunted lines of Whitman to create a unifying meaning between disparate stories. The "specimen days" of Cunningham's imagination are filled with corpses, ghosts, and reanimated dead, suggesting the possibilities and limitations for representing meaning in the face of loss.

Cunningham and DeLillo experiment with fiction by drawing on other genres and forms to represent this loss. But television and film struggle to make meaning through a more visual medium. Ghosts haunt these novels in the echoes of Whitman and "organic shrapnel" while, in television and film, visual and acoustic effects can reanimate the dead, with a play of light and sound, with transparent forms and disembodied voices. Written language also allows such variants, and theatre provides the physicality of staging to produce such effects. Yet, cinematography enables a different type of play to connect (or divorce) words from images in the representation of death. What emerges on television and film, from the 1990s to the present, is a story of reconceptualizing the face of death, the site of loss, and offering a new means of storytelling that signifies the absent presence of the dead.

Television series such as *Law & Order* (1990–), *Crossing Jordan* (2001–2007), *CSI* (2000–), *Without a Trace* (2002–), and *Cold Case* (2003–), along with their spin-offs, *Law & Order: Special Victims Unit* (1999–) and *Criminal Intent* (2001–), *CSI: Miami* (2002–) and *NY* (2004–), plus the even more recent *Bones* (2005–), all demonstrate a keen interest in forensics and new ways of knowing the body. One *CSI* episode in particular stands out as being self-consciously aware of how it is performing the detective plot. In "Who Shot Sherlock?" the examiners attempt to solve the murder of a man acting as Sherlock Holmes in a role-playing group, or, as they call it, "a serious literary society." The episode establishes and then undoes connections to the originary texts and constantly questions its own premises while examiners misidentify clues along the way. As Sherlock Holmes/ Dennis Kingsley's murderer (Irene Adler/Kay Marquette) says, she has created the "the perfect puzzle. A mystery worthy of the master." This episode suggests connections between its character examiners and those playing at being Holmes and Watson, showing how performative the show actually is. The members of the society even mistake the crime scene for their society's role-playing game, as Professor Moriarty/Josh Frost says when they encounter the CSI unit: "Oh, a scenario created for our own entertainment, yes?" The dead body of Sherlock Holmes at the show's center establishes connections to other narratives, other representations, and yet also severs most of the ties.

TV shows like *CSI* play with the plot of detective fiction, which Brooks argues is at work in all narratives. But they also highlight how narrative re-presents the body, particularly the dead body, as an object of study. The proliferation of these forensic shows suggests a cultural obsession with controlling the mysterious threat of death through crime scenes and studies of the body. Consider the teleology of a typical *CSI* episode as an example: discovery of a dead body and placement on the medical examiner's table, study of the body with close-up shots of body parts and evidence, recreation of crime scenes and reenactments of violence, and then the revelation of the killer(s). In his foreword to *Bodies We've Buried*, Bill Bass writes,

> I know of only two areas of science in which you must destroy in order to find out what is there. The first of these is an archaeological excavation, where you must dig up the site, interpret the stratigraphy, check for intrusions, and analyze the artifacts. The second of these is a crime scene search.... In both cases you have only one chance to do your investigation, and if it is not done correctly the first time you never have a second opportunity, because you have destroyed what you were trying to solve. (xi)

Bass goes on to note the importance of photography in documenting the scene before it is touched and in noting changes made during the investigation, thus highlighting some of the workings of forensic television series.

The spectacle of dissecting the body—peering into it, studying it—is a consistent trope in contemporary film and television, yet it has an extensive history. According to Elizabeth Klaver, "The Greek roots of the word 'autopsy' (auto+opsis) contain the dead metaphor of vision together with the empirical thrust of Western epistemology since the Renaissance—*to see with one's own eyes*.... Yet the initial idea lodged in the metaphor of 'seeing for oneself' as an epistemology, absent human dissection, still operates frequently today, even if it is not consciously attached to the word 'autopsy'" (2–3). This highlights how the autopsy becomes an effective (albeit obvious) trope: "The trope of autopsy as a searching gaze deployed by the subject to ferret out meaning and significance essentially descries the position of the Western spectator, whether at a microscope, in the theater, or reading a book" (Klaver 3). Klaver quotes the medical examiner's comment—"This is my theater. It is where I perform" (37)—from Patricia Cornwell's novel, *The Last Precinct*, to illuminate the performative aspect of the autopsy. Such a comment succinctly describes what is at work in *CSI* as well as other texts that represent death through autopsies. Yet, forensic TV shows also cross such boundaries.

In viewing *CSI*, Deborah Jermyn argues that "the 'boundaries' which had once governed how much crime drama could show us of the corpse, and how it looked, would never be the same again" (79). It would have been unimaginable a decade earlier that a "programme built around the gruesome clues, secrets and promises embedded within, and articulated across, the image of the corpse could become the most successful television series in the world" (Jermyn 79). Television series like *CSI* demonstrate how boundaries surrounding what is (and even can be) represented of death, of the corpse, have been altered in postmodern culture. *CSI* does more than perform as autopsy; the corpse, though mute, is a "speaking witness," and the pathologist/scientist is a "translator" or "decipherer" (82). The pathologist studies the body but, by reconstructing the scene of death in determining cause and accountability, in effect, also reanimates the dead, if only for a final show. As Charlie Gere argues, *CSI* crosses the law of genre to be more than a police procedural drama. It becomes a type of ghost story; through spectral technologies the dead crime victims are able to "haunt the living and are able to continue to speak" (Gere 133), whether it be through a recording or as the result of forensic investigation.

As critics have noted, *CSI: NY* performs a different function than *CSI* (set in Las Vegas) and *CSI: Miami*. Its landscape is post-9/11 New York: the setting, plots, and characters are haunted and attempt to re-member the dead in a different way than the Las Vegas and Miami storylines. Janet McCabe argues that "*CSI: NY* is based on the founding trauma of an absent body; and the series—formulaic narrative, generic patterns, aesthetic forms, thematic concerns, cultural politics, industrial conditions—participates in rituals of re-remembering and forgetting 9/11. At the same time, it *is* a melancholic text, constituting a space verbosely concerned with trauma and recovery" (168). While the *CSI* franchise focuses on knowing "everything about the corpse in establishing truth and restoring order (until the next episode at least)," *CSI: NY* "endlessly repeats personal (and social) trauma involving the body and recuperation." The characteristic, high-tech looking "*CSI*-shot" defines the three programs, with its effect of re-presenting the cause of death and reversing the teleology of the death drive. But it also reanimates the dead in complicated ways in *CSI: NY*, given that show's particular contexts. Like DeLillo's novel experimenting with performance art as a metaphor for the spectacle of 9/11, *CSI: NY* and similar forensic shows suggest what is at work in other genres by way of interpreting (and thus re-presenting) the dead body.

Forensic TV shows offer models for "Studying the Corpse," but another strand of contemporary television focuses on ghosts and the reanimated dead. A new cult-classic of sorts, *Buffy the Vampire Slayer* (1997–2003), is concerned with the transformation of humans into vampires, with doubles, and with the liminal transactions between the living and the dead. Its lead character, a Slayer who fights vampires, dies (twice) herself and is then reanimated, along with the show. Buffy dies at the end of season five in the episode "The Gift" only to return from the grave at the beginning of season six (and on a new network, UPN), offering another story about narrative closure and syndication. In "Apocalyptic Apocalypses: The Narrative Eschatology of *Buffy the Vampire Slayer*," David Lavery writes,

> As a television narrative, every episode of *Buffy* offers us a variety of "little deaths," mini-apocalypses as well: the distinctly televisual ends, allowing for commercial breaks, that come within the narrative itself; the ending of each episode (my primary concern here); the endings of narrative arcs; the ending of each season. And finally, we have the final narrative eschatology of *Buffy the Vampire Slayer* itself. (3)

Here Lavery explores the types of closure and, perhaps more importantly, the deferrals of closure that the series offers. Returning to H. Potter Abbott's categorization of narrative closure as satisfying expectations and answering questions, Lavery writes that the episode "The Gift" and the series' final episode "Chosen" achieve the first as they resolve multiple plot entanglements. He goes on to say that "No single episode of *Buffy the Vampire Slayer* can be characterized as closurey (at the level of questions). Indeed, not surprisingly, the final line of the show, spoken by Dawn, is in fact a question" (34). As the individual episodes, seasons, and series itself play with endings, with continually present yet deferred apocalypses, the series plays at reanimating its own body, the text of *Buffy the Vampire Slayer*.

As Buffy evades death and returns from the grave, she becomes the reanimated dead, like the vampires she slays. Her first death at the end of season one in "Prophecy Girl" leads to the calling of a new Slayer, a doubling of the one such girl in the world. Another episode, "The Gift," leads to the appearance of the Buffybot meant to stabilize Sunnydale with its presence (warding off an apocalypse once demons realize the Slayer is dead). But the bot instead highlights her absence; it will never really be Buffy. And yet, at the series' end, Buffy is replicated, reanimated, transformed for and by the viewers who inherit the narrative. In the final episode, "Chosen," all potential Slayers are called forth, reanimating these young women, empowering them to act.

Beyond the plotline of the original Buffy series, the spin-off *Angel* (1999–2004) gave new life to the storyline. After the character Spike on *Buffy the Vampire Slayer* dies, he appears on *Angel* as a ghost, reanimated, in a new form and on a new series, reenacting and performing like the Buffy plot and her return from the grave. Other metaphysical TV series intersected with and followed in the wake of *Buffy the Vampire Slayer* and *Angel*. In *Six Feet Under* (2001–2005), *Tru Calling* (2003–2005), *Dead Like Me* (2003–2004), *Rescue Me* (2004–), and *Pushing Daisies* (2007–2009), death is not final. The dead are reanimated and ghosts guide the living.

As Alasdair Spark and Elizabeth Stuart discuss in their chapter here, the series *Six Feet Under* completed its narrative arc in 2005 and, in its final episode, provided endings for all of its characters. Its website, in an intertextual loop, gave the kinds of clues that DeLillo's character Lianne was looking for regarding Falling Man, by listing obituaries for its characters. After offering a continuous narrative of trying to understand death from both metaphysical and objectivist stances, the series begins and ends with the death of the patriarch, suggesting not only that death is inevitable (as all of the characters die at the end) but also that it is somehow cyclical, performative.

Serial television, by its very nature, demands a continuous narrative arc. *Tru Calling*, despite its short lifespan, exemplifies this play with beginnings and endings that we see in *Buffy*'s reanimation of its lead (and its loops in syndication) by focusing on how the protagonist, Tru, as a worker in the morgue, is able to hear the reanimated dead person's request for help. She is then able to return to the previous day and save that person's life. In a way, episodes of *Tru Calling* begin like those of *CSI* and *Six Feet Under*: with a shot of the "corpse of the week." Yet while the reanimation plotline that drove the series was innovative, it became predictable and was then altered. Tru's attempts to save lives usher forth a counterforce in the world: Death. Jason Priestley's character is thus introduced as a stabilizing (yet destabilizing) force in the series. Although Tru can still prevent death, Jack introduces new deaths that she cannot control. Despite such innovations the series could not prevent its own death by cancellation, though reruns continued to appear on the Sci Fi network. Another series, *Pushing Daisies*, bloomed in its wake as a comedy with a similar premise. Yet, that series was also soon cancelled, becoming another site of mourning for its fans.

While television offers serialized representations of the cycles of life and death, of ghostly hauntings and reanimations, film compresses these complicated issues to offer innovative experiments in representing death and deathlike endings. In film, voice-overs often serve to reanimate the dead who tell the stories of their lives and deaths—performing like the lead character in Alice Sebold's 2002 novel, *The Lovely Bones*, a bestseller touted for being original in its beyond-the-grave narration. For example, Sam Mendes's 1999 film, *American Beauty* (like the 1950 Billy Wilder classic, *Sunset Blvd.*), begins with the narrator's account of the events leading to his death, offering a backward glance at the entangled relations of death and desire. Beginning and ending with Lester's death, *American Beauty* suggests that death encompasses life in suburban American culture. As Spark and Stuart note in the current volume, Alan Ball wrote the screenplay for this film and then created *Six Feet Under*. Thus, individual episodes in the TV series begin with a character's death, just as *American Beauty* begins with Lester's death and his prospopoetic narration.

If *American Beauty* became monumental with its success (earning an Oscar for Best Film in 2000) and representative of a prevailing episteme at the end of the twentieth century, Sofia Coppola's first feature film *The Virgin Suicides* (1999) bears a more subtle marker. This adaptation of Jeffrey Eugenides's work is consistent with the novel's attempt to remember the lives and deaths of the Lisbon girls. Like the narrator, Lester, in *American Beauty*, adult males in this film use voice-overs to reflect on their past. But the dead here are not the narrators. They are the Lisbon girls, the virgin suicides, who are the absent, yet present characters that the movie's plot revolves around but can never grasp. The narrators knew the three girls at a similar adolescent age, when the girls committed suicide, thus providing them with a "still point in the turning world," a knowledge of their own mortality in the midst of desire. These two twentieth-century films show the haunting that is prevalent in American films at this time, a sense of awakening desire and mortal limitations. Like Eugenides's 1993 novel, Coppola's film is a meditation on suburban American culture, its destabilization in the face of loss. But rather than mourning the loss of the patriarch as both *Six Feet Under* and *American Beauty* do, *The Virgin Suicides*, in a sense, kills *American Beauty*'s cheerleader, Angela, and leaves Lester to mourn. Yet, both films ultimately experiment with the effects of loss on the suburban community—as others try to retain meaning for their lives and keep a community intact.

Although the 2001 film, Irwin Winkler's *Life as a House*, was released after 9/11, it was produced prior to that tragedy and is thus similar to the pre-9/11 films mentioned above. Like *American Beauty* before it, *Life as a House* begins with a posthumous narrator. But this time, rather than being symbolized by the red rose petals that are connected to the enfleshed memory of desire for a young girl, a house is made representative of the protagonist's life and death. As a site of mourning, the house becomes a monument that bridges the divide between absence and presence. The narrator's son is brought into a new community, and transitions into manhood by building a house with his terminally ill father, George, an architect. The father is able to impart his wisdom and leave a legacy to the next generation before he dies. His memory in others' minds is made tangible with the completion of the house. Yet, a subtle shift occurs here with the insistence of memory. While Lester mourns the loss of his own life in *American Beauty*, George is mourned by others in *Life as a House*. The house becomes a symbol of both pervasive loss and the recovery of meaning.

There was yet another film in the early twenty-first century that focused on the loss of a father, providing more insights about the representation of death during this period. The 2003 film, *Big Fish*, is an adaptation of Daniel Wallace's 1997 novel, experimenting with the representation of death by way of reanimation through storytelling. Edward Bloom ostensibly evades death by gaining and preserving his immortality through the stories he tells. Director Tim Burton uses cinematography to transform Edward Bloom into another symbol of life, a large fish that is itself the story, so that it offers not the "fiction of finality" that Brooks describes but a return, a recovery. In this way, *Big Fish* is like *Tru Calling*; it begins with the study of death and dying (and the corpse) but transforms it into something other, through a phenomenological approach to the body. (The TV series *Pushing Daisies*, conceptually like *Tru Calling*, was produced by those behind *Big Fish*.) Although the narrators in *The Virgin Suicides* lament that the puzzle pieces of the girls' actions never come together, that they can never find closure to the girls' lives and deaths, in *Big Fish* the pieces do connect and make meaning. This film transforms its deathbed scene so that Will Bloom does, in fact, bloom. Will's ability to tell his father the story of his own death transforms Edward into a symbol that remains with the family: the big fish story told by Edward's grandson to his friends years later in one of the final scenes, and viewed by the audience as it, too, sees the big fish continue to swim after the patriarch's death.

I have considered the deaths of patriarchs in such films as a reflection of a shifting center in twenty-first century America, continuing a trend that Spark and Stuart identify in television. But a recent film adaptation of a novel offers another perspective on representations of death and dying. Angela is the object of Lester's desire before he dies and the Lisbon girls, in life and death, are the objects of the boys' desire. But Susan Minot's 1998 novel, *Evening*, and Lajos Koltai's 2007 film (from the screenplay Minot and Michael Cunningham wrote) focuses on the death of the mother, her sense of life ending and the moments of happiness throughout. Haunted by the ghost of her lost love, Ann contemplates her life's meaning: "She woke and thought of what was left. She had always believed in the accepted wisdom that what was important would endure and in the end survive and what mattered would last and be recognized and saved. But she saw now that was not true" (166). And yet, throughout the novel and film, Ann comes to learn that she has never lost anything. In the end, she orders her own narrative and it is almost as magical as Edward Bloom's.

At the end of *Specimen Days*, Michael Cunningham writes, "They had buried their dead.... They had harbored unreasonable hopes. They had built cities that rose and fell and might for all he knew be rising again" (333). While the figure of Falling Man represents death and performance, the "specimen days" signify a cultural moment of crisis and opportunity, for new ways of interpreting and understanding death, for new means to mourn—like an autopsy or a postmortem chapter:

> Autopsy is also a form of memorialization, for the procedure substitutes the plastination of language for the flesh of the cadaver, before the cadaver slips away. Autopsy is a way of "doing" something with the corpse, of retrieving it from the garbage can of the abject, whether that "doing" turns out to be utile, spectacular, thought-provoking, or beautiful. (Klaver 155)

Representing the desire to mourn, to remember, and to memorialize, texts and performances in our recent turn of the century offer sites of reanimation in the suspension of death and the recovery of meaning. As Brooks writes, "Any final authority claimed by narrative plots, whether of origin or end, is illusory....

It is the role of fictional plots to impose an end which yet suggests a return, a new beginning: a rereading" (109). This chapter, then, is a postmortem that fails to yield definitive answers; instead it raises more questions. Likewise, Eugene A. Arnold argues that an autopsy is more than "seeing with one's own eyes"; instead it consists of "informed observation with deductions based upon the accumulated knowledge of our antecedents" (15). Arnold highlights the as-if space where autopsy, like death itself, exists: "In many ways we are the beneficiaries of this interaction between the deceased and the observer and will continue to be in the future, if we will only listen." At the conclusion of this hybrid chapter, which reads as postmortem, eulogy, and exercise in reanimation, I return the text to you for rereading. In this way, I too avoid the deathlike ending and offer this textual body for the reader's doing or undoing, whatever the case may be.

Works Cited

Allen, Michael, ed. *Reading* CSI: *Crime TV Under the Microscope*. London: Tauris, 2007.

Arnold, Eugene A. "Autopsy: The Final Diagnosis" in *Images of the Corpse: From the Renaissance to Cyberspace*. Ed. Elizabeth Klaver. Madison: University of Wisconsin Press, 2004. 3–15.

Bass, Bill. "Foreword" in *The Bodies We've Buried: Inside the National Forensic Academy, The World's Top CSI Training School*. Ed. Jarrett Hallcox and Amy Welch. NY: Berkley, 2006. xi–xiv.

Brooks, Peter. *Reading for the Plot: Design and Intention in Narrative*. New York: Knopf, 1984.

Cunningham, Michael. *Specimen Days*. NY: Picador, 2005.

DeLillo, Don. *Falling Man*. NY: Scribner, 2007.

Gere, Charlie. "Reading the Traces." Allen 129–139.

Holland, Sharon Patricia. *Raising the Dead: Readings of Death and (Black) Subjectivity*. Durham: Duke, 2000.

Jermyn, Deborah. "Body Matters: Realism, Spectacle, and the Corpse in *CSI*" in Allen 79–89.

Klaver, Elizabeth. *Sites of Autopsy in Contemporary Culture*. Albany: SUNY Press, 2005.

Lavery, David. "Apocalyptic Apocalypses: The Narrative Eschatology of *Buffy the Vampire Slayer*." *Slayage*: *The Online International Journal of Buffy Studies* 9 (2003). 22 February 2009. http: www.slayage.tv

McCabe, Janet. "Mac's Melancholia: Scripting Trauma, 9/11 and Bodily Absence in *CSI: NY*" in Allen 167–180.

Minot, Susan. *Evening*. NY: Vintage, 1998.

Index